Voices of Emancipation

Voices of Emancipation

Understanding Slavery, the Civil War, and Reconstruction through the U.S. Pension Bureau Files

Edited by
Elizabeth A. Regosin
and Donald R. Shaffer

NEW YORK UNIVERSITY PRESS
New York and London

NEW YORK UNIVERSITY PRESS
New York and London
www.nyupress.org

LIBRARY OF CONGRESS CATALOGING-IN-PUBLICATION DATA
Voices of emancipation : understanding slavery, the Civil War, and Reconstruction through the U.S. Pension Bureau files / edited by Elizabeth Regosin and Donald Shaffer.
p. cm.
Includes bibliographical references and index.
ISBN-13: 978-0-8147-7586-8 (cl : alk. paper)
ISBN-10: 0-8147-7586-1 (cl : alk. paper)
ISBN-13: 978-0-8147-7587-5 (pk : alk. paper)
ISBN-10: 0-8147-7587-X (pk : alk. paper)
1. African Americans—History—1863–1877—Sources. 2. African Americans—Social conditions—19th century—Sources. 3. Slavery—United States—History—19th century—Sources. 4. Slaves—Emancipation—United States—Sources. 5. United States—Armed Forces—African Americans—History—19th century—Sources. 6. United States—History—Civil War, 1861–1865—African Americans—Sources. 7. Reconstruction (U.S. history, 1865–1877)—Sources. 8. African American soldiers—Pensions. 9. African American sailors—Pensions. 10. United States. Pension Bureau—Records and correspondence. I. Regosin, Elizabeth Ann. II. Shaffer, Donald Robert.
E185.2.V65 2008
973'.0496073—dc22 2007045953

New York University Press books are printed on acid-free paper, and their binding materials are chosen for strength and durability.

Manufactured in the United States of America

c 10 9 8 7 6 5 4 3 2 1
p 10 9 8 7 6 5 4 3 2 1

For Tom, Anna, and Eleanor

* * *

For Jennifer, David, and Laura

Contents

Acknowledgments

We'd like to thank the History Department at St. Lawrence University for two generous research grants that enabled us to collect materials at the National Archives. In addition, we'd like to thank the Sponsored Programs and Academic Research Center and the School of History, Philosophy, and Political Science at the University of Northern Colorado for additional research funding.

In the early stages of collecting documents, Madeline Kenney, who was then an undergraduate student at St. Lawrence University, helped us enormously both by collecting documents in the National Archives and by helping to organize and catalog them. A kindred spirit, Madeline shares our deep attachment to the Civil War pension files.

We owe Deborah Gershenowitz, our editor at NYU Press, a deep debt of gratitude for her long-time support and enthusiasm for this project.

We would like to thank *Prologue,* the quarterly of the National Archives, for generously sharing document images they produced for an article we published with them in December 2005 for use in this book. Similarly, we would like to express our gratitude to the University Press of Kansas for sharing images from Don's book *After the Glory: The Struggles of Black Civil War Veterans* and for allowing them to be published here.

Liz would like to thank her colleagues in the dean's office at St. Lawrence University—Karin Blackburn, Nancy Bovay, Lorie MacKenzie, and Grant Cornwell—for their unrelenting encouragement and support. On countless occasions, it was they who sent Liz off to the library so that she would get her work done and they who would let her interrupt their work so that she could read them passages from the files or ask them to comment on her writing. Don would like to thank his former colleagues at the University of Northern Colorado for their advice and support through the early stages of this project. Finally, we wish to thank our respective spouses and children for their support and for giving us the time away from them to complete this work.

Abbreviations

GAR: Grand Army of the Republic

GPO: Government Printing Office

RG 15: Record Group 15, Records of the Veterans' Administration, National Archives, Washington, D.C.

RG 94: Record Group 94, Records of the Adjutant General's Office, 1780s–1917, National Archives, Washington, D.C.

USCC: United States Colored Cavalry

USCHA: United States Colored Heavy Artillery

USCI: United States Colored Infantry

USCLA: United States Colored Light Artillery

Frank Nunn (alias Nearn, alias Charles Franklin Crosby), 86th U.S. Colored Infantry

Introduction

In an oral account of his life, black Civil War veteran Frank Nunn (alias Charles Franklin Crosby), described the circumstances under which he enlisted in 86th United States Colored Infantry (USCI):

> I enlisted in 1863. . . .
>
> I was not free at the time of my enlistment. I ran away and enlisted. No sir they did not examine me much. Just asked my age and I told them I was eighteen but I was not that old. I told them that because I wanted to get into the army. Q. How old were you at the time? A. Somewhere between twelve and thirteen years of age but I was big for my age. I can't tell you how tall I was but not near as tall as I am now.[1]

During his service in the USCI, the young runaway slave experienced combat. Crosby (who went by his alias after the war) continued:

> They swore me in and gave me my blue uniform and gun and drilled me. That was at Barrancas [Florida]. My gun was a Springfield. When I was discharged, I turned it in. It used a cap and ball and we had to bite the end off the cartridge. I cannot tell how long we stayed at Barrancas. I had been in the service probably one week when we had a battle. It was at a place called Pollard, Ala. That was not much of a fight, just a kind of brush but after we started back to Barrancas, we had a fight that lasted two hours and a half at Pine Bairn, a creek. I do not know, but I was told that there were only 1200 of the enemy and that we killed 800 of them, including their general, Clanton. We had only about five killed and wounded, I do not know how many of each.[2]

Crosby's narrative also describes his role in the Union effort to take Montgomery, Alabama.

After the war, Crosby lived in Texas for a number of years. He explains that he did not settle in any one place: "In 1880, I was in Texas but was not permanent anywhere as I was engaged in driving cattle to market before they began shipping them to market on the railroads. I used to drive from Texas to Kansas."[3] By 1890, Crosby had moved to Mexico, where he married Francisca Robia. The two had six children together, of whom four survived.

Whereas stories abound of the Civil War and life after it in the voices of white soldiers and civilians, illiteracy, poverty, and racism all contributed to a relative dearth of source materials on slavery, emancipation, the Civil War, and life after the war from the perspective of African Americans. Crosby's account begs the question: where does such a prize autobiographical account of a former slave's life come from? Crosby's life story did not appear in a published slave narrative, nor can readers find it among the thousands of interviews of ex-slaves collected by workers of the New Deal–era Federal Writers' Project of the Works Progress Administration (WPA).[4] Instead, Crosby's story, told in his own words, constitutes part of his Civil War pension file, housed in the National Archives in Washington, D.C.

Like Crosby, millions of Americans applied to the federal government for pensions in the late nineteenth and early twentieth centuries. The U.S. Pension Bureau, a government agency, evaluated these applications or "claims" (as they were often called). In 1862, Congress assigned to the U.S. Pension Bureau the task of administering pensions for white and black men disabled in federal military service and the survivors of the Union war dead, widows, orphans, or other dependent family members. The enormous scale of Union service during the Civil War (about 2.1 million men) and its tremendous human cost (about 360,000 Union dead) meant the Pension Bureau generated a vast collection of paperwork on each pension claimant, and its volume grew as Congress steadily expanded pension eligibility over the years.[5]

The pension system changed significantly in 1890, when Congress dropped the requirement that a veteran's disability had to be service related. After 1890, any disability that impaired a former soldier's or sailor's ability to earn a living qualified him for a pension. Thus, nearly any veteran who was not in perfect health was eligible for at least a partial disability rating. A major result of the 1890 law and its generous implementation by the federal bureaucracy was that by the mid-1890s, the federal government spent over 40 percent of its annual budget on

Civil War pensions.[6] To provide some contemporary perspective, in fiscal year 2005 the U.S. government spent a little under $2.5 trillion; 40 percent of that amount is $1 trillion. That sum is nearly twice U.S. defense expenditures for fiscal year 2004, the most recent year for which data is available at the time of this writing.[7]

Black Union veterans and their families were among the beneficiaries of the federal pension system. Nearly two hundred thousand African American men served as soldiers and sailors during the Civil War. In the decades after, families of these soldiers who died during the war, veterans themselves, and veterans' dependents obtained pensions from the Pension Bureau based on the service of over eighty thousand black soldiers and sailors.[8] African American men, women, and children made tens of thousands more claims but ultimately did not succeed in acquiring a pension. In former slaves' claims, the pension process generated a virtual treasure trove of documents—pension applications, letters from claimants and their representatives, correspondence from government officials, claimants' and witnesses' depositions and affidavits—all firsthand accounts that offer invaluable insight into the experiences of slavery, African American military service and civilian life during the Civil War, the experience of emancipation, and postwar experiences of former slaves.

Black pension "claimants," as the Pension Bureau referred to applicants, experienced unique challenges as they pursued their pensions. One considerable problem for black claimants was a lack of documentary evidence that might establish the facts of a claim. For example, slavery and illiteracy contributed to a lack of documentation of births and marriages among African Americans. Thus a veteran who needed to prove his age to receive particular benefits or a widow who needed to establish the date of her marriage to a soldier struggled to verify these basic facts. These and other similar problems, coupled with the racism of federal bureaucrats, meant that the Pension Bureau scrutinized the applications of African Americans to a greater degree than it did those of white claimants. Nearly half of African American pension files contain at least one instance of "special examination." By contrast, only about a quarter of the files of white Southern Unionists received this treatment.[9] A pension claim underwent special examination in cases when the Pension Bureau felt it needed stronger evidence than the affidavits and other documentation that the claimant had submitted him- or herself. It sent a "special examiner" or field investigator to take sworn depositions from the applicant and key witnesses, examine any records outside Washington, D.C., that might be relevant, and then submit a report to headquarters summarizing the findings.

Although the special examinations were sometimes an ordeal for black pension applicants, they provide scholars with an unparalleled opportunity to explore the applicants' lives. Special examiners usually went into the field with a list of specific issues to investigate, but they often conducted what amounted to fishing expeditions, recording any information that applicants and their witnesses revealed. In the case of African Americans, practically speaking, this meant that the depositions amounted in some cases to virtual life stories, comparable and in some ways superior to the WPA slave narratives. For instance, most of the special examinations took place from the 1880s into the 1910s, making them much more contemporaneous to the Civil War than the WPA interviews, which did not occur until the mid- to late 1930s. The timeliness of the documentation in pension files and the sheer number of applications suggests that pension files might greatly enhance and expand our knowledge of African American lives, especially when combined with the material that the WPA interviews generated.

Pension files also usually contain much of the documentation produced prior to or in conjunction with the interview: affidavits and other evidence submitted by the claimant and witnesses in the initial application process; reports from the War Department concerning records of service and any other relevant official documents; the internal correspondence of bureau personnel discussing a particular case's evidence; letters exchanged between the applicant (or the applicant's attorney) and the Pension Bureau; and materials related to any special examination, foremost among them depositions and the report(s) of the special examiner.

The themes of Charles Franklin Crosby's story reflect an array of topics revealed in African Americans' Civil War pension files. These topics include experiences under slavery; family and community relationships both during slavery and after; African Americans' military service, postwar geographic mobility, postwar employment and economic status; and the general health and welfare of former slaves. *Voices of Emancipation* aims to share a small sample of the documents found in the Civil War pension files of ex-slaves, with an emphasis on depositions from special examinations. But before this can be done, it is essential to provide more information on the nature of the files, their limitations, and their advantages.

Initially, as was the case for all applicants, most of the documents of ex-slaves in Civil War pension files emerged from a distinctly legal context. For instance, among the most common items found in most pension files besides special examination depositions are affidavits. Both the depositions and affidavits are reductionist by their very nature: they concentrate on particular issues (i.e., disability, marriage, etc.), and the persons responsible for recording testimony usually shaped the words and language of the person testifying to address those issues clearly and directly. Depositions gathered under special examinations, in particular, are usually summary; special examiners took testimony and expressed it in formalized legal language, rather than providing a verbatim transcript of what the witness said (indeed, sometimes the witness's exact language is inserted in quotation marks for clarification or illustration). Occasionally special examination depositions were written in question-and-answer form (as in the Crosby deposition), but most often special examiners rendered them in narrative form, as if they represented the uninterrupted soliloquy of the witness. Yet because it was standard practice to read back the summary to witnesses before they signed or made their mark to swear to the truthfulness of what they said, the special examinations arguably reflect the thoughts and feelings of those people who testified every bit as much as the WPA slave narratives are an accurate reflection of the thoughts and feelings of ex-slaves. The WPA slave narratives were themselves often as much the product of the interviewer who wrote them as they were of the ex-slave who was interviewed.

Certainly one finds other types of influences in Civil War pension documents. The Pension Bureau called on the expertise of medical professionals, for example. Even after the passage of the 1890 law, the pension applications of black veterans routinely dealt with matters of health and disability; thus, medical documentation is common in the files, both in the form of affidavits and special examinations of doctors, and even more ubiquitously, by the evaluation forms of surgeon's boards employed by the U.S. Pension Bureau to evaluate the alleged disabilities of men applying for pensions.

Also permeating the contents of pension files are bureaucratic mores, which were a reflection of white, middle-class Victorian culture. The employees of the U.S. Pension Bureau lived in a world of calendar dates, a world where applicants had one identity from birth and had the ability to prove events in their lives from official records or clear-cut eyewitness testimony. Theirs was a world that assumed that middle- and upper-class morality and patriarchal family relations were the norm. Bureaucrats often had a hard time understanding or sympathizing with black claimants who did not know their birthdates, let alone other vital dates. Not surprisingly, these bureaucrats looked dubiously and sometimes suspiciously at the surname changes that slaves underwent after emancipation; they found the lack of written records or credible witnesses in African American cases irritating; and sometimes they proved openly contemptuous of the failure of former slaves to live up to their own standards of morality. Yet it is a testament to the slow, grinding doggedness of the bureaucrats and the virtually unlimited resources available to them that many African American pension applicants succeeded in the end and that they left behind a mass of valuable paperwork documenting their lives.

Of course, that begs the question of how we have chosen the documents on former slaves in *Voices of Emancipation* from the masses of documents available in Civil War pension files. The book contains but a small fraction of the total number of pension files—probably about one hundred thousand files, many containing multiple claims—of black soldiers and sailors available at the National Archives. Our first criterion for including a pension file in this book was that the document allow former slaves to speak for themselves. This explains why most of the documents in this collection are depositions from special examinations and affidavits submitted by ex-slaves. Certainly other voices are present from time to time, especially those of special examiners, when they can provide helpful observations of a contextual nature. Our second criterion was that the document be novel in nature, speaking to previously little-known or poorly documented aspects of slavery, emancipation, and postwar experience of ex-slaves. Although some documents in this reader will seem familiar to persons familiar with slavery and emancipation, we aim to make *Voices of Emancipation* accessible to ordinary readers as well as experts. We have also made the decision to excerpt the documents in most cases rather than to provide full documents. Since this book is aimed at a lay as well as academic audience, we have attempted to use material that is interesting as well as trenchant. We have kept our selections relatively short, and most documents have been edited or excerpted to help preserve reader interest. To remain true to the documents, we have kept all the original spelling and punctuation as we found it. We have noted illegible words by writing "[illegible]" and have offered the correct spelling of a word in brackets if the word appears unrecognizable. Verbatim transcripts of several of the documents excerpted in *Voices of*

Emancipation, and some not excerpted here, are included in the appendix. We hope that the appendix will provide readers with a sense of the broader context within which the excerpts exist.

Ultimately, we have excerpted documents to address important aspects of the experience of slaves of the Civil War generation. Chapter 1 addresses slavery and emancipation, subjects that ex-slaves speak to in pension files as they related their biographies in special examination. Chapter 2 deals with the Civil War years, with an emphasis on the military experience of black soldiers. Since the pension system was premised on military service, this is a dominant topic in most pension applications. Chapter 3 focuses on patterns of movement, economic issues, and mortality in the postwar period for ex-slaves. Finally, chapter 4 addresses marriage and family among ex-slaves before, during, and after the Civil War. Since the primary concern of soldiers' families in the pension claims was to prove a legitimate familial relationship to the soldier, pension files are particularly informative on these issues, especially marriage.

Civil War pension files speak to much more than simply the war itself. Because the Civil War drew so deeply on the American population, including slaves, it represents perhaps the greatest encounter between ordinary Americans and the federal government in the nineteenth century. The emergence of the federal pension system for Union veterans and their survivors perpetuated this encounter well into the twentieth century. In the process of attempting to gain its largess, these Americans inadvertently revealed much about their lives in years before, during, and after the Civil War. *Voices of Emancipation* essentially takes a first glance at what ex-slaves said about their lives as they sought the beneficence of the government that they, or a family member, had fought to protect in the deadliest war in U.S. history.

1

Slavery and Emancipation

Slavery is a persistent theme in Civil War pension files. The testimony of Civil War veterans, their survivors, and their witnesses contain frequent references to the "peculiar institution," since it touched on so many issues of pension eligibility: identity, age, disability origins, and others as well. It was hard for former slaves to prove their worthiness for a pension without revealing information about their prewar lives, and that fact made the subject of slavery unavoidable. For ex-slaves, to testify about the period before the Civil War was to talk about slavery.

Civil War pension files are not the first source on slavery from the slaves' perspective. As discussed in the introduction, historians have long had access to published slave narratives and the 1930s interviews of the WPA's Federal Writers Project. However, the firsthand testimony of ex-slaves in pension files is particularly strong in documenting two particular areas of slave life: slave communities and slave identity.

First, even decades later the contours of prewar slave communities are apparent in the affidavits submitted by would-be pensioners and solicited by the U.S. Pension Bureau during special examinations. After all, in determining factual information about a black applicant in the prewar period, who better to ask than other former slaves who had once been and often still were closely associated with that same person in the postwar period? Although special examiners preferred the testimony of former slaveholders and other whites, believing that their testimony was more comprehensible and therefore presumably more reliable, testimony from former slave owners often was unavailable because slaveholders had died or were inaccessible. In the hundreds of thousands of pages documenting black applicants' lives, readers of Civil War pension files can find important insight into the structure and experiences of slave communities.

Second, the question of identity and its relationship to slavery emerges as a strong theme in the testimony about former slaves in pension applications. By identity, we mean the name by which ex-slaves referred to themselves or the name other people used for them, last names in particular, and what names reveal about familial and other social relationships. Names can expose a great deal about status, power, and relationships and about how these things changed in the era of emancipation. Identity often became an issue in Civil War pensions because the first requirement for a successful claim was for the applicant to demonstrate to the Pension Bureau that he or she was the veteran or his eligible survivor. This task was not always an easy one for ex-slaves because of the ambiguity of slave identity before and during the war, and in the transition to free identities that began during the Civil War and continued afterward. The problem was compounded by the preference of the Pension Bureau for documentary evidence that former slaves usually did not possess such as birth certificates, baptismal records, and marriage licenses. Likewise, former slaves often were further hamstrung in their pension applications by their illiteracy, a condition stemming from bondage that prevented them from knowing how to spell their names or record their birth dates by the Christian calendar—itself a consequence of the need to control slaves by attempting to deny their humanity and their worth as individuals. As Frederick Douglass poignantly explained regarding a slave's age, owners withheld from slaves the critical elements of identity:

> I never met a slave who could tell me how old he was. Few slave-mothers know anything of the months of the year, nor the days of the month. They keep no family records, with marriages, births, and deaths. They measure the ages of their children by spring time, winter time, harvest time, planting time, and the like; but these soon become undistinguishable and forgotten. Like other slaves, I cannot tell how old I am. This destitution was among my earliest troubles. I learned when I grew up, that my master—and this was the case with masters generally—allowed no questions to be put to him, by which a slave might learn his age. Such questions are deemed evidence of his impatience, and even of impudent curiosity.[1]

White claimants, too, had trouble producing material evidence in their claims, though not to the extent that former slaves did. The U.S. Pension Bureau was aware of this difficulty experienced by African American applicants and, to its credit, tried to ameliorate it. Pension officials sought evidence in the form of oral testimony, both from the applicant and from witnesses who knew them and could affirm, deny, or furnish anew important facts about the claimant's history. In this testimony, we find stories about slavery from the perspectives of former slaves, former owners, and other witnesses to the life of the peculiar institution. Some of these stories are mere snippets, a mention of having been hired out to another master on a particular date as a means of establishing one's age, for example. Some stories appear in greater length. In order to explain why he and his son possessed different surnames, for example, a father had to recount the history of his ownership and how his family was divided by slavery. Taken together, these stories provide a vast and varied portrait of the institution through the eyes of those having recently, and not so recently, lived within its bounds.

The sections of this chapter focus on community, personal identity (naming and age), and emancipation. Emancipation in Civil War pension files is often inseparable from slavery. Indeed, many of the excerpts that are featured in a particular section might speak to more than one element in the experiences of slavery and freedom. The subjects sometimes overlap significantly.

Community

Historians tend to use the phrase "the slave community" to refer to slaves as a collective body. The phrase can mean both slaves' physical proximity to one another (the "community" of slaves living in a particular locale) and their social relationships (the "community" of slaves connected by a core sense of belonging to one another, a sense of a shared situation). The notion of "the slave community" can also have even deeper meaning for historians, as it invokes the dramatic shift in thinking about the lives of slaves that occurred in the late 1960s and the 1970s. Prior to that time, historians of slavery studied the institution through the eyes of slaveholders, seeing slaves as their masters saw them. Historian John W. Blassingame explained why this perspective was distorted: "The clearest portrait the planter has drawn of the slave is the stereotype of Sambo, a submissive half-man, half-child. Such stereotypes are so intimately related to the planter's projections, desires, and biases that they tell us little about slave behavior and even less about the slave's inner life, his thoughts, actions, self-concepts, or personality."[2] Blassingame's own study of slavery, first published in 1972, used the WPA slave narratives and other firsthand sources to look at the institution from the perspective of slaves in an effort to understand how they experienced slavery and to examine the rich lives they created for themselves within slavery's bounds. Blassingame titled his study *The Slave Community*. Since that time, the use of the phrase "the slave community" has evoked the work of Blassingame and many other historians who explored the humanity of slaves, who saw slaves not as victimized automatons responding to the circumstances of slavery but as active human agents in their own right, developing their own cultural and social institutions within the confines of slavery.[3]

Former slaves' Civil War pension files contribute to the understanding of the concept of "the slave community" by offering specificity to some of the meanings attributed to it. For example, we might take it for granted that slaves living in the same locale were part of the same community. Yet, as witnesses in former slaves' pension cases describe how they came to know a claimant and the context within which a relationship was formed, we come to understand how a "community" was constituted. Some of the examples in this section illustrate that slaves were not isolated on a single plantation or farm but had contact with one another precisely because of their proximity to other slaveholders and/or because their masters were related. This contact allowed them to forge broader relationships beyond the holdings of their own masters. Readers of Civil War pension files also come to better understand how the exterior circumstances of slave owners' lives shape the interior lives of slaves and how these circumstances thus affected both the spatial and social dimensions of slave communities. One key theme that emerges from the pension files is the dispersal of communities resulting from changes in slave owners' personal or economic situations. Pension files also offer glimpses of the work that dominated slaves' lives. As historian Charles Joyner notes, "From the slaves' point of view, toil from sunup to sundown was part of the natural rhythm of the land and was a constant part of their collective experience."[4] As the pension files highlight the kinds of labor that slaves performed for their masters, the kinds of labor that they performed for themselves, and the hierarchies of labor among slaves, they provide insight into this collective, or social, dimension of work that played a role in the construction of social life in slave communities.

In a striking example, Anderson Logan, the father of Civil War soldier Boley Travis, lived in the same locale in Warren County, Missouri, all his life. To ascertain his financial condition (for much of the history of the Civil War pension system, a parent had to have been dependent on his or her dead son prior to the son's service to be eligible) and information about his relationship to his son, special examiner A. B. Casselman interviewed a number of people in 1882, black and white, who had known Logan during slavery and after. Taken together, the depositions of Logan's neighbors reveal the intersection of lives, black and white, slave and free, that shapes a community. Although the stories are not necessarily always clear as to how it happened, they show that in an area where owners often had smaller holdings (which tended to be the case in Missouri), slaves of different masters grew up together and knew one another all their lives. The lives of slaves and owners intersected one another as slaves married among the farms, visited their spouses and children, and worked as "hired hands" on neighboring holdings.

Excerpt from the Deposition of Abram Welsh, May 8, 1882, Civil War Pension File of Boley Travis, 65th USCI, RG 15:

Ques. How long have you known Anderson Logan?

Ans. I think it is not short of fifty years.

Ques. By whom were you owned and how near did you live to him when you first knew him?

Ans. I then belonged to Goren Spiers, and lived about 8 or 9 miles from Campbell Logans, where he was owned.

Ques. Was he married or single at that time?

Ans. He was then single. He afterwards married my wifes daughter, my stepdaughter, Sarah Travis.

Ques. Were you present at the marriage?

Ans. No sir. My wife was present but I was not.

Ques. How long ago was that?

Ans. It must have been fully thirty years ago, perhaps longer.

Ques. How many children did they have

Ans. They have had eight.

Ques. Did they live together as man and wife continuously after they were married

Ans. Yes sir.

Ques. Were either of them married before that

Ans. No sir, not that I know of.

Excerpt from the Deposition of Allen Powell, May 10, 1882, Civil War Pension File of Boley Travis, 65th USCI, RG 15:

Ques. How long have you known Anderson Logan?

Ans. I have known him at least thirty five years, ever since I was a lad of a boy. . . .

Ques. How long did you know Bowley before the war, how far did you live from him and how often did you see him.

Ans. I knew him ever since I was a small child, and lived about fifteen miles from him and I saw him about once in every three weeks when I went to see my wife, who lived close to him.

Ques. Did you serve in the same company with him in the army?

Ans. Yes sir, we all left Warrenton together, and I served with him until he died.

Excerpt from the Deposition of Robert Aistrop, May 9, 1882, Civil War Pension File of Boley Travis, 65th USCI, RG 15:

Ques. How long have you known Anderson Logan and what has been the nature of your acquaintance with him

Ans. I have known him a great many years, at least thirty years. I knew him as the slave of one of the Logans, I am not certain which one. His wife belonged to Thomas Travis, who lived about two miles from me.

Ques. Did he live with his wife, or how do you know that she was his wife?

Ans. He was there a great deal on Sundays in slave times. I have frequently seen him there on Sundays and then they lived together as man and wife after they were free. I do not know whether they were ever married but I do not doubt that they were.

Ques. Were they recognized as man and wife by their neighbors and masters,

Ans. Oh, I think so. They were thought a great deal of.

Ques. Were there any children who were recognized as being their children, by the neighbors

Ans. Yes sir, there were a good many, I do not know how many.

Ques. Can you name any of their children?

Ans. There is Sam, George, Birch, and the one that he is contending for a pension for. Bolick I think, and Bill and some girls.

Ques. What name do these children go by now

Ans. They go by the name of Logan, and have ever since they were freed.

Ques. How many slaves did Thomas Travis have

Ans. I think there were two families of slaves. Logans family and one other family.

Ques. What was Anderson Logan's physical condition or ability to do manual labor at the time he was freed

Ans. He has been a cripple, a right bad cripple ever since I knew him, and has been lame.

Ques. Was he then able to support himself?

Ans. Oh yes sir. He was able to make a support for himself. He worked at his trade. He was a factory hand, working at the tobacco factory. He was hired out all the time when he was a slave and got very good pay.

Ques. Did he work at that trade after he was freed

Ans. I don't think he ever did. I have often thought that he ought to have went at it. His sons have kept him since his wife died.

Ques. Has he any property, or has he had any since he was freed.

Ans. He has a horse, is all I know of.

Excerpt from the Deposition of John A. Aistrop, May 9, 1882, Civil War Pension File of Boley Travis, 65th USCI, RG 15:

Ques. How long have you known Anderson Logan,

Ans. I have known him about as long as I can recollect.

Ques. Has he been married during your acquaintance with him, If so who was his wife

Ans. His wifes name was Sarah, and she belonged to Thomas I. Travis ever since I can recollect.

Ques. Had they any children, and can you name them

Ans. I can name several of them. There was Sam, and Birch, George, Bill, Martha, Bowley, Fanny, and Kitty. I don't recollect any others?

Ques. Did these all pass as the children of Anderson Logan, among the neighbors

Ans. So I always understood.

Ques. What was his physical condition or his ability for manual labor at and prior to the time he was freed?

Ans. From the time he was freed I don't think he could hire out for his board, except among his children. I know I would not give him his board. He has been a cripple ever since I can recollect, being lame, and walking

> sideways. About 1859 I hired him about five months, from his mistress and gave twenty five dollars a month for him to roll tobacco and as a kind of boss in my tobacco factory. He knew a great deal about tobacco, and was very skillful in a factory. But he would be of no account at farm labor.
>
> Ques. Has he ever worked in a tobacco factory since he was free.
>
> Ans. Not to my knowledge.
>
> Ques. Would his labor in a factory have been as valuable since you hired him as at that time
>
> Ans. No sir, it would not. I doubt if he could have hired after the war for more than his board. His style of rolling tobacco had gone out of date.
>
> Ques. Has he supported himself since he was freed or been able to do so.
>
> Ans. No sir, not to my knowledge. He has lived with his children, and he depended on his wife when she was living.

Although not nearly as comprehensive as the evidence from Anderson Logan's claim, the following excerpts echo the depth of intimacy that characterized relationships between former slaves who knew each other over many decades. The nature of this intimacy is especially evident in the testimony of witnesses for Allie Green, the widow of Humphrey Green, who point to knowing Allie all their lives because their masters were father and son. These excerpts further demonstrate a variety of contexts within which slaves came to know one another and forge the bonds of community. For example, one witness for veteran Wiley Johnson explains that he knew Johnson in the context of belonging to the same owner and laboring together on the same plantation in Columbus, Georgia. The other suggests that as the foreman on a large plantation, Johnson was known among slaves in the locality in general. Also, William Estell, a witness for veteran Green Colyar, explained that he knew the claimant during slavery because his master and his master's sister lived near each other in a small town in Tennessee and that their slaves knew one another very well.

Excerpt from the Deposition of Marshall Gibson, Feb. 13, 1911, Civil War Pension File of Humphrey Green, 120th USCI and 6th USCC, RG 15:

> In slavery time we [Gibson and claimant, widow Allie Green] lived on joining farms and she belonged to my masters son. I have known her from the time I can remember knowing anyone.

Excerpt from the Deposition of Weston Gibson, Feb. 9, 1911, Civil War Pension File of Humphrey Green, 120th USCI and 6th USCC, RG 15:

> In slavery time she [widow Allie Green] belonged to William Gibson who was my masters son, I have known her from the time I first knew anyone. . . .
>
> Humphrey Green's former wife, Mariah belonged to the same man I did in slavery time.

Excerpt from the Deposition of George Powell, Feb. 9, 1911, Civil War Pension File of Humphrey Green, 120th USCI and 6th USCC, RG 15:

> I have known [widow Allie Green] from the time I was big enough to know anyone. We were both owned in the same neighborhood in slavery time.

Excerpt from the Deposition of Cornelius McElvy, Jan. 27, 1894, Civil War Pension File of Wiley Johnson, 136th USCI, RG 15:

> I have known [Wiley Johnson] ever since I can remember. I knew him long before the war. We both lived here in this neighborhood. Claimt [Claimant] was raised in Washington, Ga, and was owned by Gabriel Toombs, and Mr. Toombs owned a plantation near here and this claimt worked on that. He was working on that plantation at the time of his enlistment. This claimt was foreman on the plantation.

Excerpt from the Deposition of Ned Gressom, Jan. 27, 1894, Civil War Pension File of Wiley Johnson, 136th USCI, RG 15:

> I knew this claimt long before the war, was intimate with him during the war, and have known him ever since the war. . . . This claimt and I belonged to Gabriel Toombs, who lived in Washington, Wilkes Co., Ga. who owned a plantation here and a great many of his negroes worked here.

Excerpt from the Deposition of William Estell, July 27, 1887, Civil War Pension File of Green Colyar (alias Collier), 15th USCI, RG 15:

> I am 43 years of age. I am a native of Lincoln Co. Tenn. and lived at Winchester. I was born a slave & became the slave of Dr Henry Estell the brother-in-law of Col A.S. Colyer the editor & proprietor of the large "American" newspaper of this city. My master & his sister Mrs Colyers

> slaves were intimate all in the same small town. And I was with those Col A.S. Colyer bought. When the late war came up at the Murfreesboro fight we went South Col A.S. Colyer became a member of the Confederate Congress. I was with him at Richmond. Col Colyer left several of his slaves at home among them Green Colyar a youngster who was perfectly sound & well when we left home.

The very existence of slave communities in the sense that historians have come to understand them, as vibrant and thriving social networks, is all the more incredible in light of the tenuous nature of that existence. The experience of being human chattel punctuates former slaves' pension files, especially in the sense of how contingent slaves' daily experiences were on the economic and social circumstances of their owners' lives. When an owner died or went into debt or married off one of his children, his slaves' lives were altered. Being bequeathed, sold, or offered as a gift resulted in separation from families, friends, and often entire communities. In this section, readers can see more generally how separation affected communities by shaping and reshaping their constitution and social interactions. We will return to the theme of separation in chapter 4, where we will examine closely the effect of separation on slave families in particular.

Although the following two examples focus on the experience of single individuals, they shed light on the internal slave trade so prevalent in the decades prior to the war, which was a major source of disruption and dispersal of slave communities. For reasons unexplained in his pension file, Hiram Kirkland went through six masters before his last. The high price paid for him by that last master suggests that Kirkland, a Tennessee veteran, had been a strong and/or skilled worker. In the crude reckoning of the slave trade, that made Kirkland a valuable commodity and unlikely to be traded. However, a particularly telling comment suggests why he was traded so often: he appears to have been unwilling to submit to the will of slaveholders. One Pension Bureau questionnaire intended to establish identity asks, "Are there any permanent marks or scars on your person?" Kirkland responded, "some scars on my back made in slave times," suggesting that he had been whipped or punished in some other violent manner.[5] Charles Washington was one of hundreds of thousands of slaves sold from Florida west to support the expansion of the flourishing cotton kingdom before the Civil War (in his case to Louisiana). Although both Kirkland and Washington were silent on the issue of being separated from their families, the fact that they were sold numer-

Hiram Kirkland (alias Kirkham), 101st and 110th U.S. Colored Infantry

ous times suggests that they were. When Washington went off to war, he was separated from his wife and children. As the war approached, Washington's master moved his slaves to Texas, a practice common among slaveholders who hoped to retain their slaves by keeping them away from the path of Union forces.

Excerpt from the Deposition of Hiram Kirkland, Nov. 26, 1902, Civil War Pension File of Hiram Kirkland, 101st USCI and 110th USCI, RG 15:

> My first master was John Casson. I was born "low down in Miss. My next master was Mr. Lively. Milton McClure was my next after him came Latham then Hamilton Pickens who sold me to James Kirkland for \$1700^{00}. . . .
>
> Mr Kirkland only owned three negroes, myself wife (decd) and Don Bishop. Don Bishop was still living with the old master when I was down there about 20 years ago

Excerpt from the Deposition of Charles Washington, Dec. 18, 1905, Civil War Pension File of Charles Washington, 47th USCI, RG 15:

> I was born in the state of Flordida [sic], and lived there until I was quite a lad of a boy and then I was sold to a man by the name of Thompson, who sold me to a man by the name of Randolph, and was then put into the trad-

> ers yard at New Orleans, La., and there a man by the name of Dr. Vincent, who lived on Joe's Bayou, who lived eighteen miles from Lake Providence, and he owned me for a long time, until I was a grown man, and had a wife and three children, and th then Dr. Vincent, or Dr. Vinson, sold me to Mr. James Berry, who livnd on the Mississippi River, up Lake Providence, not far from Longwood plantation. He lived there, but he owned the Vincent plantation. I never lived on the place where Mr. Berry lived. I was there on the place sometimes, would go there to take his wife home when she would come down to the plantation, and would occasionally drive his carriage home, when he would be on the plantation. I had been the slave of Mr. Berry for about four years when I went into the service, and he was my owner when I enlisted. Mr. Berry bought Dr. Vinson's plantation and all of his slaves. Did not any one of his slaves who went into the army with me. After I left home to go into the army, Mr. Be[rry] carried all of his slaves who had remained at home, to the state of Texas, and I have never heard of any of them. I was a married man, and had three children and he carried them to Texas, and I have never heard of them since. My wife was called Julia Ruffin all the time, but my boys went by the name Washington. When I enlisted I did not personally know any member of my company before I enlisted. I was not asked how old I was when I enlisted, if they did I have forgotten it. They asked me who owned me. They did not tell me how tall I was when they measured me, and do not know how tall I was. Do not know what year I was born. Question. How then do you arrive at your age. Answer. My mother told me one Christmas, that I was twelve years old, and I have been trying to keep my age as near as I could ever since. Do not know long I had been married before I went into the service, but had been married long enough to be the father of three children when I left home. Have no idea how old I was when I was married. I think I was a slave of Dr. Vinson about thrity or forty years, and he bought me as a boy eleven years old. No sir, I did not have any peculiar marks about me. My color was light brown. When I enlisted I had a little mustasche, and some chin whiskers, but they had not "growed" to do any good, "they have growed out since." I have never shaved but one time, and never had shaved when I enlisted.

The experiences of Benjamin B. Manson and Austin Waters exemplify ways in which slave owners used slaves as currency and how that practice contributed to the disruption of communities as individual members were arbitrarily removed to suit their masters' needs. After having been bequeathed to one of his master's heirs, Manson was later used to resolve a financial problem for his new owner. Waters belonged to his young master, Zachariah, a boy who possessed slaves before he was even old enough to bear that responsibility. Waters's mother served as the payment to Zachariah's grandfather for raising and educating him, while her children remained the young man's property.

Excerpt from the Deposition of Benjamin B. Manson, July 1909, Civil War Pension File of John White, 14th USCI, RG 15:

> I am a colored man, now 83 years of age. I was born in the State of Va as the property of Mrs Nancy Manson of said State. When I was about 11 years of age my owner, Mrs Nancy Manson, moved to the State of Tennessee, bringing her slaves with her. When she died her slaves were divided up among her children. In this division I fell to her son Joseph Manson. When I was about 18 or 19 years of age I married Sarah who was the property of Dr L.B. White, of Wilson County, Tenn, in which County my owner lived. John was our first child. As was the costom in that day and time, John went by the name of his owner and grew up and was known by the name of John White.
>
> Joseph Manson, to whom I belonged, married a daughter of my wifes owner, Dr L.B. White. Several years before the civil war, my said owner became financially involved in some way and I became the property of Dr White. After the death of Dr White and a few years before the civil war, in some sort of a family settlement, I again became the property of my former owner . . . Joseph Manson.

Excerpt from the Deposition of Austin Waters, Jan. 19, 1914, Civil War Pension File of Austin Waters, 15th USCI, RG 15:

> I was born near Shelby Bedford Co. Tenn. I do not know the date. I was a slave. Belonged to Zachariah Waters then and belonged till the war started. I lived with a [man] named Cleggett, grandfather of Waters. Zachariah was not of [age] when I was born. When I was a small boy Cleggett moved to Centerville Hickman Co. Tenn. We stayed a year at Shelby Tenn., and then moved to Hickman Co. too. I lived there with Zachariah Waters who had come of age meantime till the war came on and I got with the yankees. My father was Fairfax Claggett. He belonged to Mr. Cleggett grandfather of my master. My mother was Ada. Belonged to Cleggett too. She was sold

> [to] Cleggett as pay for raising and scholling [schooling] my master and all her children belonged to Zachariah Waters. My father died in time of the war. Mother died between Springfield and Nashville Tenn., after the war while I was in the regular army. I do not know the date of her death. I had four brothers; George, John, Jim, and Burton, John went by the name of Cleggett, and the balance went by the name of Waters.

Just as communities of slaves lost members, they gained them, too, as their owners purchased or otherwise acquired new slaves. An example of the broadening of slave communities, from the file of Isaac Perkins, also underscores the institution of slavery's indifference to slave families. Caesar Perkins was sixty-five in 1891 when he offered the following testimony in support of his brother's widow. He described being taken from Virginia to be sold into the Deep South with his brother, each to a different owner. Perkins's testimony suggests that the rest of the family was left behind. In this instance, however, brothers Caesar and Isaac may have considered themselves fortunate since they were sold in the same location (Louisiana) and saw each other regularly. As each was introduced to a new plantation, Caesar and Isaac's bond to each other may have brought two communities together or may have strengthened the connection within a community that already crossed plantations.

Excerpt from the Affidavit of Caesar Perkins, May 9, 1891, Civil War Pension File of Isaac Perkins, 58th USCI, RG 15:

> I was the brother of Isaac Perkins who went in the U.S. Army as private Co. F 58 USCol. Infty. We came together from Virginia. We belonged to D[r] Tom Martin who lived in Hartford, Va. We left Virginia on the 22d day of March, 1850 & we were brought 12 miles below Baton Rouge & after 6 weeks we were brought to Natchez, Miss, and were sold to planters in Concordia; I was sold to Alfred Davis and Isaac Perkins was sold to D[r] Sanderson on Hill Place 15 miles from Natchez Miss. I know that Isaac Perkins was a single man when he first met Jane Perkins who was on the Hill place when we were brought there. He never had been married to any other woman before he married Jane his widow. She was only single and had never married. I know this of my own personal knowledge because I was present and saw them nearly every day up to his enlistment in the U.S. Army.

Labor shaped slaves' lives not only because it was their primary activity but also because it determined with whom they spent their time and it created hierarchies of relationships among them. Most former slaves simply described their occupations before the war as that of field hands or farmers, indicative of the fact that most slaves toiled in the fields. Yet the pension files also illustrate a complex hierarchy and variety of occupations on many plantations, with some slaves holding jobs that denoted special skills, privileges, and a position of trust. (For example, recall that Wiley Johnson was a foreman on his master's plantation.) Even decades after slavery's end, former slave Alexander Porter, who lived in Kentucky after the war, seemed defensive about his position as a house slave, a personal servant of his owner. Porter's insistence that he could have performed the more strenuous work of field labor suggests that there may have been some rivalry between slaves who worked in the master's house and slaves who toiled in the fields or performed other kinds of skilled labor. These rivalries no doubt influenced the way slaves within a community interacted with one another. Clearly more confident about his occupation during slavery, Benjamin Courtney, who lived in Illinois after the war, testified that he was a blacksmith by the time he was just eighteen years of age. Blacksmithing required both skill and strength, and the price of two thousand dollars at which he was sold indicated that Courtney possessed both.

Excerpt from the Deposition of Alexander Porter, May 3, 1900, Civil War Pension File of Alexander Porter, 58th USCI, RG 15:

> I was born and raised near Meadvillle, Franklin Co., Miss. and lived there up to enlistment. I only had one master and his name was Wm. Porter (dec'd) I have not heard from my old mistress Mary Porter directly since I enlisted, but I think my old mistress was still living at Meadville, Miss., about 3 years ago. She was a little older than myself. . . .
>
> I worked on my master's plantation but I did not do much hard work. I was a carriage driver and house man. It was not because I was not able for hard work but because I was raised around the house that I was kept from that work.

Excerpt from the Affidavit of Benjamin Courtney, Apr. 28, 1908, Civil War Pension File of Benjamin Courtney, 51st USCI, RG 15:

> I was a man stout and healthy over 27 years of age when I enlisted in the war of the Rebellion, and that I was a large healthy Robust man when I enlisted in the army Shoeing horses and Blacksmithing at the time and my master [was] Robert Marshal at Fayette Co. Lexington, Kentucky and was sold to J.F. Wilkinson in about the year 1856, and I was then large enough and man enough that I was Blacksmithing and Shoeing horses the reason why the party wanted to buy me and they paid $2,000 for me at that time I am unable to furnish any other evidence except this mentioned on account of my Master is dead and all the parties that new anything about me at that time is dead. . . .

In the evenings after the sun went down, on Sundays, and on holidays, slave owners gave their slaves "free" time, time for themselves, their families, and their communities away from the watchful eyes of whites. It would be a mistake to think of this as leisure time; clearly much of the slaves' "free" time was spent in pursuit of daily survival. In this small space of time that was their own, slaves participated in what historians have identified as an independent economy, one in which they produced, bartered, bought, and sold goods and food among themselves and with whites. Historians have identified how slaves benefited from this independent economy. Slaves were able to improve their diet through the crops they grew on provision grounds provided by slaveholders, sometimes got paid for overtime work, and found other ways to earn money, in some cases accumulating enough money to purchase their freedom or that of their family members. In testimony supporting her mother's claim for pension, Juda Gray, a former slave from Virginia, describes how her son, Alfred, used this time away from work to produce goods to sell and, in turn, bought his mother food and clothing to help make her daily survival more comfortable. Gray's testimony and that of her master's daughter, Margaret C. Wood, offer insight into how some slaves spent their time in the few hours away from work. Wood's testimony also illustrates what it meant for slaves to be "hired out" from one owner to another. In this instance, after her father's death, Wood's family hired Alfred out to another man. While Alfred toiled for this man, his master's heirs received the pay.

Excerpt from the Deposition of Juda Gray, Apr. 21, 1886, Civil War Pension File of Alfred Gray, 42nd USCI, RG 15:

> I have never been married. I was a slave until freed by President Lincoln, and was the property of Alexander Gray, now dead. I have had twelve

> children, two girls and ten boys. Only four of these children are living at the present time, so far as I know. I haven't seen any of the other children since the war, and I don't know whether they are dead or alive. . . . All my children were illegitimate. Alfred lived and worked at Alexander Hall's until the war,—and James also. I cannot remember just when he left here, but it was not a great while before the war closed. He went to Kentucky and enlisted. . . . Alfred helped me a good deal before he left. He used to help me along. He game me clothing, and things to use. He used to give me handkerchiefs occasionally. He gave me two dresses during the war. He bought coffee and one thing and another and gave me: this was during the war, and while he was in bondage. I was a slave also at the time, and my master provided clothing, and supported me, every bit as he did the other slaves. Slaves always had their Sundays to themselves; and Saturday Evenings, and during those times he would work, earn money and help me.

Excerpt from the Affidavit of Margaret C. Wood, date unknown, Civil War Pension File of Alfred Gray, 42nd USCI, RG 15:

> That when Alfred Gray the soldier worked at home he worked for his master, except when he worked of holidays and sometimes of wet days and sometimes of Sundays and sometimes of long winter nights at such work as making horse collars and baskets and split broomes which he was allowed to sell and use as he pleased. after the death of his master he was hired out to work for the heirs of his master Alexander Gray The soldier Alfred Gray did not receive or get the pay.

Personal Identity: Names and Ages

Questions about names resonate throughout former slaves' pension files because no formal system by which surnames were determined existed in slavery. Slaveholders generally did not assign slaves their own surnames, though they referred to slaves by their owner's surname as a means of signifying to whom they belonged. As evidence from the pension files illustrates, slaves' practices with regard to assigning or choosing surnames varied. Since the surname was considered a significant marker of identity in free society, the fact that former slaves had none or had several surnames over the course of a lifetime was a subject of much discussion in their pension claims. Age, too, was a crucial element of identity and the fact that most slaves did not know their date of birth made establishing their identity difficult. What is evident in the following excerpts related to both names and age is the inextricable nature of the relationship between literacy and identity.

Identity

As he searched for witnesses who could attest to Frank Finley's health prior to the war, special examiner Thomas MacBride lamented that name changes made it difficult to find former slaves. His comments are a reminder that changing names after emancipation was a frequent practice among former slaves. Under slavery, whites often identified slaves by using as the slave's surname that of his or her owner. For whites, this signified a relation of property. Slaves used their owner's surnames sometimes out of convenience, sometimes because for them it marked a familial relationship or broader ties to other slaves of the same owner. MacBride attaches a kind of arbitrariness or a lack of much thought to former slaves' practice of changing their names. For a few, perhaps, this was the case. Most chose new names purposefully. As is evident in the following excerpts, changing a surname had varied meanings, from casting off slavery's bonds to making connections to family members.

Excerpt from Thomas MacBride, Special Examiner, Lexington, Ky., to the Commissioner of Pensions, Washington, D.C., Sept. 22, 1889, Civil War Pension File of Frank Finley (alias Brown), 119th USCI, RG 15:

> If [witness] Thomas Walker is living in or about Lexington, Ky., he is probably living under an assumed name. No such person appears to be known here—there are many Walkers but no Thomas Walker. Negroes, hereabouts, change their names frequently. Many have resumed their family names who served under the name of their respective masters—Others again assume any name to which they take fancy—and in some instances have assumed another Christian name.

The two examples that follow, from Smith Jackson of Alabama and Glenn Booker of Arkansas, illustrate the predominant practice among male former slaves of taking one's father's surname. In many cases, this act provided a means of honoring family lines in face of slavery's unfeeling disregard for them and asserting patriarchal connections.

Excerpt from the Affidavit of Smith Jackson, Apr. 7, 1906, Civil War Pension File of Smith Buchanan (alias Jackson), 136th USCI, RG 15:

> My father's name was Gilbert Jackson, and after I was set free I took the name of my father, and have been known by the name of Smith Jackson. I took the name of Jackson for the reason that I prefered to go by my father's name, rather than the name of my last owner.

Excerpt from the Deposition of Henry Lock Rollie, Dec. 19, 1908, Civil War Pension File of Glenn Booker, 2nd USCLA, RG 15:

> I have known Harriet Booker, the claimant named above about 40 years and knew her husband, Glenn Booker, about 45 years. I was a soldier in Co. E 2nd U.S.C.L.A., the same company in which Glenn Booker served.
>
> I did not know him till we were mustered [out] in November 1865. I served as Henry Lock the Lock being my "Old Massa's" name but since the War I have taken my father's name of Rollie.

In some cases, former slaves did not necessarily know fathers to whom a surname connected them. As Dick Lewis Barnett (who lived in Alabama before moving to Oklahoma) explains, taking one's father's surname signified the act of a free man since, in free society, surnames reflected the paternal line. So in Barnett's case, taking his father's last name was a purely symbolic act since he did not even know the man's identity until returning from the Union army at the end of his Civil War service. It did not matter that he was not on intimate terms with his father or that his father was white. What mattered most to Barnett was being known by his father's surname, for that was the badge of a free man in a time and place where patriarchal identity was integral to a man's status and self-respect.

Excerpt from the Deposition of Dick Lewis Barnett, May 17, 1911, Civil War Pension File of Lewis Smith (alias Dick L. Barnett), 77th USCI, RG 15:

> I was born in Montgomery Co. Ala. the child of Phillis Houston, slave of Sol Smith. When I was born my mother was known as Phillis Smith and I took the name of Smith too. I was called mostly Lewis Smith till after the war, although I was named Dick Lewis Smith—Dick was the brother of John Barnett whom I learned was my father after I got back from the war, when my mother told me that John Barnett was my father. . . .

Lewis Smith (alias Dick Lewis Barnett), 77th U.S. Colored Infantry, and his wife, Eliza

> When I got home after the war, I was wearing the name of Lewis Smith, but I found that the negroes after freedom, were taking the names of their father like the white folks. So I asked my mother and she told me my father was John Barnett, a white man, and I took up the name of Barnett.

Many slave women, such as widow Julia Clark, used their master's surnames in slavery and their husband's surnames in freedom, which underscores the profound transformation that freedom wrought for slave couples. When free women married, they took their husband's surname, a practice that reflected both the patrilineal and legal nature of marriage and family in the free society of nineteenth-century America. The laws of slavery failed to recognize or to protect slave families; marriages between slaves existed only as long as owners allowed. Thus, although slave women may have used their husband's names, theirs was a practice that lacked formal standing in the eyes of free society. As we will see in chapter 4, freedom (and subsequent legislation in Southern states) afforded former slaves formal recognition of and protection for marriages.

Excerpt from the Deposition of Julia Clark, Apr. 17, 1894, Civil War Pension File of Mark Clark, 2nd USCLA, RG 15:

> Before the war I belonged to Enoch Steward about 18 miles East of Friar's Point in Coahoma Co. Miss. I lived on his place until the Monday after the fight on Big Creek, Ark when I came here to Helena—Ark. No Sir, I never was married before I married Mark Clark. I got the name of Steward from my old master—

Mollie Russell, wife of a Kentucky veteran, applied for a widow's pension after her husband died in 1906. Some question arose as to Russell's proper first name, a problem that could have jeopardized her claim if it somehow hampered her ability to prove she was the soldier's widow. The widow's account of how she acquired her name exposes the fact that slave owners, who named their slaves as they desired, in some cases tried to continue this practice after freedom. It reveals that some former slaveholders had still not accepted symbolically the full personhood of freed people. However, Russell's deposition also reveals the agency that former slaves found in taking names for themselves.

Excerpt from the Deposition of Mollie Russell, Sept. 19, 1911, Civil War Pension File of Phillip Russell (alias Fry), 114th USCI, RG 15:

> Q. Tell me the name you were called before you met Phillip Fry?
>
> A. Lottie Smith was my name and what they called me before I met Phillip and was married to him.
>
> Q. Who called you by that name and where was it done?
>
> A. I was first called by that name in the family of Col. Morrow in whose service I was in Louisville, Ky., just after the war. I worked for him as nurse for his children, and my full and correct name was OCTAVIA, but the family could not "catch on" to that long name and called me "LOTTIE" for short. LOTTIE had been the name of the nurse before me and so they just continued that same name. I was called by that name all the time I was with the Morrows. . . .
>
> Q. Besides the Morrows, whom else did you live with in Louisville?
>
> A. Mr. Thomas Jefferson of Louisville, bought me when I was three years of age from Mr. Dearing. I belonged to him until emancipation. They called me "OCK". They cut it off from OCTAVIA. It was after emancipation on that I went to work for Col. Morrow and where I got the name

> "Lottie," as already explained. I liked the name better than Octavia, and so I took it with me to Danville, and was never called by anything else there than that name. . . .
>
> Q. How did you ever come by the name of "Mollie"?
>
> A. After I had returned to Louisville from Danville, My sister, Lizzie White, got to calling me Mollie, and it was with her that the name started.
>
> Q. Where did you get the maiden name of Smith from?
>
> A. My mother's name was Octavia Smith and it was from her that I got it but where the name came from to her I never knew. I was only three years old when she died. No, I dont know to whom she belonged before she was brought from Virginia to Kentucky.

In noting that he took his first owner's surname, William Ballinger, a Mississippi veteran, offers a variation on the practice of taking a new surname by using that of his first master. This practice was relatively common and thus bears careful consideration. In some cases, taking a former owner's surname was simply a matter of convenience: here was a surname readily available that was distinct from a more recent experience of slavery. In other cases, taking the name might connote a personal attachment to the former owner. However, many former slaves associated surnames not with owners at all but with their family members who carried the names. Choosing that name was meant to invoke those familial connections; a first owner's name might have been considered a point of origin for family history. Former slaves' pension files demonstrate that, whatever the circumstances, if a former slave assumed a first owner's name, it was a consequence of his or her own free choice as a free person.[6]

Excerpt from the Deposition of William Ballinger, Oct. 10, 1901, Civil War Pension File of William Ballinger, 58th USCI, RG 15:

> I was born in Birmingham Co. Va. and Henry Treat, an old man was my master. I was sold to Miss. when I was a small boy and my last owner was Solomon Stampley. . . . I was 40 years old the year the Yankees took Vicksburg, Miss. . . .
>
> When I was brought here as a boy my first master was Jesse Ballinger and I took the name of Ballinger then and I have never changed it.

James Mabin, a Missouri veteran, told his special examiner two interesting stories about his different surnames. The first illustrates how names might be changed inadvertently in the military. In the second, Mabin explains that it was his master who recommended that he take his father's name, which suggests that not all former slaveholders were unwilling to accept the personhood of their former property and sought to guide them in establishing proper identities as free people. Mabin's testimony reveals that he had been sold as a baby to Uries Gordon and that Mabin's father had belonged to Gordon's cousin. Since Mabin learned of his father's identity after the war, it appears that father and son had been separated during slavery.

Excerpt from the Deposition of James H. Mabin, Jan. 2, 1894, Civil War Pension File of James Henry (2nd) (alias James H. Gordon, alias James H. Mabin), 60th USCI, RG 15:[7]

> My age is 42 My name that I am now and have been known by since the war is James H. Mabin. I am the claimant. I reside in Centralia Mo. I filed my claim under the name of James Gordon as that was the name under which I served. My name before the war was James Henry Gordon, that was the name I went by amongst the white folks. . . . They called me "James Henry 2d" when they were calling the roll. There was another man, James Henry Casanders, whose name came ahead of mine on the roll call, and sometimes when I would not answer to "James Henry 2d" they would call James Henry Gordon. Before my enlistment I belonged to Uries Gordon who lived about 18 miles southwest of Jefferson City, Mo I was born in Jefferson City Mo. as the property of Martha Gordon, and Uries Gordon bought me when I was a baby and took me out onto his farm and I lived there until my enlistment. . . .
>
> My father's name was Richard Mabin. After the war was over and I had gone back to my old master he said to me "Why don't you take your father's name? He then told me that my fathers name was Richard Mabin and that he belonged to his cousin, so I took the name of Mabin.

The long string of aliases following Mississippi veteran William L. Dickinson's name (Dixon, Dickson, and Dickerson) calls to mind the problems that illiteracy can create in the process of establishing one's identity. White scribes finding it hard to understand the pronunciation of African Americans were more likely to misconstrue or misspell their last names, and, because of their illiteracy, ex-slaves were unable to correct the error at the time it was made, creating unintentional aliases. Dickinson's testimony offers a compelling account of how such problems arise.

Excerpt from the Affidavit of William L. Dickerson, Oct. 23, 1902, William L. Dickinson (alias Dixon, Dickson, and Dickerson), 14th USCI, RG 15:

> I came to Miss. in 1866. I have lived near Oxford, Water Valy Coffeeville, Torrance, & Hardy Station, Miss. I went to Memphis to draw my bounty after the war. I cannot read nor write, and I donot know how my name was spelled when I enlisted in the army, nor do I know how it is spelled now. I did not intend to change my name, but if it is diferent from the way I enlisted it was changed by the parties that filled out my papers—I donot know of a single one of my comerades living—I always signed my name while in the army by making my mark. . . . I know my name by sound. . . .

Thomas Wilbourn, a Texas veteran (born in Georgia), had to explain to pension officials why he enlisted under one name but subsequently went by another. Wilbourn recounted that when he enlisted, he did so under what he believed was his father's name. Only after the war did he learn that he had taken the wrong name. His illiteracy probably created his situation, the fact of only hearing and never seeing written his own name. Wilbourn, who signed his own name to his 1909 deposition, told the special examiner, "I could not write in the army. I commenced studying in 1874."[8] Wilbourn's experience of using one name and then discovering that he had misheard it or misunderstood it was a common phenomenon among former slaves precisely because of their illiteracy. Often, when they learned the correct spelling of the name, former slaves adopted what they believed to be their proper names.

Excerpt from the Deposition of Thomas W. Wilbourn, Apr. 14, 1909, Civil War Pension File of Thomas Wilbert (alias Thomas W. Wilbourn), 122nd USCI, RG 15:

> I was born May 10, 1847, at Atlanta, Georgia. There is no Bible record or public record or other record of my birth that I know of. I was born in slavery times and was born a slave. L.J. Gottrell was my master. My father's name was George Wilbourn. My mother was Jane. She was raised by the Gideons and was Emancipated. But I don't know anything about it. . . .

(Ques.) By what name were you known before you enlisted? (Ans.) When I enlisted I thought my name was Thomas Wilbert, and I gave that as my name. After the war I wrote back to my mother in care of W. H. Quarles . . . who was a preacher. My mother belonged to his church. He wrote me that my mother was dead, and that her name was Jane Wilbourn and not Wilbert. That was 42 years ago or about that time. . . . My father's name was Wilbourn. That is where the name came from.

Reckoning Age

Mississippian Willis Wisher also took his father's name after slavery. In addition, Wisher's age was at issue in his case. Here special examiner F. S. Becker dispassionately notes that former slaves did not know their ages or their birth dates. Such lack of knowledge has deeper meaning than the "ignorance" to which many government agents attributed it; instead it signifies both the illiteracy of slaves, who were denied education, and, as Frederick Douglass argued, the power of owners to control their slaves by withholding from them the elements of their identity. As former soldier Benjamin Courtney put it, "there is no obtainable evidence of the correct date of my Birth, only what I have heard from my master and people I was raised with and there is no baptismal record. . . . I was a slave in that time and they would not allow us to know our own age."[9] Ex-slaves' pension claims are littered with statements by claimants and witnesses who simply did not know their age or date of birth.

Excerpt from the Deposition of Willis Wisher, Jan. 3, 1907, Civil War Pension File of Willis Fowler (alias Wisher), 2nd USCLA, RG 15:

> I was born on John Fowler's place which is about 2 miles from my present home. Bill Oden(?) owned the place when I was born but when he died we fell to Oden's son-in-law John Fowler. I lived on said place until I enlisted and when I was [mustered out] I went right back there and have never lived farther than 3 miles from my birth place. . . .
>
> I was 32 years old when I enlisted. I was 5 feet 10 inches tall. I will never forget that. . . .
>
> I recall that when I was first examined at Helena, I gave my age as 49 years, but since then I have learned from my discharge that I was older.

F. S. Becker, Special Examiner, Memphis, Tenn., to the Commissioner of Pensions, Washington, D.C., Mar. 22, 1907, Civil War Pension File of Willis Fowler (alias Wisher), 2nd USCLA, RG 15:

> claim was returned to this district for explanation of the vast discrepancy of ten years between War Dept. record and plantation record. The examiner is of course unable to explain how claimant's age happened to be recorded as 32 years at enlistment. Claimant is unable to explain. He could but guess at his age. It is clear to anyone familiar with this race of people that they do not know their age and don't know what a birthday is. . . . The plantation record is no doubt correct as it was carefully kept and the ages of all slaves were recorded therein. This was to be expected as the age of a slave had a great deal to do with his value.

The efforts of Frank Morse, a Kentucky veteran, to clarify facts about his name and age reveal the tangled relationship of literacy and identity. Morse could not read or write his own name, leaving him vulnerable to problems of miscommunication. Illiteracy also forced Morse to rely on the son of his former owner to help establish his age. In this instance, a copy of the bill of sale provides the mechanism by which Morse's age was determined.

Excerpt from the Affidavit of Frank Morse, Nov. 7, 1892, Civil War Pension File of Frank Morse, 8th USCHA, RG 15:

> my real and correct name is as above stated, and I belonged to Jeff Morse and this way acquired my name given above. I have no education and cannot read or wright & if my name was on Co. F 8th US Hevy. Art as Franklin Mass I dident know it & I couldent have told the difference If I had seen it. Persons who was intimate with my masters family tell me his name was spelled morse.

Excerpt from the Affidavit of John K. Morse, Feb. 18, 1908, Civil War Pension File of Frank Morse, 8th USCHA, RG 15:

> This man Frank Morse was purchased by my Father Jefferson G. Morse in the year Jan the 16th 1846 from a man by the name of Baley This man Frank Morse was said to be 10 years old when purchased. This Feb 18th 1908 purchased Jan 6th 1846 which would make his age 72 years one month and 12 days old.

Excerpt from the Affidavit of John K. Morse, Apr. 21, 1908, Civil War Pension File of Frank Morse, 8th USCHA, RG 15:

> Billisale [bill of sale] of Frank Morse given to J. G. Morse by James Bayley dated Jan the 6th 1846 said Frank 10 years old when purchast—so sais billiesale.

Arthur Smith, too, attempted to narrow down his date of birth by using dates he could remember. Why he remembered the date that he was hired out as a slave is unclear. Possibly, his master never told Smith, an Arkansas veteran, his date of birth, so when he heard a date that might have given him a clue, he remembered it. In any case, it shows how slaves tended to reckon the passage of time by reference to events rather than to calendar dates.

Excerpt from the Affidavit of Arthur Smith, Feb. 3, 1908, Civil War Pension File of Arthur Smith, 137th USCI, RG 15:

> Arthur Smith hearing sworn makes the falling statement in 1858 I Belong to James H. Smith . . . I was app[r]aised That year and Highered out My Master Told the man i was Born in 1835 Feby 16
>
> i have No Record other Than This

In the process of attempting to acquire an increase in his pension under the law of February 6, 1907, questions arose about Solomon Lambert's age. This piece of legislation for the first time by statute tied pension eligibility for Union veterans to age instead of disability. Essentially, in passing the law, Congress codified what had been practiced for several years, which was recognizing that old age itself was a form of disability. As per the requirements of the law, Lambert needed to show that he was over the age of sixty-two to be eligible for a pension. Initially, Lambert explains why he cannot furnish information about his age to the satisfaction of the Pension Bureau. Later, he is able to obtain evidence from two former owners in the form of their short statements written on a letter that Lambert had from the Pension Bureau. Lambert's letter of explanation regarding that evidence suggests the undesirable position in which ex-slaves often found themselves when seeking help from former owners.

Excerpt from Solomon Lambert, Holly Grove, Arkansas, to J. L. Davenport, Acting Commissioner of Pensions, Washington, D.C., Oct. 4, 1908, Civil War Pension File of Solomon Lambert, 2nd USCLA, RG 15:

> When I enlisted my Capt informed me that I was 18 years of age. Which was 1864 and my former Master told me I was that age and that seems to be the proff I could Furnish the Pension office. . . . My master Jod Lambert died 1890 and That the family Bible that contained all of the Births and ages and was Burned some years after His death.

Excerpt from Solomon Lambert, Holly Grove, Arkansas, to the Department of the Interior, Sept. 3, 1910, Civil War Pension File of Solomon Lambert, 2nd USCLA, RG 15:

> Dear Sirs;
>
> You will notice on the back of your letter of the 15th . . . at the bottom of same what is stated by Judge Grant Greer and J.J. Mayo respectively and if their statement will be of any benefit, please use it. You know we have once been these peoples' slaves, and it is a matter of the most delicate nature to ask them to help to obtain a pension in the cause in which they were engaged and lost. They therefore will only make written statements.
>
> Hope you will take this matter under consideration.
>
> Respectfully yours,
> Solomon Lambert

If a veteran could not produce material evidence of his age, the Pension Bureau encouraged special examiners to find other means of determining as accurately as possible his date of birth. In a section entitled "Colored Claimants" in the Bureau's *General Instructions to Special Examiners of the U.S. Pension Bureau,* agents were instructed, "In claims by colored persons it will generally be necessary to call the attention of the witnesses to some important event, holiday, &c., to enable them to testify with any approach to accuracy in regard to dates. For example, a witness may be able to tell how long before the war or after the capture of Port Hudson, or some other important event, a marriage, birth, &c., occurred."[10] In other words, the Pension Bureau tried to approximate calendar dates by tying them to the major events that the ex-soldier or other black witnesses could remember.

The Pension Bureau's tactics in determining birth and other dates reflects the importance of the oral tradition among slave communities. The absence of literacy did not mean an absence of memory or history among slaves, who have been noted by historians for a rich oral culture that featured storytelling, music, and spoken language as a means of passing on significant information from one generation to the next.[11] As indicated in the Bureau's instructions to its special examiners, slaves used major events as markers by which to recall the details of their personal and collective experiences, a typical practice among oral cultures. Thus, for example, a memorable natural event, a disease epidemic, or a momentous personal event such as being hired out for the first time or getting married might serve as a means by which slaves could date other events in their lives.

Henry Haddox, a Tennessee veteran, could not offer an accurate guess of his calendar age. Special examiner W. L. Sullivan talked to a number of Haddox's relatives, most likely trying to approximate Haddox's age by reconciling events in his life with events in their lives. Although their testimony did not help much in the effort to determine Haddox's age, it does offer us tantalizing glimpses of his life as a young slave, as well as of family and community in slavery.

Excerpt from the Deposition of Henry Haddox, Dec. 13, 1905, Civil War Pension File of Henry Haddox, 17th USCI and 101st USCI, RG 15:

> I don't know how old I was when I enlisted. I don't know whether I was 18 years old or 25 years or 40 years I belonged to Dr. Haddox of Spring Hill, Tenn. None of his family are now living.

Excerpt from the Deposition of Delia Bond, Nov. 6, 1906, Civil War Pension File of Henry Haddox, 17th USCI and 101st USCI, RG 15:

> I was about 22 years old when I married. I married 8 years before the war.
>
> Henry Haddox of Columbia Tenn. and I belonged to the same master.
>
> Henry Haddox was about 10 years old when I married, as near as I can recollect.
>
> My master, Dr. Haddox killed himself about 6 or 7 years before I married.
>
> Henry Haddox was hired out before I married; when he was a little bit of a chap, only old enough to pick up chips.

> I do not know exactly how old Henry Haddox is.
> His father was my mother's brother

Excerpt from the Deposition of Ellen Haddox, Nov. 9, 1906, Civil War Pension File of Henry Haddox, 17th USCI and 101st USCI, RG 15:

> I am one of the Haddox colored folks I don't know my age. I was married and had two children when the Civil War began. I reckon that I was 21 years old when the war began I understand that Henry Haddox is my cousin. I think that Henry Haddox is some younger than I. I do not know what the difference in our ages is.

Excerpt from the Deposition of Margaret Grant, Nov. 10, 1906, Civil War Pension File of Henry Haddox, 17th USCI and 101st USCI, RG 15:

> "I am 70 years old last Christmas morning."
>
> Henry Haddox is my cousin I belonged to the Sanfords. Dr. Haddox married my young mistress I went to Miss. when I was seven years of age, and never came back to Tenn. until after the close of the Civil War. On my return to Tennessee I found that I had a cousin Henry Haddox. I saw him several times. . . . I can't say whether he is older or younger than I. I do not know whether he was born before or after I went to Miss.

Pension officials commonly sought out former owners to establish or corroborate evidence in former slaves' pension claims. Generally, it appears that pension officials considered former owners to be a vital source of information in former slaves' claims because of their literacy, which meant that they established dates by calendars and recorded significant information, unlike most slaves. Typical of even the most sympathetic whites, pension officials also simply presumed former owners to be more intelligent than former slaves and hence more reliable as witnesses. Common among whites in the postbellum era was the belief that both African Americans' previous condition of servitude and inherent racial inferiority made them unintelligent, dishonest, and superstitious, among other negative stereotypes. Although federal military pension legislation was "racially neutral," offering black soldiers and their families the same right to pensions as whites, these racist attitudes nonetheless colored the Pension Bureau's efforts to award such pensions. Thus, Bureau officials tended to treat black claimants with greater suspicion, making their claims that much more difficult to prove, especially in the context of having minimal documentary evidence to begin with. Additionally, these same attitudes informed the manner in which individual Bureau agents pursued their work to varying degrees, from the blatantly racist to the more egalitarian.[12] Ultimately, the relentless quest for accurate evidence in former slaves' pension cases resulted in the occasional appearance of former owners' testimony or that of their children and other relatives in former slaves' files. As the two following cases from Washington, D.C., and Louisiana illustrate, it is difficult to know when the knowledge shared was derived from a true closeness between masters and slaves, from records of the business of slavery, or from a kind of forced intimacy derived from the proximity of slaves and owners on the plantation or farm.

Excerpt from the Affidavit of Emily Burnley Tolson and Charles Thorton Burnley, Nov. 15, 1916, Civil War Pension File of Erastus Green, 1st USCI, RG 15:

> Eliza Stevenson [Erastus Green's widow] . . . was born a slave in the family of their parents, and who was born a short time after Charles T. Burnley, and was raised in the family, and so remained until after the slaves were freed by the war. That Mrs. Tolson will be 73 years of age her next birthday, and that Chas. T. Burnley will be 71 years of age March 10th, 1917; and while they have no record of the exact date of the birth of Eliza, they know positively that she is over 70 years of age, and will be 71 years of age on her next birthday, which will come sometime shortly after that of Charles T. Burnley. They have known Eliza since her birth and were raised children together on the old Burnley place, now occupied by Charles T. Burnley. There can be no doubt but that Eliza is over 70 years of age at this time.

Excerpt from the Affidavit of General Walker, July 18, 1905, Civil War Pension File of General Walker, 88th USCI and 97th USCI, RG 15:

> [General Walker] was born in the month of May 1830. that he was given this information by a grand daughter of his old Mistress: that the memoranda enclosed herewith was given to him yesterday July 17th 1905 by the Grand daughter of his former Mistress (owner) at Smoke Bend near Donaldsonville, La. and he is certain that this is the correct date of his birth, that the lady who gave me this memoranda was raised up on same plantation and is 3 years older than I am.

In the following instance, the testimony of Mary A. Harvey, David Edwards's former young mistress, helped special examiner W. L. Sullivan to pin down Edwards's age. Edwards, an Arkansas veteran, himself testified, "I really don't know what year I was born. It was about 1848 or 1850. I have never had my right age. There is no way I can prove my age."[13] Undaunted, Sullivan cross-referenced the date that Harvey gave for when the family moved its slaves with Edwards's sense of his age at that time to arrive at 1847 as the year of his birth. In her recollections of that time, Harvey shares a tragic story about a young slave boy.

Excerpt from the Deposition of Mary A. Harvey, Sept. 18, 1912, Civil War Pension File of David Edwards, 88th USCI, 9th USCHA and 3rd USCHA, RG 15:

> Tom Claiborne was my father. His full name was Thomas Burrell Claiborne.
>
> I remember the boy Dave who belonged to my father. He had a brother George, and a sister Jane that I remember.
>
> Dave was older than George.
>
> I do not remember the age of Dave. He was some younger than I.
>
> We have no record of dates of birth of our colored folks.
>
> We moved from Williamson Co Tenn. . . . in 1849. I was 13 years of age when I came here to the county of Haywood near Brownsville, Tenn.
>
> George Claiborne lost a lower limb when a small boy. He had a fit and fell off a stump into the fire and was so badly burned that his leg was amputated. He left this vicinity years ago and I do not know what ever became of him.

Emancipation

Interestingly, there is a casual character to former slaves' stories of emancipation in their pension claims. That is not to say that emancipation was not significant or that freedom did not matter but, rather, that in the context of making a bid for a pension, emancipation was a piece of a broader story rather than the focus of the story itself. As such, former slaves' pension claims offer an insight into the specific advent of freedom, what it was like to be a slave one day and free the next, and what were the concerns of that very moment. This section also includes two stories of slaves freed before the war, one by manumission and one by running away.

Freedom by manumission came to precious few prior to the war. The massive tide of manumissions associated with the period of the American Revolution was stemmed significantly in the antebellum era as the institution of slavery reestablished its footing. Peter Grumer was fortunate enough to reside in Missouri at the time of his manumission; Missouri, Delaware, and Arkansas were the only slave states that still allowed manumissions by the 1850s.[14] Grumer was one of 2,618 free African Americans living in Missouri in 1850, making up approximately 3 percent of the entire African American population in the state at that time.[15] Although there is no specific mention of Grumer's experience as a free person of color living with slaves, we can only imagine the precariousness of his existence. As a black man living in a community that associated blackness with slavery, and whiteness with freedom, Grumer's free status was probably questioned at every turn. It would not have been unusual for Grumer to carry "freedom papers"—official documents confirming his freedom—at all times. In addition to whites' viewing free blacks as undermining their very sense of freedom and the distinct gap between themselves and blacks, they often regarded free blacks as potential fomenters of slave revolution. Whites addressed both concerns by limiting free blacks' freedom through legal means. Historian Ira Berlin explains that "whites legally prohibited Negro freemen from moving freely, participating in politics, testifying against whites, keeping guns, or lifting a hand to strike a white person 'except in defense against wanton assault.' In addition, they burdened free Negroes with special imposts, barred them from certain trades, and often tried and punished them like slaves."[16] Berlin notes that although many free blacks found a measure of prosperity in the skilled trades and crafts—especially free blacks that lived in their own communities and managed to set themselves apart from slaves—most of them lived in poverty as they competed for work against slaves and poor whites.[17] Grumer most likely fell into the latter category, living with his slave wife, Jane, on her master's plantation. Rather than constantly searching for work in order to survive, however, Grumer appears to have been steadily employed by Jane's master. In this instance, then, although living among slaves may have constantly called his freedom into question, Grumer's direct association with them provided some measure of stability in his daily survival.

Excerpt from the Affidavit of Jane Groomer, May 30, 1872, Civil War Pension File of Peter Grumer (alias Groomer), 67th USCI, RG 15:

> Jane Groomer . . . declares that she is the widow of Peter Groomer deceased. That she was first the slave of Eben Best who sold her to Joseph Courtney that her husband was the slave of Garrett Groomer, who in the year 1850 or thereabouts was set free by will of his master. he then hired to Joseph Courtney and lived with Courtney until the beginning of the war that her said husband was never the slave of Courtney but lived with the family for a number of years as a hired man.

Living in Kentucky, Warren Carter's relatively close proximity to the North no doubt provided the impetus to escape slavery by running to Illinois in the late 1850s. Historians note that the difficulty of running away increased throughout the antebellum period; some suggest that a mere one thousand slaves a year managed to reach the North by the late antebellum era.[18] Although Carter's testimony offers little information about how he escaped, it reveals how he survived once he reached freedom.

Excerpt from the Deposition of Warren Carter, May 3, 1889, Civil War Pension File of Warren Carter, 29th USCI, RG 15:

> At the time of my Enlistment I was living at Wyanet, Bureau Co. Illinois; had been living there about Eight months. Before that I lived in Chicago, Illinois; had lived in Chicago from October 27th 1858. I was a slave up to 1857; I was owned by John C. Breckenridge and lived at Lexington, Ky, until 1857, then I ran away and went to Chicago and lived there till I moved to Wyanet, as stated, and was living at Wyanet at the time of Enlistment. I followed farming after I ran away from my master, as stated, and that was principally my occupation up to Enlistment. During the time I lived at Wyanet, I chopped cord-wood. I was not married until after my discharge from the army.

How did slaves learn of their freedom? What did they do in those first days and weeks? In his claim for a pension as the father of Boley Travis, Anderson Logan gives us insight into freedom's first moments.

Excerpt from the Deposition of Anderson Logan, Aug. 3, 1882, Civil War Pension File of Boley Travis, 65th USCI, RG 15:

Ques. When did you become free

Ans. Sometime in the year 1865. It was about the time all the slaves were freed. It was in the winter, I think about January.

Ques. Who told you that you were free

Ans. My mistress's daughter and all of the family told me that I was free and that it was no use to keep it any longer and that I could go any time I wanted to.

Ques. Did you leave your mistress as soon as you were told that you were free or how long did you remain with her

Ans. I think I staid with her about three weeks afterwords.

Ques. Where did you go when you left your mistress

Ans. I went to Mr. Thomas Travis who owned my wife and family and he told me the sooner I would take my family away the better, and I took them and moved onto the farm of a german, Mr. Minnings.

Ques. How long did you live there

Ans. Four years.

Ques. Where did you live when your wife died

Ans. On Mr. Snare's farm.

Ques. How many years did you live on Mr. Snares farm and did you remove directly from Minnings' to Snare's farm

Ans. I removed directly from Minnings' to Snare's farm and lived there two years. My wife died in August of the second year we lived at Snare's farm.

Ques. Do you recollect whether your wife died about the time of the eclipse of the sun

Ans. She died the next morning after the day when the sun was eclipsed.

Ques. Did you continue to receive any support or aid from your mistress after you were freed

Ans. None at all. Her daughter said when she told me that I was free that if they were able they would give me something but she said they were not able.

Ques. Who was your mistress and is she living

Ans. Mrs. Sallie Logan, the widow of Campbell Logan. She died I think last September.

Anderson Logan himself did not offer any clue about what kept him at his mistress's home for three weeks after he had learned that he was free.

In the excerpts that follow, Silvy Granville, widow of Washington Granville, a South Carolina veteran, explains clearly why she and the other freed slaves with her stayed with their mistress after hearing about emancipation. Evident in Silvy's testimony is her sense of the scope of her freedom.

Excerpt from the Deposition of Silvy Granville, Nov. 21, 1901, Civil War Pension File of Washington Granville, 128th USCI, RG 15:

> I do not know my age, I guess I was half grown at time of freedom. I am the widow of Washington Granville, who served in the war. I could not tell where he served, but Col. Henderson has the papers. I live about 4 miles South of Walterboro, S.C.
>
> I was born in Columbia, S.C. I was owned by Mrs. Sallie Rhett. She moved all of her slaves down to Stirling, Colleton, Co S.C. when I was a little child. My father was Peter Pinkney and my mother was Peggy Pinkney both belonging to Mrs. Rhett. I called myself Silvy Pinkney until I was married. . . .
>
> Mrs. Rhett had carried all of us up to Abbeyville when the soldiers came out towards Stirling. The 2nd year of freedom all of us moved back to Stirling again, because we were free and could go where we liked. . . .

Excerpt from the Deposition of Silvy Granville, Dec. 21, 1901, Civil War Pension File of Washington Granville, 128th USCI, RG 15:

> When Mrs. Rhett told us that we were free we were in the middle of a crop. We agreed to help her make that crop for 1/3 of the crop. When that was harvested we desired to come back here. We started the first week in January when Mrs. Rhett had told us about freedom the preseeding April. I cannot give the year.

During the Civil War, some slaveholders desperately sought to hold on to their slaves by whatever means available. This was particularly true in the Mississippi Valley, a focus of Union operation during the conflict. It became a common practice for slaveholders in this region to "refugee" or ship their human property west to Texas. The deposition of Luvenia Smith is particularly valuable, then, because it offers a glimpse of what slaves in the Mississippi Valley, desperate for freedom, were willing to do to avoid being sent off to Texas.

Excerpt from the Deposition of Luvenia Smith, May 16, 1905, Civil War Pension File of Joe Smith, 83rd USCI and 78th USCI, RG 15:

I was born on the Greenwood plantation, West Feliciana Parish, Louisiana. I was a young girl when the war came on. My master and owner was Ruffin I. Barrow, long ago dead. I was a field hand and worked in the sugar cane. My father was named George Smith and my husbands father name was Lyttleton Smith. My name was Smith even before I married Joe Smith. My mother was Dorcas Smith. Both my parents are dead.

When I was married to Joe Smith, I was not more than 13 years old. . . . Barrow my master said I was too young to be married but he said if I wanted to be married to Joe he would marry us. So my master married me to Joe Smith who was my first and only husband I ever had. We were married slavery fashion our owners making us husband and wife. We never had license those days. Joe Smith was much older than I was. He owned by my owner and raised on the Barrow plantation like I was. . . . I cant say how old my husband Joe was when we were married but I know I know I had one child born to me before the war came on. Joe was half way to a settled man in age when the war came on, that is to say a young man is 20 and a settled man is 30 years old so I reckon my husband Joe Smith was about 25 years old when he enlisted in the army. The way he come to enlist was this way. When the Yankee soldier come to Port Hudson the white folks wanted to run us as refugees to Texas to keep us from the Yankees. So all us colored folks run off to Port Hudson. A lot of us ran off together. We stole mules to travel off. My husband carried me off behind him on a mule. We slipped off in the night. Ole Marse died bout that time and young Marse John Barrow ran off himself. . . .

You see I did not follow my husband when he enlisted. I left him at Port Hudson He went first with his regiment to New Orleans and I followed him on a boat and staid with him awhile in New Orleans. Then I come back to the Huston plantation, Bayou, Sara La. and staid and worked there until my husband came after me when mustered out of service.

While some slave owners clung to the institution of slavery during the Civil War, others saw its inevitable end and acted accordingly. The advance of the Union army into the South and the escape of many thousands of slaves to Union lines led owners like William Walkup to sell off slaves in order to minimize the financial loss of slavery's end. In this instance, Walkup sold one slave, Allen, as a substitute in the Union army, a practice that enabled border-state slaveholders to reap some profit from slavery. This story is revealed in testimony that sought to prove that Allen King had indeed served in Companies A & B, 122nd USCI.

Questionable in his case was the fact that King had used three names in his lifetime. (He also lived in three states after the war: Kentucky, Illinois, and Indiana.) He was known as Allen Walkup (his master's surname), Allen Walker (a distortion of Walkup, perhaps simply a miscommunication as in the case of Frank Morse), and Allen King (his father's surname). One means of determining if a soldier was who he claimed to be (or, as in this case, who his widow claimed him to be) was to circulate his picture among people he claimed to know to see if they could identify him. A piece of Allen King's story came from testimony by his former master and mistress, who recognized King's photograph shown to them by special examiner George M. Flick. King's former master and mistress corroborated his identity and also explained their reaction to slavery's impending end.

Excerpt from the Deposition of William Walkup, Apr. 23, 1901, Civil War Pension File of Allen Walkup (alias Walker, alias King), 122nd USCI, RG 15:

> I recognize the picture you show me as the likness of my old colored boy Allen. It looks very much like him indeed. I bought him at the sale of the estate of old man Strange, my wife's father in Adair Co. Ky. As well as I recollect he was about eleven years old when I bought him, and he was about 18 years old when I sold him. It was toward the close of the war, and the negroes were running away, and I took a small price for him, as he was threatening to leave. I sold him to a man in Columbia, Adair Co. Ky to go as a substitute into the army, and it seems to me that it was to Ed. Russell., a young lawyer in Columbia that I sold him; but I think he was buying him to go in as a substitute for some one else. I cannot now recall who it was. . . . He went by the name of Allen Walkup. I do not know whether he was called Walker in the army. I think his father was a King. It was said that his father was Beverly King, but his parents were not married to each other.

Excerpt from the Deposition of Elizabeth Walkup, Apr. 23, 1901, Civil War Pension File of Allen Walkup (alias Walker, alias King), 122nd USCI, RG 15:

> I recognize the picture you show me as our old colored boy Allen Walkup. It is a good picture of him. My husband bought him when he was a lad from the sale of my father's estate, Archelaus A. Strange. His father was

Allen Walker (alias King), 122nd U.S. Colored Infantry

> supposed to be Beverly King, but his parents were not married. My husband sold him about the close of the war to go as a substitute for some one into the United States army. I have forgotten who it was. . . . There was some one drafted, and he was bought up to go in their place.

As a whole, the details of slavery that emerge from former slaves' Civil War pension claims offer readers a fascinating lens through which to view the institution and the lives of all those who lived within its bounds. Clearly, individual pension files vary as to the depth of information that they convey on the subject. Yet each piece contributes to a broader understanding of the personal experience of slavery. Ultimately, what makes the collective story that emerges from the pension files so valuable is that it is a story that former slaves tell to us themselves.

Pension files illustrate how communities came into being as slaves on single farms and plantations came to know each others' lives intimately; they grew up together, worked together, spent their off time together, and celebrated each others' marriages and the birth of children. Broader communities of slaves formed as their masters' relationships with families, friends, and neighbors brought them together. Former slaves' pension files also reveal the near constant state of flux that characterized many slave communities as individual members were sold and bought, bequeathed and inherited, hired away and hired on. A most poignant element of the community experience was the separation of families and friends that commonly occurred as slave owners tended to their own financial and familial needs.

A key theme of the pension process, personal identity also clearly played an important role in slaves' transition to freedom. As many slave owners denied their slaves the basic elements of identity, asserting one's identity by choosing a name for oneself or reclaiming family ties through naming became a significant act of freedom. Additionally, the Civil War pension system, rooted as it was in a preference for documentary evidence, brings to light the role that the denial of literacy played in slaves' and former slaves' lives. Pension files show how illiteracy contributed to the challenges of establishing identity, especially of determining one's age. Yet former slaves' testimony also reveals the persistence of the rich oral culture of slavery and the tradition of recalling and passing on history through the spoken word.

In their personal accounts of emancipation, former slaves shed more light on the variety of means by which they came to be free. Whereas some slaves took freedom for themselves, running away during slavery or running to Union lines during the war, others came upon freedom by manumission or by virtue of the war's end. In their pension files, former slaves recount stories of asserting their freedom, of hearing from their masters that they were free, and in freedom's first moments, of making their own choices about where to live and how to make a living for themselves.

2

The Civil War

Since military service justified the government's pension system, the Civil War is a central topic in the files, especially prior to 1890, when every pension was premised on war-related death or disability. Yet even after the passage of the 1890 law, veterans' Civil War experience remained central to their claims; former soldiers were often required to provide sworn testimony about their military service or the service of comrades through private affidavits or depositions given to special examiners of the U.S. Pension Bureau.

In either case, this testimony is particularly valuable for African Americans because of the dearth of accounts of Civil War service in their own words. Their relative silence is understandable. Whereas the vast majority of white troops on both sides were literate, many black soldiers could not read and write, especially in regiments recruited among slaves. Further, the writings of white soldiers were more likely to survive and become available to scholars, which has resulted in the creation of an immense body of work on their Civil War experiences. White Americans more often put their thoughts to paper than did African Americans, particularly illiterate slaves, and archives and historical societies more often preserved the letters, diaries, and other documents of whites than of African Americans.

Nevertheless, historians have recovered the letters of African American soldiers published in newspapers during the Civil War, mined government papers relevant to black military service, and uncovered the handful of memoirs written by black men who served the Union.[1]

Pension files add both breadth and depth to our understanding of the black military experience in the words of the soldiers themselves. Whereas special examiners, lawyers, pension agents, and other third parties involved in the application process had their own agendas in the testimony concerning the war, veterans of the U.S. Colored Troops were able to comment on a wide variety of subjects related to African American service in the Civil War. Likewise, because special examinations tended often to be autobiographical in nature, it is often possible to see a particular man's military service in the context of his prewar life and postwar activities. Undoubtedly, pension files have their challenges as a source. If there is a gap in this source material, it is in the lack of testimony on combat, which might have offered a richer understanding of that experience. In part this lack arises simply because the Union army used black troops less in combat than it used whites, leaving less to discuss. Black veterans with serious disabilities tended to apply for and receive pensions soon after the war, their cases proven through War Department records (meaning no special examination was necessary). Black veterans who did discuss combat in their claims tended to do so in the context of proving that a disability was service related, and they thus focused more on the nature of the wound itself than the circumstances of the battle or skirmish. Later applications tend to be questionable, especially those submitted after the 1879 Arrears Act since that law gave former soldiers a significant financial incentive to make specious disability claims because successful claimants would receive not only a future pension but also a lump sum for all the pension money that they should have received since the time they were wounded or otherwise disabled. Taken as a whole, however, pension files provide a fertile source on the Civil War from the perspective of ordinary black veterans, virtually all of whose words on the war would not have been recorded or survived without the existence of the federal pension system and the vast bureaucracy that kept it running.

Although in some ways African American soldiers' service was comparable to just about any Civil War soldier, Union or Confederate, their pension files reveal that, not surprisingly, their military experience was quite distinctive from that of white soldiers. In how they came to enlist, the nature of their camp life, their experience of combat, and their postwar military service, African American soldiers experienced the Civil War differently than did their white counterparts. These differences are hardly surprising, but it is compelling and valuable to learn about them from the mouths of former black soldiers themselves.

Commonalities

Although the black military experience was fundamentally different from that of white soldiers, some aspects of their military life were quite universal. The discipline hammered into recruits left a lasting impression on many black veterans. As the following excerpt from the 1907 deposition of Milton Denny (alias Charles Davis) shows, this ex-soldier could readily recall the identity of his former leaders (officers and noncommissioned) and the minutiae of military life decades after leaving service. Pension Bureau officials revisited Davis's claim, even after its approval, because it had come to their attention that while he had applied for and been granted a pension as "Milton Denny," he was also calling himself "Charles Davis." The government wished to determine whether Denny and Davis were the same man and dispatched a special examiner to question him.

Excerpt from the Deposition of Charles Davis, Nov. 1, 1907, Civil War Pension File of Milton Denny (alias Charles Davis), 65th USCI, RG 15:

> I am 64 years of age, P.O. and residence, Homochitto St., No. 33, or rather in near of where 33 ought to be, Natchez, Miss. I am the person who served as a private in Co. G—65" U.S.C.V.I., during the Civil war, under the name of Milton Denny. I am pensioned at $6 per a month on account of said service.
>
> I was born in Pike Co., Mo., the slave of Samuel Denny and I remained his slave until freedom. When the war came on I went to Louisiana, Mo., and joined the army. A crowd of us, about 50, went to St. Louis, to be mustered in. I enlisted in Dec. 1863, and we were mustered in at Benton barracks, St. Louis, in Jan. 1864. I was there assigned to Co. G—and our Regt. was called the 2" Mo. When we were in a short while, our Regt. was changed to the 65 U.S.C.T. We went to Donaldsonville, La., then back to Port Hudson, then to Mantganza, then to Baton Rouge, where I was discharged; but I have lost my discharge paper. When I went to join the G[rand].A[rmy of the].R[epublic]., the A[djutant] G[eneral] of the U.S.A. sent me this paper: (Here affiant presented a paper from A.G., which shows: Milton Denny, enrolled Dec. 27, 1863, and discharged Sept. 1, 1866. G—65 U.S.C.V.I.) I was discharged to enable me to enlist in the regular army. I enlisted in the regular army on the same day that I was discharged from the volunteer service. I was assigned to troop B-9-U.S. Cav. I served in the regular army until April, 1867, when I deserted while on detached service in the Q.M. Department. When I was relieved from detached duty in New Orleans, and given transportation to my command, at Fort Stockton, Tex., instead of joining my command, I went home, and never returned.

I was Milton Denny in my regular service. . . . When I left the regular army, I took my father's name, Davis. My baby name was Charles. There was another man on the place named Charles, and they nick-named me Milton. Charles Davis is my proper and correct name. . . . I am known in pension matters only, as Charles Davis, no I mean as Milton Denny.

Our Col. was named Brown. Our Lt. Col. was named Horn. Our Major was named Baldwin. I speak now of my volunteer service. My Capt. was Olney. The 65" and 67 consolidated, when Olney resigned, and Frost was our Capt. Reed was 1" Lt. Tillison was 2" Lt. Henry Jones was Ord. Sergt. He was a dark-brown, medium size and wore chin wiskers. Joseph Clark, Lewis McPherson, Henry Wright were the only duty Sergts. I can name. Henry Wright was the tallest man in the Co. Henry Myers was the shortest man. Richard Groves, General Johnson, Edmund Pepper were corporals.

We had dress parade in the morning, reverse arms at a funeral, and fired a salute in the grave. We had three reliefs on guard. Each stood two hours and rested four. We carried water in a canteen, grub in a haversack, clothes in a knapsack. (This man drills well and gives proper salutes.) "Taps" means lights out. The countersign is only a word, it was given only to friends and those who had the right to pass. It changed every day.

The army tried to instill discipline in black soldiers, as with all Civil War soldiers, but this effort was at best only a partial success. Like their white counterparts, most African Americans in the army were young. Their average age was twenty-five years (the same for white Union soldiers), but the largest single age group was nineteen-year-old men, most of them away from home for the first time in their lives (and away from the corporal punishment of slaveholders). Some of these men, boys really, misbehaved. They stole from civilians even when such theft was not militarily necessary and went AWOL for reasons as whimsical and unremarkable as the desire to pursue women, as the following deposition of Alfred Barksdale (alias Ward) makes clear. (Historians have documented similar misbehavior by white soldiers, Union and Confederate.)[2] Like Charles Davis's, Alfred Ward's testimony came in the context of an investigation of his identity by the U.S. Pension Bureau.

Excerpt from the Deposition of Alfred Ward, Apr. 10, 1901, Civil War Pension File of Alfred Barksdale (alias Ward), 63rd USCI, RG 15:

I am about 71 years, a farmer. res- & p.o. address, Lintonia, Yazoo City, Miss. I am the pensioner in this case. . . .

I was away from my Co. a while in service—we went away in the Spring & came back in the Fall of 1864—3 or 4 of us left the Co. when it was at Waterproof, La. Jack Nichols, Needham Smith, Alfred Davis, Harry Nichols & Adam Smith & I all left & went up to Davis Bend—left without leave—we had some women up there to be with so went on up there to see them. We went back to the Company voluntarily at Natchez—rather at Vidalia, La. opposite Natchez—they put us in jail awhile & made us lose all our pay while we were away. Abner Smith and Abe Smith were kept in jail longer than any of the rest of us.

I enlisted at Vicksburg. Our Co. was there only a little while, then went down to Davis Bend, then to Waterproof where I left the Co. & I did not get back to the Co. till it was at Vidalia where we remained till we went to Devall's Bluff where we then remained till muster out. We never had but one fight in service—one at Bullitts Bayou, La. near Vidalia. We had that after I came back to the Co. & was duly punished. . . .

My regiment was first called the 9" La. I can't recall how I gave my age when I enlisted. I was a full grown man at enlistment. I don't think I knew my age then certainly but found it out after the war from an old uncle of mine now dead. I don't know what year I was born in. I had no nicknames in the army. I can't state what height was given me when I enlisted. . . .

I told you the truth about my wives the other time[3]—I never had a wife named Minerva—I had a woman of that name for [a] sweetheart while we at Vidalia in service—I left her behind when we went to Devalls Bluff & when I came back I heard she had left with another soldier & I have never seen or heard of her since then. We were never married by any ceremony whatever. I never considered her my wife—I never heard of her being dead & I cannot understand why the person who wrote that paper for me should have so stated in that paper—I did not tell him to so state.

Differences: Confederate Service

Of course, much more of the testimony of black veterans in pension files speaks to the distinctive nature of their Civil War experience. Perhaps the most interesting thing they revealed in this regard was, ironically, that the Confederate army proved to be a common way station for black men who later enlisted in the Union army. That is, before they joined the Yankees, many of these men had been servants or laborers or had worked in other support roles for the rebels. Indeed, if pension files make one thing abundantly clear, it is that although black persons were a common sight in Confederate army camps, they were not present there as soldiers. Instead, Confederate service seems to have brought many African Americans into a position where they could more easily escape to Union lines or be captured by Union forces and, hence, be in a position to enlist as soldiers in the Union army. The latter scenario was certainly the case with John Burgess, who testified in an 1895 special examination.

Excerpt from the Deposition of John Burgess, Aug. 8, 1895, Civil War Pension File of John Burgess, 11th and 113th USCI, RG 15:

> I am 55 years old occupation farming. P.O. address Clarendon Monroe Co Ark. I served in Co B, 11 U S Inf. but we were afterwards made Co B, 113 U.S.C.T. This is my only service in the U.S. Army or Navy. I was raised in Franklin County Ala. I belonged to Ben Burgess. I was waiterman on West Burgess who was a Captain in the Confederate army but as I was small man & I don't know what regiment he was in. I was not enlisted in the Confederate army. My master was captured in Missouri in one fall Neosho I think and the Yankees turned all the darkey boys loose, and I came down to Dardanelle Ark and enlisted in the Union army in December 1863 just before Christmas. I was discharged I think in 1866. I remember it was in April I was discharged at DeVall's Bluff Ark.

Like John Burgess, Louis Jourdan served the Confederates in a support capacity before enlisting in the Union army. However, as his 1915 deposition makes clear, he worked as a military laborer not as the personal servant of a Confederate officer. Indeed, the Confederate military effort would have faltered much sooner if not for the often-unwilling efforts of laborers like Jourdan. The Union army also realized early in the war the value of black laborers, which explains why well before the Preliminary Emancipation Proclamation (September 1862) and even before the First Confiscation Act (August 1861), Union officers were giving refuge to escaped slaves. Although most "contraband" escaped directly to Union lines and never looked back, Jourdan shows that the process of going from slave to Confederate laborer to Union soldier could sometimes be a bit more complicated.

Excerpt from the Deposition of Louis Jourdan, May 27, 1915, Civil War Pension File of Louis Jourdan, 77th USCI and 10th USCHA, RG 15:

> I am 75 years of age; my post-office address is No. 1920 St. Anthony Street, New Orleans, La. Occupation—laborer. I am pensioned under Cert. No. 839,270 under the name of Jourdan, Louis Jourdan for service in Co. F, 77" U.S.C.I. and Co. K, 10" U.S.C.H.A.
>
> I was born in Washington Co., Md. near Boonsborough, I was only a few miles from Hagerstown too. I was born the slave of Ed Butler. . . . There were ten children of us in all, the whole family was sold to the slave traders about five years before I enlisted in the army and were brought here, no that is wrong only three were brought here to New Orleans, viz. my brothers, Nelson Jourdan, John Jourdan and myself, we were sold to Dr. Martin whose plantation was about a mile below Paicourtville, Assumption Parish, La. My age was given as 18 when I was sold, John's age was given as 19, and Nelson's as 20 past. I remained on the Martin place until about the time there was a battle near Paincoutville, I then went with soldiers to Thibodaux, I was then a married man and had four children, my slave wife was named Ellen Thomas, my children then were Alfred, Solomon, and two dead. From Thibodaux I came with my family to Algiers, and was in a Contraband Camp and living here awhile, my wife belonged to Madam Lestree, and she came or sent some one to the Contraband Camp and took my wife and children back to Bayou Lafourche, later I went out to visit them and while there the Confederates run in on us and took me with them and made me dig trenches and breastworks, I escaped from them just this side of Morgan City and came back to Thibodaux via of Houma, then I came on back to this city and went down to the Tauro Building and enlisted in Co. F, 77" U.S.C.I. . . . I was in that regiment a little over a year then my regiment was consolidated with the 10" U.S.C.H.A. and I served with that regiment in Co. K, for a year or more and was discharged at Baton Rogue. . . .
>
> After my discharge I went out to Bayou Lafourche and got my slave wife and brought her here and lived with her until she died, this wife died in the Charity Hospital in this city I cannot give the date but she died a year before I married my second wife. . . .
>
> I have lived with this wife ever since our marriage and we never have been separated nor divorced. These two are the only wives I have ever had and they are the only women I have ever lived with.

Differences: Recruitment

The cases of Jourdan and Burgess reveal the very act of enlistment often to have been more adventurous for African Americans than it was for whites. For a white soldier, North or South, enlisting usually was easy; he merely had to visit the local recruiting station. Joining up was more challenging for African Americans, who often had to escape the clutches of slaveholders opposed to their enlistment. The result was that slaves who joined the Union cause often had dramatic recruitment stories that they sometimes shared during special examinations. A particularly interesting, though not typical, case is that of George Madison (alias Seymour) who testified in 1914 about his encounter with William Quantrill, the infamous Confederate guerrilla leader whose band was active in the Kansas-Missouri border region for most of the Civil War. On October 6, 1863, Quantrill and his men ambushed a Union column led by Maj. Gen. James G. Blunt near present-day Baxter Springs, Kansas, killing many of Blunt's men (Blunt himself barely escaped). The timing of this engagement is consistent with Madison's account of escaping from Quantrill at Baxter Springs and enlisting at Fort Scott four days later, on October 10. Fort Scott is about fifty-eight miles north of Baxter Springs.

Excerpt from the Deposition of George Madison, Mar. 6, 1914, Civil War Pension File of George Seymour (alias Madison), 83rd USCI (New), RG 15:

> I am 68 past, years of age; my post-office address is #1215 "O" street, Atchinson, Kansas. My occupation has always been laborer. I was a soldier during the Civil War, member of Co. A, 83 U. S. C. Inf., enlisted October 10, 1863 and was discharged October 9, 1865 at Camden, Arkansas. I hand you for inspection my original discharge certificate from that organization. (Original discharge certificate shown-RSM) That was the only time I was ever in the service. I was never in the United States Navy nor Marine Corps. I am pensioned at the rate of $17 per month under the old law for chronic diarrhea and resulting disease of the rectum and am claiming pension at the rate of $30 per month under the disability clause of the Act of May 11, 1912. . . .[4]
>
> I was born in Lafayette county, Mo., close to what is Higginsville now but it was not much of a town then; I was born in slavery. . . . At the time

of my enlistment (and I enlisted at Ft. Scott, Kansas) I was a farm laborer on the place of Dr. Seymour, I do not remember his first name; I was a young boy, 18 years old, black hair and black complexion, black eyes. I had no scars on my face or hands; my teeth were good then; I was beardless. rahther heavy set, weighed about 130 or 140 pounds.

Q. Did anyone else from that neighborhood enlist at the same time? A. Not around my neighborhood that I know of.

Q. How did you happen to go to Fort Scott, Kansas to enlist? A. Well, it was this way; I was with Quantrell in 1863 at the time he cut Blunt's bodyguard up at Baxter Springs, Kansas and I got away from him there, went to Ft. Scott and enlisted.[5] He had my brother Charles with him too. And I have never heard of him since.

A more common enlistment story for a black Civil War soldier comes from the 1903 deposition of William Cullens, who ran off from his Mississippi plantation and served under the name Peter Williams to avoid being reclaimed by his owner. Though not a common practice, other African American enlistees also resorted to serving under an alias, particularly in the border states, where Unionist slaveholders were exempt from the provisions of the Confiscation Acts, which allowed the seizure and then freeing of the slaves of disloyal slaveholders.

Excerpt from the Deposition of William Cullens, Nov. 18, 1903, Civil War Pension File of Peter Williams (alias William Kerling, alias William Cullens), 53rd USCI, RG 15:

I am [not stated] years of age; my post-office address is Pilchers Point, La, a farmer. I am the identical Peter Williams who served during the war of the rebellion as a private Co E 53 U.S. Col. Vol. Inf. I enlisted at Grand Gulf, Miss. can't give date and was mustered in at Warrenton, Miss. They took us to Millikens Bend, La. and our regiment was in a fight there on a Sunday morning.

I was born in Hinds Co. Miss and my master was named Kelly. . . . My father was named Bill Cullens. . . . I was going under the name of Bill Cullens when the war went on and I ran away and I was afraid my master would get me so I took the name of Peter Williams and enlisted and served in the army under that name. I never had the name of Peter Williams any where except in the army. As soon as I got out of the army I went back to my own name again, William Cullens. My name is not Kerling but Cullens.

As with white soldiers, the recruitment of African Americans into the Union army was plagued with fraud and corruption. For example, it was common for men to join the Union army in order to collect a recruitment bonus or "bounty" and then desert and attempt to join the army elsewhere in order to repeat the process—a practice that became known as "bounty jumping." African Americans, however, appear from pension files more often to have been the victims of recruitment scams than the perpetrators. (No doubt some black men also took advantage of the Union recruiting system, but they do not tend to show up in pension files). The following two depositions deal with what must have been common scenarios of deceit involving black recruits during the Civil War. Robert Harrison was defrauded by a corrupt recruiter. Austin Waters was taken advantage of by a Union officer in what amounted to a case of theft of services.

Excerpt from the Deposition of Robert Harrison, Apr. 11, 1890, Civil War Pension File of Robert Harris (alias Robert Harrison, alias John Wilson), RG 15:

> When I went to enlist . . . the recruiting officer, said to me, your name is John Wilson. I said, no, my name is Robert Harrison, but he put me down as John Wilson. I was known while in service by that name. I was a green boy right off the farm and did just what I was told to do. . . . I had no thought of joining the army but a couple of men at Hannibal, Mo. told myself and others that if we enlisted that we would get new clothes and jewelry. My mother said after my discharge from the army that the reason the officer put my name down as John Wilson was he could draw my bounty. . . . I heard at some time in the past that the recruiting officer who ever he was ran away with the money.

Excerpt from the Deposition of Austin Waters, Jan. 19, 1914, Civil War Pension File of Austin Waters, 15th USCI, RG 15:

> I am 65–66 years of age; my post address is Columbus, Ark. I am a farmer. I do [not] know my exact age but I count myself between sixty five and sixty six years of age. I am the claimant for pension for service in Co. K. 15th U.S.C.Inf. Volunteers.
>
> I was born near Shelby Bedford Co. Tenn. I do not know the date. I was a slave. Belonged to Zachariah Waters then and belonged till the war start-

> ed. I lived with a [man] named Cleggett, grandfather of Waters. Waters was not of [age] when I was born. When I was a small boy Cleggett moved to Centerville Hickman Co. Tenn. We stayed a year at Shelby Tenn., and then moved to Hickman Co. too. I lived there with Zachariah Waters who had come of age meantime till the war came on and I got with the yankees. . . .
>
> The yankees took me from home. I went out from home to get some warp[6] for the Mistress Waters, and the Yankee scouts took me to Columbia Tenn., and I did not stay there long till I was turned over to wait on the doctor. His name was Dr. Gregory and he was Major Doctor of the regiment 15th Cold. Inf. [the] same regiment that I afterwards enlisted in. I did not enlist at first but waited on him for about four or five months. Drove the ambulance and made coffee and carry messages and tended to his hoirse. He said I could get my pay by enlisting. After I enlisted I was assigned to the band as fifer for Co. K. I do not know the date of enlistment. It was either the last of Feb. or first of March in the year 1864, at Nashville Tenn. . . . I served in the band as fifer till I was mustered out of service in Nashville in 1866 near about the same time that I enlisted. I understood from the Major Doctor that I would get pay for the time that I waited on him before enlistment if I enlisted, but I do not know what they did about that when I was paid. I think I was discharged in March of Feby. 1866. I do not know exactly. I have lost the certificate of discharge. I do not know when nor where it was lost. Some one went in my Grip at Murphreesboro Tenn., and took things out and that is when and where I lost the certificate of discharge

A core part of enlistment for all soldiers was the physical examination to determine fitness for service. Veteran Wiley Johnson (whose case will be considered again in the chapter) mentions in passing that he was "stripped and thoroughly examined" at enlistment, an occurrence that comes up regularly in African American veterans' pension claims. This phenomenon appears to be at odds with conventional wisdom on the experience of white soldiers, particularly early on in the Civil War, when recruits tended to be given only a cursory medical examination. Historian Bell Irvin Wiley notes that even after the government required a more rigorous examination in late 1862, the procedures for doing so "were in large measure nullified by failure to provide anything like an adequate staff of examiners."[7] However, whether it was actually the case that black soldiers were subjected to a more thorough or invasive examination at enlistment requires more careful examination of white Civil War veterans' claims. What is clearly different is the way in which black and white soldiers might have experienced such an examination. Given the extensive nature of the domestic slave trade in the antebellum period, it is reasonable to imagine that a number of black soldiers—generally young, fit men—had experienced being sold at some point in their life under slavery. For them, being stripped and closely examined would have eerily mimicked the degrading, dehumanizing experience of being examined for sale.

Excerpt from the Deposition of Wiley Johnson, Jan. 26, 1894, Civil War Pension File of Wiley Johnson, 136th USCI, RG 15:

> I am applying for pension under the act of June 27, 1890. I am applying for pension because I am not able to work and make a living for my family. . . . No, I was not asked my age when I enlisted. Yes, I was put into a room stripped and thoroughly examined before I enlisted. Neil Speller was examined with me. No, I do not know how old I was when I enlisted. I think I was about 30 or 35 years old when I enlisted. I was working on Gabriel Toombs plantation in Muscogee Co. and run off from him and enlisted in the army.

Differences: The Presence of Soldiers' Family Members in Military Camps

The testimony of black veterans and other witnesses in Civil War pension files reinforces evidence from other sources that the presence of the families of black soldiers in or around military camps was not unusual. Certainly, one of the things social historians are rediscovering is the significant extent to which women and even children, white and black, were present in Civil War military camps.[8] However, the pension files of black veterans make clear that this phenomenon apparently was more common among African Americans than whites. The presence of so many black civilians in Union military camps should not be all that surprising. Many family members escaped with men who subsequently joined the Union army. Escaped slaves found Union army encampments to be a refuge where they could not be reclaimed by slaveholders, a place where available rations, clothing, and money could sustain families. In addition (as we will see in chapter 4), Union army encampments served as places where slave families could find legal sanction and protection. In the following 1893 affidavit, Hannibal Sibley, the son of black soldier Solomon Sibley, substantiates this reality. The affidavit was in support of his mother's application for a widow's pension.

Excerpt from the Affidavit of Hannibal Sibley, Jan. 11, 1893, Civil War Pension File of Solomon Sibley, 63rd USCI, RG 15:

> The said Hannibal Sibley states—I am the son of Solomon & Lucinda Sibley. I was present & saw my father & mother the said Solomon & Lucinda Sibley married by Rev. J.R. Locke on the 15 of May 1864. It was at the Camp of Co D 63 USC Inf. near Helena Arkansas My father was at that time a soldier in Co. D 63 USCI & my mother & her children were living in the camp called Contraband, which was connected with the Camp of said Company. My said parents had lived together many years before that time & continued to live together up to the date of fathers death about 11 years ago.

Some family members not only lived in close proximity to black soldiers; they actually lived with the troops in their encampments. Such was the case for Martin Campbell, a Tennessee resident and the son of Dennis Campbell, who served and died in the 63rd U.S. Colored Infantry. Martin's testimony about being with his father came in an 1889 affidavit, part of an unsuccessful application seeking a pension as the child of a Union soldier. Campbell's claim failed because a child of a deceased soldier (or veteran that died of war-related causes) could only receive a pension if he or she was younger than sixteen. Children lost their pension when they turned sixteen and could not claim a lump sum as an adult to cover the pension that they might have received if they had applied during childhood.

Excerpt from the Affidavit of Martin Campbell, June 10, 1889, Civil War Pension File of Dennis Campbell, 63rd USCI, RG 15:

> I am the only living child of Dennis Campbell deceased who was a member of Co "D" 63rd Reg U.S. Col Troops and who died at Davis Bend Miss. of chronic diarrhea in the year 1865 while in the service. My Father, Dennis Campbell married my mother Jane Bowline before the late war, the exact date of the marriage I do not know. They were married in Corinth, Miss. My Father went into the army in 1863 at Corinth Miss and after-

wards served through Miss and Memphis Tenn, then came went to Davis Bend, Miss and died there. I was with my father when he joined the army at Corinth and went with him everywhere and grew up in the regiment, was with him when he died at Davis Bend Miss

Martin Campbell was not the only son of a black Union soldier to follow his father into the army. Another son who went with his father, James Keebler, tried to avoid the fate of Campbell's unsuccessful application by using his intimate knowledge of his father's military service to impersonate his father with the Pension Bureau. He might have succeeded; since he had been there, Keebler was highly knowledgeable concerning his father's military service, and perhaps he hoped to use the ambiguity of ex-slaves' ages to fool the government. However, he was unable to simulate his father's age convincingly. Bureau personnel uncovered his ruse when they met him because Keebler simply appeared too young, even for a black man, to have served in the Civil War. In response to this ruse, the Bureau brought up Keebler on charges of falsely impersonating a soldier, making and filing a fraudulent claim, and perjury. Keebler accepted a plea deal from the U.S. Attorney in which in return for pleading guilty he was sentenced to a year and fifteen days at the federal prison in Brooklyn, New York, and had to pay a one-thousand-dollar fine. The facts of his fraud were described by H. L. Williams, a special examiner, in an 1895 report to the commissioner of pensions in Washington, D.C.

Excerpt from the Report of H. L. Williams, Special Examiner, Johnson City, Tenn., to William Lochner, Commissioner of Pensions, Washington, D.C., Nov. 11, 1895, Civil War Pension File of George Deadrick, 1st USCHA, RG 15:

Johnson City, Tenn.,
Nov. 11th, 1895

Hon. Wm Lochner
Commissioner of Pensions,
Washington, D.C.

Sir:
I have the honor to forward herewith a letter addressed to me from Hon. J.H. Bible, U.S. District Attorney for the Eastern District of Tennessee, in

reference to pension claim No. 906,968, of George Deadrick, Co. G, 1st U. S. C. Hv'y Artillery. Inclosed with Mr. Bible's letter were the papers in said claim.

As suggested by the District Attorney I had a warrant issued for the arrest of the claimant. He was arrested on the 9th inst. and brought before the U.S. Commissioner, at Johnson City for a preliminary hearing.

The trial lasted through two days, and was not concluded until this afternoon. The defendant was represented by able counsel, but the evidence on behalf of the Government was conclusive, and he was held for trial, at the January 1896 term of the Federal Court, at Knoxville, Tenn., upon the charge of falsely personating a soldier, making and filing a fraudulent claim, and for perjury. His bail was fixed at $1,000, and being unable to furnish same he was placed in jail.

The case is as follows: George Deadrick is shown by the records of the War Department to have served in Co. G, 1st U. S. C. Heavy Artillery from May 11, 1864, to March 31, 1866, when he was honorably discharged.

On Aug. 18, 1890, a claim was filed under Act of June 27, 1890, by a man who claimed to be the said soldier, the claim was rejected on the ground of no pensionable disability; then on July 17, 1894, the same claimant filed a new declaration under said Act.

It has been proven that the soldier George Deadrick was a man at least 40 years old at enlistment, he was Commissary Sgt. of the Company, and was known as "Uncle George" among his comrades, also that he died in Washington Co., Tenn. in 1869. It was also shown that he was born in Virginia, and was a low, heavy-set man.

It was proven that the claimant's name is and always has been John Keebler, that he is a son of the soldier George Deadrick, that he was born in Washington Co., Tenn., May 4, 1852, and was therefore less than 12 years old when George Deadrick enlisted.

Several of the soldiers' comrades testified positively that they saw the claimant at Knoxville when the lad's father was in the service, and that he was but a boy or so 12 years old. A number of witnesses testify positively that there was but one George Deadrick in Co. G, 1st U. S. C. H. A. and that he died soon after the war. All the above facts were fully set forth in my report made in the case, and which now among the papers.

It will be seen however that the District Attorney expressed the opinion that "there is not much of a case against Deadrick." It is my opinion however that if the case is prosecuted with any vigor that the conviction of Keebler is certain. I cannot conceive of a plainer case of attempted fraud.

On Oct. 18, 1895, I submitted to the Bureau the deposition of James Noel in reference to the case in a supplemental [illegible] said report is not among the other papers of the case. The witness testified fully before the Commissioner however, and the deposition taken by me will not be needed in the further prosecution of the case.

At the request of the U.S. Commissioner, I have retained all the papers in the pension claim, and will have them at court when the case goes to the Grand Jury. The District Attorney also, some time ago, requested that whenever any pension papers were needed in a trial the Special Examiner take charge of them until they should be needed at Court. Unless otherwise instructed therefore, I shall keep the papers I have receipted to the District Attorney for them.

Very Respectfully,
H L Williams
Special Examiner

Differences: Black Union Soldiers and Military Service

Just as the recruitment and camp life of black soldiers was different from that of their white counterparts, their testimony in Civil War pension files also demonstrates that their experience of combat was dissimilar. Most notably, compared to whites, relatively few African Americans saw combat. When the subject of combat experience came up in special examinations, most black Union veterans indicated that they had not been in battle or had only seen limited action, such as skirmishes and expeditions. A typical example is that of veteran Cuffee Simmons, who testified that his regiment moved around a lot in his year and a half of service but that it participated in only a couple of skirmishes.

Excerpt from the Deposition of Cuffee Simmons, Apr. 18, 1901, Civil War Pension File of Cuffee Simmons, 128th USCI, RG 15:

26 years of age as near as I can make it, I went to Beauford, S.C. and enlisted in Co. B—128 U.S.C. Vol Inf I enlisted in Febr. Could not give the year. No one recruited me, but Gen Littlefield swore me in to the service at Hilton Head.

I was discharged at Morris Island, Oct 4, could not give year. I served something less than two years. I had no other service, military or naval, federal or confederate.

I was never on detached service. . . .

We were in no battles. We were in skirmishes on Morris Island and Folly Island. No one was killed or wounded in my Co.

We remained in Beauford about 4 months or more, when we went to Hilton head. We remained there about 2 months, than we went back to Beauford, when we remained there about 3 months. Than we went to Sullivan Island. We remained there about one month. Than our Co went to Morris Island where we remained about 6 months or until we were mustered out.

Black veterans testified that they were more commonly used as garrison troops or military laborers. For example, Alexander Daughtry, a Georgia veteran, told a special examiner in 1911 that he had been recruited to support William Tecumseh Sherman's famous march through Georgia and the Carolinas in 1864–65. Also, interestingly, he claimed to have marched in the Grand Review in Washington, D.C., a parade in which black troops were conspicuously absent, except for some laborers like Daughtry. White soldiers of Ulysses S. Grant's and Sherman's great eastern and western armies dominated this two-day event on Pennsylvania Avenue in May 1865, meant to celebrate Union victory in the Civil War. The event featured a who's who of personalities from the major Union armies, as well as masses of soldiers, but except for a few black labor units attached to Sherman's western army, no other black Union soldiers participated in the review.[9]

Excerpt from the Deposition of Alexander Daughtry, Nov. 5, 1911, Civil War Pension File of Alexander Daughtry, 135th USCI, RG 15:

I am 64 or 65 years of age; my post-office address is Egypt, Effingham County, Georgia. I live about two miles south of Egypt.

My full name is Alexander Daughtry. From my birth, my given name has been Alexander but I have all the time been called Alec. I have learned to write Alex as my given name; I haven't learned to write the name Alexander. It hasn't been very long since I learned to write what I can write.

I served as a private soldier in Co. C, 135th Colored Infantry. I am not certain as to the time I enlisted. I was discharged in the fall of 1865 and I had enlisted early in the same year. I had been before in what was called the pioneer corps—we built roads and prepared the way for the army to go. We had no uniform thou; had no company nor regiment but we had squads. I didn't get any pay, I think, for the time I was a pioneer corps. I got three hundred dollars by the time I left the army and I don't know whether the pay was partly for the time I was in the pioneer corps or not.

I have not been in the service of the United States—not the army nor navy—at any time other than while I was a member of Co. C, 135th U.S. Colored and in the pioneer corps just before I came into the 135th.

I have the certificate of discharge that I received when I was mustered out of the 135th. (Deponent produced the original certificate of discharge of Alexander Daughtry from Co. C, 135th U.S.C. Infantry. Examiner). I am the person named in that certificate as Alexander Daughtry and I received that certificate at Louisville, Kentucky, when I was mustered out of the 135th Colored Infantry. In 1871 or 1872—somewhere along there—I sent that certificate to Washington to get some money. . . .

I was born in Scriven County, this state at the time I enlisted my age was given as 20 years. I remember that was the case. . . . I had been doing farm work. I don't think that there was a noticeable mark or scar on me when I enlisted [in] the army. There was no peculiarity of person or of feature in my case. There was no picture of me taken while I was a soldier. There is no small picture of me now.

Through the years just before I entered the army, I lived with a Mr. Tom Daughtry, near Scarboro, Scriven County, this state. I went from his place to the army, and I joined Sherman's army a little below Scarboro. I went with it to Savannah, working on the roads; there we went to Beaufort; then through South Carolina & North Carolina. While we were in the woods in South Carolina we were organized as soldiers but I don't remember at what place we were given guns. We were at Kingston, Goldsboro, and Raleigh, North Carolina. I don't think that we had any guns at Kingston—I don't remember that we had any guns until we [were] at Louisville. I don't remember a place called Jones in North Carolina. We were at Raleigh but once. From Raleigh we marched north; we just went along with the rest of the army, not having guns or other equipment to carry. We went to Virginia—to Richmond—then on to Washington. I don't remember the name of any town near Washington. We stopped near Washington and then on the day the soldiers marched through Washington we marched through too, but I don't remember that we had any guns. After that parade, our regiment went into camp a little distance from Washington and it stayed there for a little space of time; then it took [a] train from Washington and went, as I

> remember, to a place called Parkersburg on the Ohio River. From Parkersburg, we were in tents during the summer; when colder weather came we were in barracks in Louisville. We were armed at Louisville and we were drilled. We were discharged at the barracks in Louisville.

Like Alexander Daughtry, Alexander Porter never saw any combat. Instead, he reports in his 1900 deposition, he spent his military service principally on garrison duty at various points in Mississippi. This pattern of black military service in the Civil War was quite common in the western theater, where Union commanders were particularly reluctant to use African Americans in combat, instead preferring to use them to free up white soldiers for such duty.[10] Despite the success of black troops at engagements like Fort Wagner, Port Hudson, and many others, some Union officers remained unconvinced of their reliability in combat. Hence, they preferred to use African American soldiers in labor-intensive, noncombat roles, which allowed white soldiers to focus on fighting. Porter gave his testimony in support of his claim for a service-related pension under the original 1862 pension law. At the time of his testimony, he already was receiving the maximum monthly rate under the 1890 pension law, which did not require disabilities to be service related. Because of the lack of official army records substantiating his claim and his inability to produce reliable eyewitnesses that might substantiate his claim for a service-related disability, his application was rejected.

Excerpt from the Deposition of Alexander Porter, May 3, 1900, Civil War Pension File of Alexander Porter, 58th USCI, RG 15:

> I am 62 years of age; my post-office address is [Clinton, Hickman Co., Kentucky]; residence 3 1/2 miles N.W. with Wash Vincent; occupation gardening and working around the house.
>
> I am the identical person who served as a private in Co. A, 58 U.S.C. Inf. I do not remember the dates of my enlistment and discharge. Not even the years. I think I enlisted in August in the third year of the War, and served 2 years and 8 months, but I do not remember the month I was discharged but it was in the Spring. I was a private during my entire service. I served in no other company or regiment. I am pensioned at $12 per month under the act of June 27, 1890.
>
> I claim pension under the general [1862] law on account of disease of eyes as a result of smallpox contracted in service and line of duty. . . .

I was born and raised near Meadvillle, Franklin Co., Miss. and lived there up to enlistment. I only had one master and his name was Wm Porter (dec'd). . . . I was strong and well at enlistment. I never had anything wrong with my eyes before enlistment. Never even had sore eyes before enlistment. I enlisted at Natchez, Miss. and was mustered in there about 3 months after enlistment I think. The only examination I was subjected to at enlistment or muster in was that a doctor looked at my teeth to see whether I could eat hard tack. . . .

The regiment remained in barracks at Natchez, Miss for two years after enlistment. We had nice comfortable barracks there. From Natchez we marched to Brookhaven, Miss where we lived in tents for about 6 weeks. We then marched on to Corinth, Miss where we were encamped in tents about 2 months. We then marched to Vicksburg, Miss where we were encamped in tents for 5 or 6 weeks or until muster out and discharge.

I was not engaged in any actual battles.

We had one hard march from Natchez, Miss to a place near 'Homachita River' near where it empties into the Mississippi River. We started at 4:00 p.m. and marched until 5 a.m.

I contracted the disease of the eyes as a result of small pox, 10 or 12 months after enlistment at Natchez, Miss. . . . I was in ranks at roll call at 6 PM when it was discovered that I was broken out with small pox. It was raining then I was ordered out of ranks and sent to the pest house at Natchez Miss. I reckon I was in the Pest house about 6 weeks. I did not notice my eyes being affected while in the pest house. I did not notice anything wrong with my eyes until after I had returned to duty and was standing guard. The night wind seemed to affect my eyes then. Capt. Willis McGrew excused me from duty with out my seeing a doctor on account of my eyes, but I know he did excuse me from guard duty and I stayed around the barracks. . . .

I never was treated in hospital or at sick call on account of my eyes. I never was treated at any time except when I was in the small pox pest house. I had attended sick call in service before I had the small pox on account of a little fever or diarrhea.

Differences: Black POWs

Of course, not every black Union soldier's service in the Civil War was as uneventful as that of soldiers who saw no combat. Although combat narratives are rare and often unreliable, an unusual number of former black prisoners-of-war show up in Civil War pension files, and these accounts further demonstrate the chaotic reality that existed behind formal Confederate policies toward captured African Americans. Officially, black Union soldiers taken as prisoners by the rebels were to be treated as rebellious slaves, meaning that they could be put to death summarily and that their white officers were subject to the same penalty for inciting a slave rebellion. However, surviving black POWs in pension files reveal that their treatment at the hands of the Confederates varied according to the whim and will of their captors. Certainly in some cases, most infamously the Fort Pillow massacre in April 1864, Confederates killed captured black Union soldiers. At Fort Pillow, an earthen fort on the Mississippi River about forty miles north of Memphis, Tennessee, Confederate raiders under Nathan Bedford Forrest surprised and overwhelmed a garrison of African Americans and Tennessee Unionists guarding the fort. Several hundred black soldiers were killed in this incident, many of them after they allegedly tried to surrender. Some black troops were spared and carried off by Forrest's men. At least two African American prisoners-of-war lived long enough after the war to tell their stories to special examiners. One survivor of Fort Pillow was Allen James Walker. He stayed alive, Walker testified in 1902, because he was claimed by a Confederate Orderly Sergeant that valued a living servant for himself more than another dead black soldier. Even more fascinating is the case of Revel Garrison, a black cavalryman, who was captured by the Confederates in Virginia. He testified in 1888 of being forced by his captors to dig entrenchments before his harrowing escape back to Union lines and freedom.[11]

Excerpt from the Deposition of Allen James Walker, Feb. 5, 1902, Civil War Pension File of Allen James (alias Allen James Walker), 11th USCI and 7th USCHA, RG 15:

> I am 59 yrs old near as I can tell—occupation odd jobs of any kind. P.O. 239 Ala. St. (Alabama St.) [in Memphis, Tennessee].
>
> I am the identical Allen James who served under the name Allen James in Co. D 11 US Col Vol Inf. I enlisted in Nov 1863 at Corinth Miss and mustered out at Memphis Tenn at Fort Pickering in Jan. 1866. . . . In Dec of 1863 or Jan 64 we came to Memphis—to Fort Pickering bringing our siege guns with us and shortly after reaching Memphis we were sent to garrison Fort Pillow Tenn about 60 or 75 miles up the river. We left our

siege at Fort Pickering and had smaller cannon at Fort Pillow Here (Apr 12) in the forepart of 1864 Forrest run in on us—and killed and captured us nearly all of us—I was captured there.

I was not treated like the other prisoners but a John Peary, a Sergeant, Ord Sgt. of Willis' battalion McCullough's brigade—Forrests command took me and made me his servant. Made me change my US uniform for confederate clothes and Kept me with them for nearly a year—and I went with them all over Tenn, Ala, and Miss. About Dec 64 or Jan 65 he—John Peary—sent me with his brother, Dallas Peary who also belong to the same Co. to their home in Gonzales Texas, or rather on their little farm near there and here they made me practically their slave and I put in a crop that spring for them. About July 15, 1865 we learned of the surrender and hearing some US soldiers coming through there I ran off and got with a wagon train—I don't know from whose command and they took me to Columbus Texas where I was turned over to head quarters and given transportation to Galveston. Here I was sent to New Orleans by ship. Then to New York and falling in with a crowd—numbers of many regiments scattered about they sent us all round in Va and N.C. dropping each man off as they reached his command and finally wound me up at Baltimore Md. Here I was given transportation by rail to Cairo Ill and from there by boat to Memphis Tenn where I arrived about Nov 14, 1865 and found my regiment camped on Vance St. and then known as the 11 US Col Vol Inf, commanded by Col. Turner. I remained with it—Co. D of said regt till mustered out about Jan 12, 1866.

Excerpt from the Deposition of Revel Garrison, Sept. 10, 1888, Civil War Pension File of Revel Garrison, 2nd USCC, RG 15:

I am 63 years old occupation laborer P.O. address Pungoteague Accomac Co Va. I served in Co H 2 U.S.C. Cav.

I have never belonged to any other organization. I cant remember exactly when I enlisted but I think it was in 1864. I never was in the Naval service. I claim pension for rheumatism and got my toe broke and I was struck in the side with the breech of a gun breaking my ribs on the left side. For several years before the war I lived here in Pungoteague and I have lived near here ever since the war. . . .

I had my toe next to my great toe broken and my left side injured while a prisoner or rather I had my toe broken while escaping from the rebels.

> I was captured at Deep Bottom Va. . . . I was out getting fodder for my horse as we had orders to do, when I was taken prisoner. We were out on picket and having come in we went to the reserve post and slept—There were five or six of us at the reserve post. When I waked up in the morning I found the rest of the boys had gone after fodder for their horses so I started out and met the other boys coming back. I went on to get the fodder and was captured by two rebels. I was taken to prison at Richmond Va. I was there some time when they took me out and put me to work digging trenches on the James River quite a distance from richmond. While digging down in the pit one day I got warm and took off my blouse and asked the rebel soldier guarding us to lay it up on the bank for me. He got mad at me and said what giving me your lousy dirty Yankee blouse to handle and he hit me in the left side with the breech of his gun. I knew something in my side broke when he hit me. They carried me to camp this was late in the evening and I made up my mind to get away or die. That night I went down to the river and rolled in a log and swam across. The rebels shot at me before I got across. I hurt my toe down to the river but I first noticed it was broken when I rolled the log into the river I was alone when my toe was broken. There were many present when my side was hurt but no members of my company and I did not know any of them No one examined my side while with the rebels but I know that side has always been deformed since and I never was hurt there at any other time. I was not sent to the hospital until two or three weeks after I rejoined my company None of my comrades examined my side then. I think some of them saw my toe was broken when I pulled my shoes of.

Differences: Postwar Service

The black military experience did not come to an end with the Civil War. African American soldiers served disproportionately compared to white Union soldiers for occupation duty in the postwar South. As most black troops enlisted in 1863 or 1864, their three-year enlistments had not expired at war's end, making them ideal to retain to garrison Southern cities. Indeed, the 1894 deposition of Wiley Johnson shows that as the war was winding down in the late spring of 1865, Union recruiters still were active among African Americans, especially in states such as Alabama and Georgia that had heretofore seen little black enlistment in the Union army, since they were far removed from Northern lines until quite late in the war. It is likely that the recruiters aimed to enlist fresh black troops for postwar duties so that war-weary white Union soldiers, recruited in 1861 and 1862, could be more quickly released from service.

Excerpt from the Deposition of Wiley Johnson, Jan. 26, 1894, Civil War Pension File of Wiley Johnson, 136th USCI, RG 15:

> My age is 72 years, occupation farmer, residence and P.O. address Fort Mitchell, Ala.
>
> I am the identical Wiley Johnson who served during the late war as a member of Co H- 136 U. S. C. Inf with the rank of private. I enlisted in May or June 1865 and was discharged Jany 1866.[12] I enlisted at Columbus, Ga. but was mustered into the service at Atlanta, Ga, and was discharged at Augusta Ga. . . .
>
> Q. How long did you remain in Atlanta after you were mustered into service.
>
> A. We remained there in Atlanta until About October 1865—when we were sent to Augusta where we went into quarters for the winter, and remained there until I was mustered out.
>
> We did guard duty all the time we were in Atlanta. After we were enlisted at Columbus, Ga. we went direct to Macon, to garrison that city and we stayed there six or eight weeks, and went from Macon, Ga. to Greenville, Ga. to work on the R.R. and went from there to Atlanta and was mustered into service No, we never had any fighting to do. We got to Augusta, Ga. about October 1, 1865 and did guard duty all the time we were there until we were mustered out of service, along about the first of January, 1866

Besides helping to garrison the postwar South, black troops were held in service after the Civil War for another reason. Many black soldiers were sent to Texas as part of a large force assembled on the Mexican border to pressure France to end its occupation of Mexico, where it had set up the Austrian prince Maximillian as its puppet emperor. Pension files make it clear that many black soldiers detailed to Texas reacted fearfully to the news of their reassignment. One such account came out in the testimony of Henry Ford (alias Charles Newton) to a special examiner in 1902. During his special examination, it emerged that Ford was a deserter from his unit, the 2nd U.S. Colored Cavalry. Ford initially claimed that he had been sick and absent without permission but that by the time he tried to rejoin his Virginia-based unit, it had been shipped off to Texas, so he had returned to his family. Later he admitted that this account was false and that the real reason he had deserted was because of rumors that black troops being shipped out of Virginia were not really being sent to Texas but were instead being shipped to Cuba, where slavery was still legal, to be sold into bondage. Given this change of story, it might be possible to dismiss Ford as lacking credibility and to dismiss his stories of the rumors circulating among black troops in Virginia in 1865 as false. However, one of the few autobiographies written by a black Civil War veteran, Alexander H. Newton's *Out of the Briars*, describes this same rumor circulating among African American soldiers on a Texas-bound transport.[13] If these rumors reveal anything, they are a poignant reminder of just how tenuous in 1865 some former slaves believed their freedom to be and how fearful they were of being reenslaved.

Excerpt from the Deposition of Henry Ford, Apr. 5, 1902, Civil War Pension File of Henry Ford (alias Charles Newton), 2 USCC, RG 15:

> I am about 64 years of age; my post office address is 1032 County St Portsmouth, Norfolk Co, Va, and residence same, occupation, laborer in U.S. Navy Yard at Portsmouth, Va, but they dropped me last Monday.
>
> I was born in Perquimans Co, NC, near Woodville but I can't give you the year of my birth. My father's name was Augustus Sawyer and he was a slave to the Sawyer family at first and then fell to the Joe Granby estate. My mother was Angie Ford and she was a slave to Dr. Ford to whom I was a slave also. My full and correct name is Henry Ford, but I am also called sometimes—Charles Newton and Newton Charles. My full name was Henry Charles Newton Ford before the war and that is where my name Charles Newton came from. I have never gone under any other name, I am known mostly as Charles Newton and married under that name.
>
> I was about 20 years of age when I enlisted as a private of Co A 2 U.S.C.V. Cav, at Newbern N.C. in Dec, 1863. I can't recollect the name of the recruiting officer as I volunteered I was stripped and given a thorough physical examination at Newbern and again Fort Monroe, Va, where I was sworn in.
>
> I was discharged at Portsmouth, Va, in 1865 along about June 16. I really wasn't discharged till got my discharge certificate from Wash, D.C. and now show this discharge certificate. . . .

Q. Why did you not receive a discharge certificate when your company was mustered out and discharged?

A. I was not with it but absent at Portsmouth, VA, with my people and was sick. We came down from City Point to Portsmouth to go to Texas and stopped there, I took off without permission to my aunt Clarkie Ford (dec'd) in the country and as I was sick remained there quite awhile Anyway when I got to Portsmouth the ship had gone on its way to Texas. I didn't bother any more but stayed at my aunt and never rejoined my company and regiment because I didn't think I was needed

Q. Well, I will now ask you if it is not a fact that you made no effort to get back to your company and regiment and that you left your command at Portsmouth with the careful and deliberate purpose of quitting or giving up the service and never again returning to it?

A. No I intended to join or rejoin my company the day but didn't get to Portsmouth until three days after I quit it and then the company was gone. Yes, I admit that I took "French leave" and skipped out without permission of my superior officer. I had been sick ever since the Deep Bottom fight I was better when we reached Portsmouth but was up and down

No, I never had been in a hospital but was treated in camp I had [illegible]

No, I never was in the service before, or since.

No, I never deserted from a previous or subsequent service and never served in the Confederate Army or Navy. . . .

Q. Now I am going to ask you a question and desire you to tell me the true facts Did you not take this name Charles Newton or Newton Charles on account of your desertion from the army?

A. Yes, sir, I did.

Q. Did you not assume the name of Charles Newton alias Newton Charles immediately after you left your company at Portsmouth?

A. Well, within five days after I came out of the army or skipped from it

Q. I will now ask you if it is not a fact that you took the name of Charles Newton alias Newton Charles because you were afraid the authorities, the U.S. or Federal authorities would arrest you?

A. Well yes sir, that is so.

Q. Then you did not want to return to your company and took that name Charles Newton alias Newton Charles to avoid service in the U.S.A. after you deserted?

A. Yes sir I did. That is so.

Q. Didn't you take the name Charles Newton or Newton Charles immediately after you left the service?

A. No, I didn't until five days after While I was in the army I heard talk at City Point and all the way down to Norfolk that we were to be taken South to Cuba and placed in slavery. Well it was on account of my hearing talk at being put in slavery in Cuba that I deserted, I admit that to you now.[14]

It is also clear from Civil War pension files that service in Texas, after the end of the war and often a long way from home, was more than some black soldiers could take. This situation is understandable given the difficult environment that African American troops found along the Mexican border. A shortage of drinking water, extreme heat, insects, reptiles, and a lack of firewood all contributed to the harsh conditions under which many men fell ill and died at an alarming rate. In the case of Joshua Helm, these appalling conditions and the separation from his family literally drove him crazy, as an 1874 affidavit from two former comrades, made in support of his widow's pension claims, makes clear. (Helm never recovered and died in a federal insane asylum in 1871.)

Excerpt from the Affidavit of Harrison Caldwell and Mester Talbott, Feb. 6, 1874, Civil War Pension File of Joshua Helm, 116th USCI, RG 15:

State of Kentucky
County of Boyle

On this the 6th day of February A.D. 1874, personally appeared before me Jon B. Nichols Clerk of the County Court a Court of record in and for the County and State aforesaid Harrison Caldwell and Mester Talbott known to me as persons of respectability and entitled to credit, who being duly sworn according to law, declare that they were both members of the 116 regiment U.S.C. Troops, the said Harrison Caldwell a Sergeant in Co. E and the said Mester Talbott a Private in Co. F that were acquainted with Joshua Helm deceased who was also a Private in Co C in said regiment; that they were intimately associated with said Helm whilst in the service and knew him before his enlistment in the U.S. service; that he was a man of sober, temperate habits, sound in mind and body, never exhibited any signs of insanity before enlistment nor after, until about the time or immediately after the surrender of the Confederate Army by Genl. Lee.

> The regiment was, at this time, stationed in Virginia, and after the surrender many of the colored Soldiers became impressed with the belief that they would be discharged at once and sent home, and the said Helm among them, that the regiment instead of being discharged was ordered to Texas, which caused the said Helm to become much depressed in spirits which soon terminated in total derangement of his mind. He soon began to talk wildly about his wife, children, and home, saying that his wife and child, or children were all dead, said he had received letters to that effect, when in fact no such letters had reached him; that he at one time applied for a furlough and failing to get it, he became worse and talked more wildly and foolishly than ever; that his whole manner was changed, and his conversation on any and all subjects became extremely wild and nonsensical; that his condition finally became so bad as to render it absolutely necessary to send him to the Asylum at Washington; that they are perfectly satisfied from their knowledge of this case, the insanity was produced by an inordinate desire to return home, in other words, was the result of a most violent attack of Nostalgia (Home sickness) and originated whilst said Helm was in the service and in the line of duty, that they believe that if said Helm could have been discharged and allowed to return to his family, all simptoms of derangement would have passed away, and he would have been entirely, restored, and that they have no interest whatever in this claim.

As the case of Joshua Helm demonstrates, even for black soldiers who did not serve in combat, Civil War service still entailed significant stress and sacrifice. This was certainly not exclusive to African American troops. Indeed, much about the service of black Union soldiers was not unique to them but also was true about white soldiers, North and South, and in some cases soldiers before and since. The Union army inculcated soldiers with the customs and discipline of the military so thoroughly that decades later, an elderly African American veteran could readily recall them for a federal bureaucrat. Yet it was also the case that young black soldiers who were confronted with temptation, in particular the company of young women, acted as irresponsibly as their white counterparts did on occasion.

Still, pension files also show that there was much special about the black experience in the Civil War. For white Union soldiers the enemy army was not a common avenue into Union service. For many African Americans their presence in Confederate military camps as servants, laborers, and in other support roles brought them near enough to Union lines to make service in the Union army more feasible than it would have been if they were on plantations deep in rebel territory. Neither did as many whites in Union service have as many adventurous recruitment stories, assume an alias to keep from being reclaimed by a slaveholder, get defrauded as often by recruiters, or bring family members with them into the army. Black soldiers also clearly saw less combat than their white counterparts, having been used more often for labor and garrison roles. Still, their service often was a great burden, especially for those men sent to Texas in the wake of the conflict. As will be seen in the next chapter, pension files also demonstrate the unique nature of the lives of African Americans following the Civil War.

3

Postwar Patterns

Civil War pension files provide a revealing firsthand perspective of former slaves' lives after the war and emancipation. Their stories reveal how they experienced their new freedom of movement and some reasons that prompted them to travel and relocate. The pension files also offer readers a sense of how freed people described their work, as well as how a significant minority came to enjoy a modest degree of affluence, while the vast majority of their peers remained in desperate poverty. Finally, former slaves' Civil War pension files bring to light many important issues around marriage and family in postwar life, chief among them the preindustrial view of time common among former slaves, especially in rural areas, and how high mortality ravaged postwar black communities.

The information that freed people provide in pension files about the patterns of their postwar lives offer important insights into the aggregate data that defines the overall picture of former slaves in the decades following freedom. The statistical portrait of African Americans during this period contains a few encouraging facts in a mostly depressing picture. The postwar censuses reveal a population still overwhelmingly Southern and rural, as the Great Migration to Northern cities that began during World War I was still years away. The 1890 census, for example, counted only 7 percent of the black population in the United States residing in the Northern states.[1] It also reveals a poor people still mostly engaged in manual labor but with a small but significant group beginning to accumulate wealth in the form of land, livestock, and personal possessions. For example, the 1880 census found about 20 percent of black farmers as land owners, an impressive figure given that the Civil War had ended only fifteen years before and most slaves emerged from bondage penniless.[2] But the 1900 census reveals that the death rate of black Americans was significantly higher than for whites: thirty per one thousand blacks died each year, as opposed to only seventeen per one thousand whites.[3]

Such statistics constitute the big picture, but what the census cannot uncover are the countless individual stories that lay behind it. Civil War pension files capture some of these tales of geographic movement and stability, the accumulation of property and the battle to keep it, the struggle to obtain the necessities of life, experiences of family and marriage, mortality that outstripped even the lamentable life expectancy for white Americans of the post–Civil War period, and the relative isolation of many former slaves from the clocks and calendars that increasingly were affecting the way that most Americans, especially whites, reckoned time in an age of industrialization.

Geographic Mobility

African Americans did not tend to stay in one place after the Civil War. Many of them experienced geographic mobility, or in simpler language, they moved their residence. That former slaves relocated from time to time is hardly surprising. The most basic restriction that defined American bondage was the slaves' inability to leave their owner's plantation without permission. Yet after an initial wave of wanderlust, Civil War pension files also reveal that former slaves moved for many of the same reasons that made the American population as a whole in the late nineteenth century highly mobile. In addition, former slaves moved because of factors unique to their own community and condition. However, some former slaves demonstrated very little movement at all, preferring to stay close to one locale, sometimes not far from where they had been enslaved, because they considered that place home. Indeed, when freed people did relocate, the move rarely was far; in most cases it appears to have occurred fairly close to the place of departure, because they had knowledge of the general area.

Although former slaves had many reasons to relocate, the pension files demonstrate that economic motivations clearly took the lead. Albert Kelly's fascinating and truly exceptional 1882 affidavit makes clear that the primary motive for his frequent moves after the war was the need to make a living: he moved where he could find employment. A Tennessee veteran who had been a prisoner of war of the rebels, Kelly worked as a civilian laborer for the War Department, building national cemeteries for the Union dead in Murfreesboro and Nashville. Next, he apparently became a sharecropper. According to his affidavit, Kelly and his family seem to have moved to a new location every few years. Despite his stated intention near the end of the affidavit to leave soon for Kansas (where many African Americans moved, seeking a new start free from the emerging racial repression of the post-Reconstruction South),[4] Kelly and his family ended up in Oklahoma, where he died in 1903.

Two other more typical documents also reveal the connection between economic need and postwar geographic mobility: the affidavits of Columbus Kimble and Isaiah Holt. Kimble was a Tennessee veteran who, after numerous moves, was living in Kentucky when he filed his affidavit with the Pension Bureau in 1898. Holt was another ex-soldier from Tennessee, who moved to Indiana, following a common path of postwar migration that took African Americans in the border states into the southern or "butternut" regions of neighboring Northern states. These areas were economically and culturally similar to the regions they had left behind.[5]

Excerpt from the Affidavit of Albert Kelly, Jan. 2, 1882, Civil War Pension File of Albert Kelly, 111th USCI, RG 15:

> Slave of Henry Kelly of Giles County Tennessee now alive & there
>
> 1st. For 5 years before and up to my enlistment in Co A, US Col, Infs, Vol, I was his slave and living on his place and doing his part and was perfectly Sound and well. . . . I was clear of *Hernia* or *Piles* or *Aches* in the Stomach which has attended me Since my blow up at Mobile Ala 1865. . . .
>
> 2. I remained Sound & well all the time of my enlistment till Blown into Bay of Mobile and there treated by Confederate Sergeans in a *Confederate Hospital* till I was released from my imprisonment by U.S. Soldiers and then treatment was at *Kingston Springs*, on the North Western R.R. of Tenn, where the escaped men of our Reg, had been for Some time and where we as late prisoners refreshed were clothed & armed had a temporary Hospital. There reclothed & well fed with nourishing food I got out of the Hospital to go with Reg, to Murfreesboro Tenn where Reg, Camped till ordered to Nashville, & was discharged. . . .
>
> 3. I was promoted Corporal at Murfreesboro fer though letter & could do duty & was steady all the time. I would get so weak at times from fainting Spells like [illegible] would make a noise & Piles hurt I knew who was coming. I would hold on to my Syde & care for myself. So I was the day I was discharged.

4. Discharged I went at once to Murfreesboro was promised & got as job at the Cemetary for the Nation there and at it Six months. . . .

5. Capt McTige came to Nashville and opened this Cemetary at a place 6 miles out of Nashville where the books will no doubt Show I stayed 3 years and having gotten my family with from Giles Co and the Cemetery finished I carried them into Hadleys Bend 10 miles of Nashville, and there lived 4 years, and had 3 children Sons getting up able to help me. . . .

6. I then moved to Kneelie's Bend, and lived on Chodnells place one year, he was a clerk in court house here, Madison Station was the mail PO.

7. I then moved to Capt William Waltons place near Hendersonville, and 3 miles South of it, with my family [illegible] & helpers and Stayed there 3 years

8. I then lived the remainder of my time on S.R. Doxeys farm 3 miles South of Hendersonville Sumner Co, Tennessee, and will leave there soon to go to Kansas with my family.

Excerpt from the Affidavit of Columbus Kimble, Nov. 9, 1898, Civil War Pension File of Columbus Kimble, 101st USCI and 110th USCI, RG 15:

[Columbus Kimble states] that after he was mustered out of the U.S. Army he lived in Giles County Tenn, his post-office address was Pulaski Tenn for about 3 years. Afterwards Lenville Sta. Giles County was his post-office for about 4 years he then went to Marshall County Tenn, his post-office was Cornersville his post-office about one year. He then went to Buford Station in Giles Co. post-office Reynolds Sta. he lived there 2 years. he remained there in Giles County for about 7 years when he moved to Franklin Simpson County Ky where he has lived until the present time.

Excerpt from the Affidavit of Isaiah Holt, Nov. 2, 1889, Civil War Pension File of Isaiah Holt, 13th USCHA and 72nd USCI, RG 15:

My Post Office address is Rockport Spencer County Indiana I first went to Nashville Tenn after my discharge followed sawing wood remained there two years then I went to Evansville Ind. done Job work as I could find it stayed there seven or Eight years then Came to Rockport Spencer County Indiana where I have been ever since Sometimes Sawing wood when Rheumatism did not effect me and doing other chores I am now almost totaly unfit for the performance of labor by reason of Rheumatism and have been for the past three years

Historians have long known that many slaves were eager to see the cities once they became free. For one thing, in urban areas, "freedom was freer."[6] Although Southern cities certainly were not free of discrimination, life proved less onerous there, and former slaves could avoid efforts taking place in the countryside to institute new forms of coercive labor through the Black Codes and antivagrancy laws. They also found that cities were more interesting than rural areas, with more opportunities for entertainment and social life, as well as access to black institutions (schools, clubs, mutual aid societies, etc.) and other resources that were scarce or did not exist in the plantation districts.

Civil War pension files provide first-person accounts of this rural to urban migration. John Burgess, for instance, moved to Little Rock from Holly Grove, Arkansas, in 1872, but 1877 found him back in rural Holly Grove. Burgess's return to the countryside was not unusual, for Civil War pension files suggest that although some ex-slaves stayed in urban areas, many migrants eventually returned to the countryside. This helps to explain why the 1890 census found only 11 percent of the black population nationwide in cities with a population greater than twenty-five thousand people. Indeed, in the overwhelmingly rural lower South, less than 5 percent of African Americans could be defined as "urban."[7]

Excerpt from the Deposition of John Burgess, Aug. 8, 1895, Civil War Pension File of John Burgess, 11th USCI and 113th USCI, RG 15:

> When I was discharged I went down near Holly Gove [Arkansas] and worked for Jerry Dial for five years Daniel Dial, Austin Moore and Tommy Roberts of Holly Grove worked with me and they know what I am telling you for one day my leg got to bleeding and I fainted in the field. These men have known me ever since and we see one another most every Sunday, excepting the old white man Jerry Dial and he may not remember me.
>
> I staid in Little Rock from 1872 to 1877 and the rest of the time I have lived in this neighborhood. I went to Little Rock so that I could go to Hot Springs and cure my leg but after I staid in Hot Springs for three months I found I could not cure it I came back here.

Alexander Daughtry of Georgia and David Edwards of Arkansas demonstrate the readiness of some former slaves not only to leave their old environs after the Civil War but to adopt a vagabond existence for a time. Both Daughtry and Edwards bounced around from place to place until both men settled down in rural settings not terribly different from the places in which they had grown up. Their experiences demonstrate that after the initial desire for travel was sated, most ex-slaves seemed to gravitate toward familiar rural settings.

Excerpt from the Deposition of Alexander Daughtry, Nov. 5, 1911, Civil War Pension File of Alexander Daughtry, 135th USCI, RG 15:

> When I left the army, I returned to my old home near Scarboro, this state [Georgia]. I was there not more than a month. I worked on a railroad from in January until in June; then I was in Savannah for awhile; then on a railroad again. I settled down in this county [Effingham], at Eaton, in 1868, I think it was. I have lived in this county since last Feb.

Excerpt from the Deposition of David Edwards, Nov. 14, 1911, Civil War Pension File of David Edwards, 88th USCI, 9th USCHA, and 3rd USCHA, RG 15:

> At muster out I went about 18 mi above Memphis Tenn with Capt Methudey & was there from April to Sept & went to Lake City, Ark & was there several years & then to Big Bay, Ark, & then West Memphis & stayed about 8 yrs & came here [Crittenden Co., Ark.] & have been here ever since.

One noteworthy and particularly mobile group in the post–Civil War black community was the clergy, some of whom were former slaves. The African Methodist Episcopal (AME) Church is especially noted for transferring ministers regularly between congregations, and in the process, the ministers moved over long distances. Clergy from other denominations also relocated frequently. Such was the case for Thomas W. Wilbourn, a Baptist minister, who lived in Texas after the war. His 1909 deposition to the Pension Bureau showed that he had moved frequently within Texas in his thirty-year career in the clergy. Wilbourn resided in Texas after the Civil War because his regiment had served there at the conflict's end. Whereas some soldiers like Joshua Helm went crazy as result of serving in Texas (see chapter 2) and others like Henry Ford (alias Charles Newton) actually deserted to avoid service there, other soldiers like the Georgia-born Wilbourn decided to spend the rest of their lives in the Lone Star State (as Wilbourn did until his death in 1918).

Excerpt from the Deposition, Thomas W. Wilbourn, Apr. 14, 1909, Civil War Pension File of Thomas Wilbert (alias Thomas W. Wilbourn), 122nd USCI, RG 15:

> Since my discharge I have lived in Texas all the time. Have been in all parts of the State. Have lived in Galveston 2 or 3 years, Waxahachie 7 yrs., Corsicana about 2 yrs., Celeburne 1 year, Ft. Worth about 15 years, Marshall about 1 year, here [Wharton] since 1896. I have been preaching almost 30 years. Before that I was a barber.

While some former slaves were on the move in the decades following the Civil War, pension files show that others stayed quite stable. Although people might move occasionally, as the depositions of Burrell Howell of Kentucky and Nancy Fee of Louisiana demonstrate, they tended to remain in particular localities for long periods. Such people no doubt felt stronger connections to place, had better personal situations, or simply did not want to move.

Excerpt from the Letter of Burrell Howell, Maxon's Mills, Ky., to John C. Black, Commissioner of Pensions, Aug. 10, 1887, Civil War Pension File of Burrell Howell, 8th USCHA, RG 15:

> For nine years, my post office address was at Paducah, Ky. The remainder of the time it has been at Maxon's Mills, Ky. The first year, or in 1866, I worked in Paducah, driving a team; all the time since, about 20 years I have attempted to run a farm in McCracken County between this place and Paducah.

Excerpt from the Deposition of Nancy Fee, July 19, 1909, Civil War Pension File of Romeo Fee, 10th USCHA, RG 15:

> Soon as he was discharged he [Romeo Fee] came at once to the Lonestar plantation & found me there & we lived right there on the Lonestar place till 6 or 7 years ago when we moved to Magnolia St. [New Orleans] this city & lived [here] till he died. . . . After the war on the Lonestar place soldier made crop, plowed, ditched & chopped wood.

Although she ultimately ended up living in Illinois, former slave Sally Wallace describes living with and then near her former owner in Kentucky for a number of years after the war. Wallace does not explain why she did so, nor does her testimony shed light on why she and her family followed her master back to his plantation after the war. However, Wallace's testimony reveals that her former master, a doctor, provided her husband with medical care for illnesses incurred during his service, which may have factored into her decision about where to live.

Excerpt from the Deposition of Sally Wallace, Nov. 27, 1899, Civil War Pension file of Berry Wallace (alias Gordon), 8th USCHA, RG 15:

> That soldier was never in any other service than in the 8 Hvy Artillery and that his enlistment was forced as near as she understands. General Paine took the whole county of negroes away to Paducah Ky and they enlisted there and she never saw soldier again til after the war ended and then he came to Mound City after her and remained but a few hours when her master came from Kentucky and took her and her family and soldier back with him and they all remained on the plantation til soldier died. . . .
>
> Q. When soldier came from the war what was the matter of him if anything.
>
> A. He had a misery in his head and jaws—and from that kept lingering on until he took to bleeding of the lungs and died of lung disease.
>
> Q. What do you mean by misery in his head and jaws.
>
> A. He had pain in his head and jaws and a rising inside his jaws on one side dont remember which side. . . .
>
> Q. What became of this rising.
>
> A. Dr Harris and Dr Wallace—our master lanced it and that cured the rising but he still had that misery in his head and in his left side. . . .
>
> Q. Where did you live when Dr Harris attended him.
>
> A. About 3/4 of a mile from Hurricane Island . . . on Master [William] Wallace place. . . .
>
> Q. How long did you live on that place.
>
> A. About four years then we went about four miles further up on Henry Wallace [a white man, likely related to William Wallace] land.
>
> Q. Did you have a doctor there.
>
> A. No sir but got what medicine we used from Henry Wallace (dead) and made medicine out of roots and herbs in the woods and gave him that.

Economic Patterns: Labor

The end of slavery did not mean an end of work for former slaves. Indeed, their testimony in Civil War pension files suggests that they worked at least as hard for themselves, if not harder, than they had for their owners. Although they now got to keep the fruits of their labor, ex-slaves discovered that the world of free labor could entail insecurity, humiliation, danger, and hassles both large and small. They had gained their freedom but had in one sense merely traded the struggle to be free for the struggle to survive, and perhaps do better—if they could. Yet testimonies also imply that ex-slaves had a certain degree of pride in working for themselves and that they had absolutely no desire to return to the "security" of slavery.

In 1894, James H. Mabin gave a special examiner an account of his experiences with work and relocation, which was representative of the lives of many male ex-slaves after the Civil War. His long list of employers and different types of manual labor highlights the insecure world of work that confronted many African Americans in the late nineteenth century, as does his lament, "I have worked for so many people at odd jobs I can hardly name them all." Nonetheless, Mabin still must have taken comfort in the fact that now he was working to benefit himself and his family, instead of for a slaveholder.

Excerpt from the Deposition of James H. Mabin, Jan. 2, 1894, Civil War Pension File of James Henry (2nd) (alias James H. Gordon, alias James H. Mabin), 60th USCI, RG 15:

> When I was discharged I staid for about eight months in St. Louis with my mother and then came to Cole Co. where I was raised and staid there about two years. I worked for John Gordon and Uris Gordon mostly. I also worked some for Crook Scruggs and I farmed for myself.
>
> I then moved to Boone Co. Mo. about ten miles South East of Columbia & staid there about three years. I worked for John Robinson while there. He is dead. . . . I then moved to Columbia & worked around there until about 1882, or for about four years. While in Columbia I worked for Sally Ann Young. She is dead. I also worked for David Guitar, who lives about 2 1/2 miles north of town. I farmed some for him. Then I

> worked in a blacksmith shop. . . . I worked there between eight and ten months.
>
> Since I have been here [Centralia, Mo.] I have worked for so many people at odd jobs I can hardly name them all. I worked for Oats and Eaton on the brick yard. Oats is in Kansas City and Eaton is dead. . . . I also worked with Jim Hulin and Jim Angel, plasterers, making and carrying mortar for them on a couple of jobs.

Like Mabin, Howard Mason, a Kentucky veteran, worked as a manual laborer in the postwar period, working on farms and supervising other farm laborers. Mason's account reveals much about the paltry wages earned by black farm laborers in the postwar period and about the fact that those wages rose and fell in response to the perceived worth of a laborer.

Excerpt from the Deposition of Howard Mason, Apr. 8, 1895, Civil War Pension File of Howard Mason, 13th USCHA and 121st USCI, RG 15:

> I enlisted in the army from this county [Madison Co., Ky.] and after my discharge returned here and began working for John A Duncan of Richmond, Ky, I worked on his farm for eight years and he paid me one dollar per day for the time I worked. Mr Duncan had been dead for some years.
>
> On the very next day after I left Mr Duncan I began working for Mr Alexander Black a farmer living near Richmond Ky, and worked for him for seven years and he paid me seventy five [cents] per day.
>
> I was Mr Duncans "boss." for the eight yrs I was at his place and he usually had from ten to twelve hands and I could always do as much as any of them and always got better pay than any of them. Mr. Black did not have any good hands and I did most of the work there myself. He is dead also.
>
> I next worked for Mrs John McDowell of this place for four years but was affected with rheumatism at this time so that I could not make a full hand. Since I left her employ I have been working around town at odd jobs and have not been able to do a real good days work for ten years.

Widow Luvenia Smith's testimony illustrates the necessity among former slaves to pool their labor to survive, especially in the case of freed women. Recall from chapter 1 that Smith was the widow of Joe Smith, 78th and 83rd USCI. As a slave in the Mississippi Valley, Smith ran off with her husband and other slaves to keep from being taken to Texas by her master. Smith's story resumes with her husband's discharge from military service, and it underscores the inextricable links between geographic mobility and agricultural labor.

Excerpt from the Deposition of Luvenia Smith, May 16, 1905, Civil War Pension File of Joe Smith, 83rd USCI and 78th USCI, RG 15:

> You see I did not follow my husband when he enlisted. I left him at Port Hudson. He went first with his regiment to New Orleans and I followed him on a boat and staid with him awhile in New Orleans. Then I come back to the Huston plantation, Bayou, Sara La. and staid and worked there until my husband came after me when mustered out of service. I was with the wives of Aleck Cary, Charles Cotton & Harry Whitaker all this time and their husbands came with my husband Joe Smith and we all went back together to the Greenwood plantation West-Feliciana Parish La. After myself and husband made 5 or 6 crops in Louisiana after the war we went to near Leota, Washington County, Miss. to work on the plantation of Mr. Bill Sterling. . . . We moved from Leota on Lake Washington in Washington Co. Miss about 4 years after the big high water (1882) and moved on the Clopton plantation 3 miles from Helena Ark about 1886 or 87. Made about 6 or 7 crops there before my husband died. He died from the effect of the bite of a mad dog. I dont know zactly what year. He died in the beginning of cotton picking time 13 years ago. He was buried on the Clopton place. No record was made of my husbands death. I do not read or write and have got no idea of time, years or dates. . . . I had 10 children by my husband when he died. All are now dead except two. The oldest is now Mrs. Patsy Harris of Helena I live with her she is about 31 years old. The other child is named Collins Smith, married, he is 29 years old. I had no children under 16 years of age when my husband died. I have not remarried since the death of my husband Joe Smith and have never lived with any man as his wife or otherwise since my husband died. When he died he owned no land and no other valuable property except a few horses. These the white folks took away for debt. I was left destitute with no one bound for my support. I have made my living by hard work since his death.

Even if former slaves could find geographic stability, it was still not certain that they would experience occupational stability. Such was the case for Alexander Porter, a slave raised in Mississippi, who lived in Louisiana and Kentucky after the Civil War. Trained as a cobbler before the war, he worked initially after the war for a carpetbagger planter in Louisiana and then, after moving to Kentucky, resumed work as a cobbler before becoming a small-time sharecropper. Porter does not explain why he quit cobbling, but it is possible that he was forced out of work by the increasing saturation of the postwar American market with cheap, factory-made shoes. It is also possible that he was forced out of business by white cobblers, who resented his competition. In any case, when he was interviewed in 1900, Porter could afford to be farming on a small scale because by that time he was already a pensioner under the 1890 law (his deposition was in reference to a belated claim under the 1862 law).

Excerpt from the Deposition of Alexander Porter, May 3, 1900, Civil War Pension File of Alexander Porter, 58th USCI, RG 15:

> For 2 years after discharge I lived with Mr. John Lynch at "Ellawah" Landing or it was sometimes called "Goodriche's" Landing, 50 miles up the Mississippi River, on the west bank, from Vicksburg, Miss.[8] I can't remember the name of the state or county. . . .
>
> I do not know whether Mr. Lynch is still there or not but he told me before I left that he was going to sell out and go back North. I do not know his home in the north but he had been a major under Gen. U.S. Grant. . . .
>
> From Ellawah Landing I came to Oakton, Hickman Co., Ky and have not lived further than 4 miles from Oakton, Ky. since then. I have been here something over 30 years. I worked on a farm at Ellawah Landing, and after I came to Oakton, Ky.
>
> I learned the shoemaker's trade before the War. I had been making the shoes for my masters family for 2 years before my enlistment. About 2 years after coming to Oakton, Ky. I began repairing shoes or cobbling and worked at it for 7 or 8 years. I have not work at my trade for 12 or 14 years. Yes it may have been since 1880. Since I quit working at my trade I have been farming a little on shares.
>
> I still make a small crop of corn, about 3 acres each year and raise a garden

The work world of former slaves involved changes not only in occupation but also of employers. This was particularly true for men engaged in manual labor, who were considered easily replaceable. When they described their work histories, they often related a succession of employers, such as in the cases of Austin Waters (Texas), Erastus Green (northern Virginia and Washington, D.C.), and Richard Breck (Kentucky). Their experiences vividly depict the insecure world of work for unskilled ex-slaves. In the case of Green, who worked at Arlington National Cemetery, Capitol Hill, and the Washington Navy Yard, the stress of contingent employment may have facilitated his alcoholism, which was noted by a special examiner in his report to the commissioner of pensions. The examiner's report also is valuable in that it reveals as much about the world of federal pension bureaucrats as the world of former slaves.

Excerpt from the Deposition of Austin Waters, Jan. 19, 1914, Civil War Pension File of Austin Waters, 15th USCI, RG 15:

> After discharge I came to Jefferson Texas, and stayed about a year. Worked on the farm. Cut wood made rails and done farm work worked for Louis Love on Ben Whitakers farm about sixty miles from Jefferson I cut wood and made rails for Mr. Arbuckle in Jefferson and worked on the farm at Whitakers farm on Red River. And then I came to Washington, Ark. in 1872, and lived here till 1908, six years ago I went to Columbus Ark. I lived out on Capt. Thomas Farm here at Washington, and at Columbus I live on Mr. Jim Wilsons place.

Excerpt from the Deposition of Erastus Green, Oct. 15, 1898, Civil War Pension File of Erastus Green, 1st USCI, RG 15:

> After my discharge I took up residence in Alexandria Va where I lived until Garfield was Elected President [1880], then moved to Washington D.C. where I lived seven years. I then went back to Alexandria Va and only returned to this City Sept 15 1898 I was Employed at the US Capitol from 1882 to 1894 not all the time as a regular employee Since 1894, I have had no regular employment prior to going to the Capitol I was for 5 years from 1867 to 1872 at the US Cemetery at Arlington VA & Alexandria VA where I was employed in the Green house—the balance of the time I have just worked at whatever I could get to do.

Excerpt from C. W. Okey, Special Examiner, Washington, D.C., to the Commissioner of Pensions, Washington, D.C., Dec. 31, 1898, Civil War Pension File of Erastus Green, 1st USCI, RG 15:

> I have held this case open for a long time and repeatedly called the attention of both the Claimant and his attorney to the weak and Unsatisfactory character of the Evidence both as to origin and continuance and the Evidence herewith appears to be the very best that can be had. I therefore do not feel warranted in recommending further Examination but on the contrary believe the Claim should be rejected. The Soldier is a man who is addicted to the Excessive use of liquor Came here to the Office to See Me about his Claim was so much under the influence of liquor that the Watchman put him out of the building he is now Employed in the US Navy Yard in this City, doing heavy laborious work and I doubt very much whether he is justly Entitled to a pension under the Act of June 27, 1890, As he receives full wage as a laborer.

Excerpt from the Deposition of Richard Breck, Mar. 25, 1890, Civil War Pension File of Richard Breck, 13th USCHA and 121st USCI, RG 15:

> Upon receiving my discharge, I came right here [Richmond, Madison Co., Ky.], and have been living here ever since, and almost *every* body knows here I *near* failed until I came home out of the war, and that I've been ailing about *all* the time since. They know this, or as many of the old citizens as are living, know it, even if I never receive a [illegible] for pension. Then there is our Colored Grand Army lodge here, I was in it. Touch any a few you please, and they'd all tell you about how I've been ever since the war.
>
> Since the war I've done odd jobs waiting on lawyers offices and such for a while I had a job of driving hearse, but had to give it up on account my health about 3 years ago, after driving about 3 years. Mr. Ulverson knows that for a fact. Then another thing I done while driving hearse. It was nasty, but I actually made $15, a night some nights, cleaning out privies, but I had to give that up too. I had to leave, but Ulverson had me hearse driving, and lent me his old furniture wagon to use in night work cleaning vaults, so I could make extra money. No Sir, my health was not made worse by frequent contact with dead bodies, or from vault cleansing. I drove two hearses, one for whites, and one for blacks. After quitting this, on account of choking up spells coming on so often, I worked considerable about the offices of Jerry Sullivan of this city.

Richard Breck's experience suggests that ex-slaves' jobs could be not only distasteful but dangerous. The American workplace of the Gilded Age was filled with perils, as employers put much greater emphasis on profits than on worker safety. And as the testimony of Robert Whiteside of Louisiana and William Herbert and Thomas Gross of Maryland make clear, former slaves were even more likely than other workers to be employed at jobs that put them in danger of workplace accidents.

Excerpt from the Affidavit of Robert Whiteside, Nov. 27, 1901, Civil War Pension File of Robert Whiteside, 89th USCI and 92nd USCI, RG 15:

> That on August 15, 1883, at Burnside, La., while he was slacking a barrel of lime, and by stirring it with a stick, some of the hot lime flashed into his right eye, which caused loss of its sight.
>
> He further declares said disability is not due to vicious habits.[9]

Excerpt from the Affidavit of William Herbert, Mar. 25, 1892, Civil War Pension File of William Herbert, 41st USCI, RG 15:

> I was a Stevedore And Whilst engaged at my work by heavy lifting from a Strain felt Something give way. Which resulted in a Rupture of the right side, this about the latter part of 1888. The injury was through no Vicious habits of Mine and are of a permanent Character, incurred as Aforesaid in Baltimore City Md

Excerpt from the Affidavit of Thomas Gross, July 20, 1892, Civil War Pension File of Thomas Gross, 39th USCI, RG 15:

> That several years ago cant Say just how many, he Steped on a nail with his left foot-While employed on a Sailing vessel as a hand, that his foot got very Sore and Kept growing worse that he went to Baltimore to the Calvert Street Hospital for treatment that he remained there a long time and the Surgeons finally amputated his leg below the knee to Save his life as they informed him that when I steped on the nail he was in the discharge of his duties as a hand on said vessel and that Said disability is not due to any vicious habits on my part—or any fault of his that he has been compelled to go on crutches ever Since he lost his foot.

Pension files demonstrate that disability among former slaves was caused not only by postwar employment but by the war itself. Although war-related disability was less common among African Americans because they saw less combat than white Union soldiers did, some black troops were wounded in battle. Moreover, there were myriad ways for soldiers in the Civil War to become disabled that did not involve fighting. Besides accidents, many ex-soldiers, such as Frank Finley, a North Carolina veteran, claimed to have developed disabling medical conditions while in service. In Finley's case, he asserted that he had begun to have blinding headaches and rheumatism while in the Union army and that these conditions had continued to plague him in the postwar period, detrimentally affecting his ability to make a living. Although the federal government rejected Finley's claim for a pension on the basis of his headaches, they did accept that his rheumatism was service related, and he was approved for a partial disability pension under the 1862 law.

Excerpt from the Deposition of Frank Finley, Aug. 20, 1889, Civil War Pension File of Frank Finley (alias Brown), 119th USCI, RG 15:

> He is at present working on a farm for seven dollars per month [near Wilkesboro, N.C.], boarding included when the average wages of good farm hands is eight dollars per month, boarding included.
>
> He has been compelled, at times, since discharge to work for less wages than good hands were getting by reason of not being able to do a full days work on account of rheumatism and trouble with his head.

Economic Patterns: Property Ownership

According to the 1880 census—taken only fifteen years after the end of the war—one-fifth of African Americans owned at least some of the land they farmed. Civil War pension files give a sense of the more complicated reality behind this impressive statistic.

In the case of Kitt Mitchell, a South Carolina veteran of the U.S. Colored Troops, the pension file demonstrates his obvious pride at being a landowner, as he boasted to a special examiner in 1903. It also is important to note that Mitchell's financial success appears tied to the ability of two generations to pool their labor and resources (see chapter 4).

Excerpt from the Deposition of Kitt Mitchell, June 9, 1903, Civil War Pension File of Kitt Mitchell, 128th USCI, RG 15:

My age about 62—Farmer P.O. Jacksonboro, S.C. . . .

I own 50 acres of land—all paid for—worth, with the house, about $250^{00}—I plant 15 acres and if I had the help I could plant 22 acres that much is cleared up—

My wife & daughters & I work the place & we make one to two bales of cotton—for which I get from $30 to 50—I make from 50 to 100 bus. of corn & from 30 to 60 bus. of potatoes—and we have a garden—We have two horses—My son-in-law lives with me & works another place—he has no horse—so I arranged with him to do my ploughing for the use of the horses on his land and I feed the horses—& he does the work as promised—I had the same arrangement with another man last year—We do very well when we have a good season, and what we make together with my pension, keeps us going very well. No sir—My wife never did do any of the ploughing, she just does a little chopping now & then, and very little of that—She looks after the garden—but she has had small-pox for two weeks & has not looked after it—My daughter helps since with the chopping & with the cotton picking—

Although Kitt Mitchell and his family could be justly proud of being landowners when they themselves had once been property, their land holdings were modest—only fifty acres. The testimony of Mitchell and other former slaves in Civil War pension files makes clear that most African Americans who held land in the postwar period almost invariably owned small parcels. In addition, the following widows' pension cases of Sophronia Latham (living in New York State) and Mollie Thompson and Ellen Bettlesworth (both of Kentucky) demonstrate that these small holdings often were encumbered with debt, making black land ownership precarious. It is no wonder, then, that Kitt Mitchell boasted that his fifty acres were "all paid for."

Excerpt from the Affidavit of Sophronia Latham, June 3, 1907, Civil War Pension File of Winslow Latham, 31st USCI, RG 15:

State of New York
Allegeny Co

. . . the claimant Sophronia Latham, who being by me duly sworn testifies as follows said soldier had no insurance of any kind—he left a will a sworn copy of which is hereto attached—

There is a farm of about 35 acres worth $\$15^{00}$ to $\$20^{00}$ per acre with a mortgage on it amounting to about $\$342^{00}$ there are other debts against the estate amounting to about $500—or more that I know of—The estate is not settled—There is no personal property except a horse worth $100—& 3 hogs—I have no income whatever & no property that I can use & had none for some time before the death of said soldier.

Excerpt from the Affidavit of George Royalty and Ed Hill, Sept. 13, 1906, Civil War Pension File of Henry Womack (alias Thompson), 40th USCI, RG 15:

Personally appeared before me a Notary Public in and for the aforesaid county [Warren Co., Ky.] duly authorized to administer oaths, George Royalty, age 80 years whose post office is Bowling Green, Kentucky, and Ed Hill, age 64, whose post office is Bowling Green, Kentucky, both of whom being duly sworn declare in relation to said case as follows: That they have known the claimant, Mollie Thompson whose maiden name was Mollie Loving from her childhood; that they know she is the widow of the soldier, Henry Thompson, alias, Walmock; that she was never married until her marriage with the soldier; that she owns no property of any kind or character whatsoever, and no one is legally bound for her support, and that she is wholly dependent upon her earnings as a washer woman for the support of herself and her infant children. They say furthermore that her late husband, the soldier left no will and had no property of any kind except two houses in Bowling Green, Kentucky, one of which the claimant and her children now live, and which is worth about three hundred dollars, and the other house is worth about One hundred and fifty dollars, and would not rent more than $4.00 or $5.00 per month. They say that they are informed that the house in which the widow lives is mortgaged for about $130.00, but they have no personally knowledge of that fact. They further state that they have been informed that the soldier left a little industrial insurance upon his life payable to his widow, perhaps about enough to bury him, but their statements in this regard is from information obtained through others, instead of personal knowledge.

Excerpt from the Affidavit of Ellen Wade, Dec. 19, 1903, Civil War Pension File of Walker Bettlesworth (alias Wade), 116th USCI, RG 15:

> [Ellen Wade states] That she is above claimant and that she owns a house and three and one half acres of land situated in Franklin County State of Kentucky and valued at three hundred dollars and one cow valued at twenty dollars and that she does not own any other and does not own any interest in any property except the above property and that she is dependent upon her daily labor for her support and that no one is legally bound for her support and that her income from all sources would not exceed forty dollars per annum.

Certification of N. B. Smith, Clerk of County Court, Franklin Co., Ky., Feb. 6, 1904, Civil War Pension File of Walker Bettlesworth (alias Wade), 116th USCI, RG 15:

> I, N.B. Smith Clerk of the Franklin County Court in the State of Kentucky and legal custodian of the tax Books, Deed Books and Mortgage Books of the County of Franklin in the State of Kentucky do crtify that I have examined the tax books of Franklin County for the year 1903 and find Walker Wade assessed for taxation in the name of said Walker Wade 3 acers of land near Sam Wade at the value of $20, and our assessments are bassed on fair voluntary sale, but in many instances it is not more than 80% of its value, and I further certify that Walker Wade and Ellen Wade his wife mortgaged 4.1/2 acrs of land to Wyatt Meaux on the 4h day of February 1896 for the sum of $50. and that he sold 2.1/2 acres of said land to Jake Jones on the 5th day of April 1897 and $41.20 was paid on said mortgage and the lien is released to that extent.

Although most of the property owned by former slaves was in the form of real estate, some former slaves also started businesses in the postwar period, as the following deposition from Mississippi makes clear. Mary Virginia Morgan owned a small restaurant catering to African Americans in the state capital of Jackson. As with land holdings, such businesses tended to be small.

Excerpt from the Deposition of Mary Virginia Morgan, Sept. 19, 1904, Civil War Pension File of Charles Morgan (alias Charles Crucell, alias Cruselle), 74th USCI, RG 15:

> I was married to Chas Morgan in this town in 1885 but cant give the month or day. We had a license from the Court House and Elder Shurm-

> furt a colored preacher performed the ceremony. . . . Chas Morgan and I were never separated or got any divorce from each other but lived together as husband & wife from the day we got married until his death. I have not since remarried—and make a living by running a small restaurant for colored folks on West St. [in Jackson, Miss.] He left me a three room house and small lot with a restaurant building of two rooms adjoining. I occupy the residence and run the restaurant myself with the assistance of Rosa Hutchison a little adopted girl fourteen years old and barely get a support out of it. I keep no books and cant say what amt income is but know it is pitiful.

Economic Patterns: Poverty

The vast majority of former slaves were poor, so the poverty apparent in their pension file testimony is not surprising. However, rarely did such people have any chance to comment on their lives in a forum where their testimony would be preserved. Their words humanize the poverty of ex-slaves in the postwar period. Perhaps the strongest theme to emerge from their words, as the following testimony in cases from Alabama, Michigan, South Carolina, North Carolina, Kentucky, and Arkansas demonstrates, besides the poverty itself, is how medical problems both contributed to and were compounded by poverty. Illness left former slaves with medical bills that they could not pay or without access to proper medical care, leaving them in a position where they had to treat themselves with herbal remedies or patent medicine, forms of therapy that sometimes ameliorated symptoms but rarely provided a permanent cure.

Excerpt from the Deposition of Wiley Johnson, Jan. 26, 1894, Civil War Pension File of Wiley Johnson, 136th USCI, RG 15:

> My age is 72 years, occupation farmer, residence and P.O. address Fort Mitchell, Ala. . . .
>
> I am applying for pension because I am not able to work and make a living for my family. . . . I have never applied for pension before because I was able to work and make a living. . . .
>
> I have no property of any kind, not even a hog. I owe about sixty dollars for doctor bills and house rent and I am not able to pay a cent of it.

Excerpt from the Affidavit of James Walton, Nov. 2, 1888, Civil War Pension File of James Walton, 102nd USCI, RG 15:

I first lived with William Harrison in West Bloomfield Mich after my discharge in 1866 I lived tow years and in 1869 I lived with Hartwell Green 5 years in the same township Mr hartwell Green said that I could live with him long as I lived if I would just help him to do his chos and keep the woman about the house and them in wood and water and in the spring you can help the woman to work in the garden and if you get so that you are able to earn wages I pay you some in 1874 I went to Toledo Ohio and work in the stores 5 years Well I was of and on all the while because I was not able to put in full time and in 1879 I was sent to the county house in ohio I was there till I was sent hear to soldiers home the store that I work in at Toledo Ohio the mans name was Winfield on Madson street—James Walton as to all the medical treatment I had I went in the woods and got it some times I would buy medicent from first one & nother & when I coulden not get to the woods as to the de evidince it empasds [?] be for me to get that I never had no attendenc of Docters for that reason it imposable for me to get.

Excerpt from the Deposition of Silvy Granville, Nov. 21, 1901, Civil War Pension File of Washington Granville, 128th USCI, RG 15:

About one year after Joseph Hamilton left me I had Washington Granville. I was married to him 2[d] Thursday in January, Could not give year. We were married by M. C. Singleton. That was before I hear that Joseph was dead. I moved down with him to Askepoo, S.C. and lived with him until he died. He died Saturday before Christmas. This December coming will make 3 years since he died.

He was only ill about 2 weeks and died from pain in his side. Prior to this illness he had been sound, except that he had chills & fever every fall. I never heard him complain of anything else He never complained of rheumatism or dysentery or diarrhora as long as I lived with him. I never had any children in my life. Soldiers youngest child was over 16 when he died. Neither of us had any land. He left a horse, which his children kept. I had three head of cattle. I have them yet. I have no land, but rent from M. C. Singleton. I work in the white mans fields for my living. I have had no man since Soldier died. I moved up to Singletons place last Febr Singletons crippled boy stays in the house with me. He cannot stand on his feet. He is crippled up with rheumatism. We have each one room, but I take care of him.

Excerpt from the Deposition of Rosa Petteway, Feb. 26, 1889, Civil War Pension File of Isaac Petteway, 37th USCI, RG 15:

Q. After coming out of the Army did your husband, the soldier, ever have any fever, or pneumonia, or was he troubled with any cough or lung disease?

A. He had a bad cough and after he was taken down with his fatal illness he had a desperate cough. He was always subject to cold and had the chills bad often.

Q. Tell me all you can about his condition from the time you say he was taken down until he died?

A. He was down in his bed 3 years, helpless as a child, and I nursed [him]. He was full of pains and misery, and that leg would pain him. He would holler so you could hear him holler along way. He had a very bad cough and complained of his side and chest, and across his breast and stomach. The ulcer on the leg would run part of the time and there again would break out again. The sore or corruption did not [illegible] above the knee. There was no running sores on his body only the old one.

I didn't think he had any hemorrhage or bleeding, not as I knows of.

Q. What did you believe was the immediate cause of his death?

A. That leg, the pain in it run up into his body and took his life away from him

Q. How do you know that it was not pneumonia or consumption he died of?

A. I don't know, only I think it was the leg.

Q. When you found your husband was dying, was there no way you could have secured a Doctor, is there no state or county provision for Doctors for the poor?

A. No Sir, You can't get a doctor here [Beaufort, N.C.] without the cash. . . . We were not able to employ any Doctor. I just treated my husband with herbs and such like—We never had any Doctor

Excerpt from the Deposition of Mollie Russell, Apr. 8, 1911, Civil War Pension File of Phillip Russell (alias Fry), 114th USCI, RG 15:

Q. What property do you possess?

A. I do not own any at all. All the things I have in the world are an old bed, wash tub, table, stove and two or three chairs. The whole outfit is not worth ten dollars. I have four hens, but the rooster died. No, I have no stocks, bonds, mortgages, real estate, notes or anything at all. My clothing and the

> things I have mentioned are all I possess. My husband left no insurance, and as a matter of fact I have not yet got through paying his burying bill.

Excerpt from the Deposition of Eliza Hudson, Oct. 5, 1900, Civil War Pension File of Albert Hudson, 54th USCI, RG 15:

> I have not remarried since Albert Hudson died, nor lived with any one as husband & wife since then.
>
> We had twelve children, only two of who were under 16 years old when he died Virgil & Annie. . . .
>
> I ain't got no property but me & the children, but I have to pay 35 cents tax on what I have in the house but I ain't got nothing but two beds. I have tried to get cotton enough to buy me a hog, but it looks like I couldn't do it.
>
> My mother Mary McDaniel grannied all the older children & she is dead. . . .
>
> I didn't have any doctor. We was too poor. I don't know who I can prove the births by. I lived off away from other people & I have no bible record nor any thing else to show when they were born.

The poverty of some former slaves was so bad that it left an impression on special examiners, many of whom were indifferent or even hostile to black pension applicants. One such examiner was John L. Paine, who was so affected by the suffering of Henry Taylor, a black Civil War veteran living in St. Louis, that he saw fit to write the following report to the Commissioner of Pensions in Washington, D.C.

Excerpt from the Report of John L. Paine, St. Louis, Mo., to the Commissioner of Pensions, Washington, D.C., Nov. 19, 1897, Civil War Pension File of Henry Taylor, 102nd USCI, RG 15:

> Sir:
>
> I have the honor to return papers in above cited case with report.
>
> An original claim under the general law on account of injury to right knee. Supplemental allegations cover injury to heel of right as of same date.
>
> The soldier was pensioned in 1892 under Act of June 27, 1890 on acct of injury of right knee & left side; dropped from the rolls in 1895 under the "Revision"
>
> He again filed, June Act, May 1896. This claim appears to have been rejected in June of this year 1897.

The Atty informs me that he is about to renew the claim under Act of June by the filing of another Application

In my humble opinion the pensioner should not have been dropped from the roll in the first instance.

It may not become me to proffer up my own opinion in opposition to the findings of those Boards whose reports left no course for the Bureau but rejection. But, I do not understand the motives of these Boards, nor can I comprehend their Certificates.

The soldier has very marked enfeeblement of Senility. He is 66 years of age. He has been a familiar figure to me for six months; have seen him time and again hobbling with his cane and rag hook, and bag, doing the alleys and gutters for rags. He does not earn two dollars a week.

He came to the door, when I called, & he did not know my business, on a crutch.

His mouth is as crooked as letter Q or I—facial paralysis, and I do not believe that the cause of same has limited its symptoms & effects to face, or mouth, alone. The man is a cripple. That is certain. He suffers neuralgia pains from broken ribs—am certain of that.

I do not believe he could lift a 50 pound weight off of the ground. His habits and character are good—much above the average of his class.

In event of his renewing application under June Act, I earnestly suggest that sp. instructions be issues to same Boards to make a report truly reflecting soldier's condition and disabilities of every character.

Poverty also meant that former slaves had precious little to pass on to their heirs. Veteran John Walker spent his last years as a resident of the Western Branch of the National Home for Disabled Volunteer Soldiers in Leavenworth, Kansas. The federal government set up a network of these homes across the country initially to care for severely disabled veterans and eventually to care for elderly former soldiers and sailors.[10] Most of the inhabitants of the homes were poor men without families able or willing to care for them. Hence, although these cases do not represent all the poor, the example of one such veteran does provide a sense of just how little some ex-slaves had in the way of possessions at the end of their lives.

Excerpt from Effects of John Walker, Western Branch, National Home for Disabled Volunteer Soldiers, Leavenworth, Ks., Oct. 18, 1918, Civil War Pension File of John Walker, 31st USCI, RG 15:

Cash deposited with Surgeon $22.00

1 watch "Elgin" 10351549 silver case brass chain and charm.

1 grip containing 1 set sleeve buttons, 1 shaving set, 1 purse, 2 handkerchiefs, 1 towel, 3 shirts, 1 suit, 1 cane, 1 pr drawers, 1 pr gloves.

1 paper box containing 1 pair shoes, 1 brush, 1 tie, 1 cap.

There is also outstanding to the credit of such deceased member, under provisions of law, pension money amounting to $102.80

Pension money can be paid under the law only to certain heirs in the order named, as follows: (1) the widow, (2) minor children or children, (3) dependent mother or father. Pension money is not payable to a legal representative, as such, under any circumstances.

Preindustrial Time Perception

Calendar dates played a major role in the work of the U.S. Pension Bureau since, in many cases, such precision was needed to determine the monthly rate a pensioner would receive and for how long. For instance, widows had to verify the dates of birth of all their children, since they received extra money per month for each child under the age of sixteen at the time of the soldier's death. (Children also lost their pension when they turned sixteen.) Yet the need for calendar dates clashed with the preindustrial perceptions of time held by many former slaves. They could not record vital dates since many of them were illiterate, as Georgia Evans's case reveals, nor were they inclined to do so since they did not reckon the passage of time by calendar dates but by the agriculture cycle, by the passage of the seasons, and in relation to other events that took place around the same time, as can be seen in the testimony of Jennie German. Finally, poverty and racism also contributed to the lack of formal birth records. In addition to underscoring the continued phenomenon of a dearth of information on dates, the following examples are suggestive of the conditions under which many former slave women bore children, conditions that contributed to high child mortality (see the next section). Lastly, the frustration of some Pension Bureau personnel with the preindustrial time perception is worth noting, and a classic example from Eugene B. Payne, the special examiner in the case of Georgia Evans, is included in this section.[11]

Excerpt from the Affidavit of Georgia Evans, May 12, 1893, Civil War Pension File of Osborne Evans, 18th USCI, RG 15:

> I am unable to furnish a certified transcript of a public or church record of the dates of births of the children claimed for in my declaration for the reason that no such record was ever made. I am unable to furnish the testimony of the attending physician at any of the births of said children for the reason that there was no attending physician at any of said births except one at which Dr. Humphrey of Moberly, Mo. was in attendance, but he is now dead. I am unable to furnish the testimony of female attendants as to the date of births of any of said children for the reason that none of them can fix any of the dates from memory or any concurrent circumstances. They are all illiterate colored women and do not think or know anything about dates. I, therefore ask that the following transcript from my mother's family Bible, as to the dates of birth of said children, be considered:
>
> "Pearl Evans Born Dec 11—2 weeks before Christmas 1879
> Willie Evans Born February the 11 1881
> Clarence Evans Born Dec th 26 1887"
>
> The foregoing is a true copy of the record of said births as read to me from my mother's Bible. I can not read myself.

Excerpt from the Affidavit of Kate Childers, Oct. 11, 1900, Civil War Pension File of Stephen Childers, 13th USCI, RG 15:

> I am unable to furnish a copy of the public or church record of the births of my children Stephen and John because no such record exists; nor of an attending physician because none attended me. I offer the evidence of female attendants in lieu thereof.

Excerpt from the Affidavit of Jennie German, Sept. 14, 1900, Civil War Pension File of Stephen Childers, 13th USCI, RG 15:

> My name is Jennie German. I am a mid-wife. I waited on Katie Childers at the birth of her two youngest children, Stephen, Jr. and John. Stephen was born September 18th 1892. I have no record of this birth, but I fix the date from the marriage of my grand-daughter which took place September 1892. Katie Childers was invited to this wedding but on account of her sickness in the birth of this child she could not go. I attended the wedding

and after it was over went immediately to her house waited upon her and the child—administering such service as she and the child needed. I also waited upon her at the birth of her child John. I have no record of his birth and no means of fixing the exact date. I am sure, though, that he was born during the latter part of the month April and that he was about three and one half years younger than his brother, Stephen.

Excerpt from the Affidavit of Florence Covington, Sept. 18, 1900, Civil War Pension File of Stephen Childers, 13th USCI, RG 15:

I have known Katie Childers widow of Stephen Childers for more than twenty years. I know when her boy Stephen was born. At that time I lived on Lewis Street directly opposite where Katie and Stephen Childers lived. We were intimate friends. My little girl, Rebecca, was born July 28", 1892, and Katie's boy Stephen was born not quite two months thereafter on Sept. 18", 1892. I know this because my bible shows the above to be the correct date of birth of my child and because she visited me after the birth of my child and before the birth of hers. We talked over the matter of the birth of our children and she several times expressed the wish that she was over with her trouble as I was with mine. Another reason I know the above date to be correct is because almost immediately after this child was born its father came over to my home after me. I went over and was the third person to take it into my arms.

Excerpt from Eugene B. Payne, Chillocothe, Mo., to the Commissioner of Pensions, Washington, D.C., Dec. 23, 1893, Civil War Pension File of Osborne Evans, 18th and 72nd USCI, RG 15:

This widow's claim under the Act of June 27, 1890 is meritorious and should be admitted. To determine the *exact* ages of the 3 children is a knotty problem—The Bible entry as to their ages is worthless because inscribed by guess *after* soldier died by a young girl assisted by Pearl one of the children It is singularly *impossible*, to get a colored person to give, the *date* of anything. And the only way I have of getting at the ages of the children of colored people is to get the mother to state how long it was from the marriage to the birth of the *first* child and then ascertain the difference in their ages.

It will be found in this case that claimant told a *reasonable* story of their ages of her children when she *went down* the line, but when she found that it would make the youngest Clarence about 7 years old . . . instead of 6—she began to crawfish in But in my opinion her first statement is correct.

Mortality

Given the widespread poverty in the post–Civil War black community, it is not surprising that mortality there was more pervasive and on average occurred earlier than for white Americans. As noted earlier, in areas of the United States with death registration in 1900, thirteen additional African Americans died that year compared to whites for every thousand people in the population. It also appears that life expectancy was significantly shorter for blacks in the late-nineteenth-century United States. For instance, one demographer found that during the period from 1870 to 1900, white males had a life expectancy of about fifty years, while for black men life expectancy was closer to forty years.[12]

Civil War pension files provide further insight into these statistics. One important aspect of death in the postwar black community, for example, was child mortality, which was more prevalent among African Americans than whites. Civil War pension files suggest that most of this mortality occurred soon after birth. One valuable set of documents in this regard comes from the case of Charles Barber, a Louisiana veteran. After the Civil War, Barber lived in Grand Coteau in St. Landry Parish, where he attended St. Joseph's Catholic Church. This church kept vital records of its parishioners, including baptisms, marriages, and deaths. Barber and his family appear in these records, during an era in which relatively few African Americans appear in vital records, whether publicly or privately kept. Of these rare documents, translated from French, four are excerpted—two baptism records and two death records. The ages of the Barber's children who died are listed in days lived. The baptism records are equally disturbing. The fact that children were baptized months after they were born suggests that the Catholic clergy in Grand Coteau waited to baptize children until it was apparent that they would not die soon after birth.

Extract of Catholic Church Records [translated from French], Grand Coteau, La., Apr. 22, 1891, Civil War Pension File of Charles Barber, 81st USCI, RG 15:

Extract from the Baptismal Registry of our Church (People of Color):

In the third book of aforementioned Registry, page 298, under the number 118, in the margin, it is written "Jean Berchmans Barber" and in the text "the 24th of December of 1871, I baptized Jean Berchmans, born the 24th of November last year, legitimate son of Charles Barber and of Marie Felvin (sic, without a doubt the maiden name of Sullivan). Godfather James Blacksmith and godmother, Dulomene Leurs"

Signed, GF Abbadie SJ

Certified to conform with registry, by me, Current Curé of Grand Coteau, 22 April 1891

CD Fris SJ

Extract from the Death Registry of our Church:

In the third book of his Registry, page 191, on the 10th number on the page, we read in the margin "Child of Charles Barber" and in the text we see "the 26 May 1870 I gave a Christian burial to a small child of Charles Barber, aged 18 days."

Signed, GF Abbadie SJ

Certified to conform with registry, by me, Current Curé of Grand Coteau, 22 April 1891

CD Fris SJ

Extract in the Death Registry for the people of color:

In the 3rd book in the Registry, page 209, under the number ten, we read in the margin "Child of Charles Barber" and in the text we see: "The 20th of February, 1875, I gave a Christian burial to a child of Charles Barber, age five or six days old."

Signed, GF Abbadie SJ

Certified to conform with registry, by me, Current Curé of Grand Coteau, 22 April 1891

CD Fris SJ

Extract on the Baptismal Record of our Church (People of Color):

In the third book in the aforementioned Registry, page 322, under the number 90, we read in the margins "Marie Marcelite Barber" and we see in the text: "The twenty eighth of August, 1873, I baptized Marie Marcelite, born the 12th of July last year, legitimate daughter of Charles Barber and of Marie Louise Lolivan (for Sullivan I suppose). Godfather Henson Barns, godmother Sarah Barns."

Signed, GF Abbadie SJ

Certified to conform with registry, by me, Current Curé of Grand Coteau, 22 April 1891

CD Fris SJ

In addition to the rare Barber church records, the more ubiquitous special examination depositions also demonstrate that child mortality was most common among newborn babies. One particularly telling deposition comes from Ella Benson, the daughter of Alfred Benson. Following the war, Alfred Benson lived in Memphis, Tennessee, where he raised a large family. Both he and his wife, Melvina, died in 1898, leaving several minor children. Ella, the oldest surviving child, was interviewed regarding the pension claim of her youngest sibling. In her testimony, it is noticeable that not only did her parents have many children, but many of them died before they could be named, so many in fact that Ella Benson found it impossible to fix their number, let alone to provide a record of their birth and death dates.

Excerpt from the Deposition of Ella Benson, Mar. 23, 1903, Civil War Pension File of Alfred Benson, 46th USCI, RG 15:

I am 32 yrs old—I wash and iron for a living—. . . . I am the oldest living child of my father and mother Alfred and Melvina Benson. My father was a pensioner—died Sept 26, 1898 and my mother died Dec 4, 1898—I was present when they died. . . . My father left this house and lot—902 DuBose Av.—worth $700 or $800 and this is the only property my mother had from his death till she died—She had no other means of support but her own labor while she was a widow and she did not remarry after my father died.

Maggie and Isaiah are the two youngest children of my father and mother—Maggie is between 17 and 18 yrs old now and Isaiah between 14 and 15 is the nearest I can come at it. Maggie's birth day is Feb 15th and Isaiah's birthday is Dec 12th but I cant give the year they were born.

From myself down all of us children were born in this house and I have no way in the world of fixing their ages except from memory. There are no neighbor children or other fact or event I can fix their ages by.

> Anna is the only other surviving child of my parents She is about 21 or 22 or 23 now. Alfred came in between her and Maggie and he got killed Nov 6, 1900—and was called 21 yrs old then—Then came Maggie there is about 2 yrs difference in their ages. Then came Freddie who was born June 10.—and died age 2 yrs and then came Isaiah—but I cant tell you how much time there was between them. Maggie must be some 3 or 4 yrs older than Isaiah is the best I can tell about it.
>
> Now Freddie died of whooping cough in the spring—he would have been three that summer June 1—and is buried in Elmwood cemetery and Isaiah was born Dec 12th before Freddie died.
>
> Dr Butt attended on Freddie, but Dr Butt has since died.—
>
> My father—mother and the other child—Alfred—are buried in Zion Cemetery.
>
> Supplemental
>
> I think my mother had 21 children in all—So many died as babies I cannot begin to give you the dates of birth—
>
> Of those who lived to be named and get any size—were Mary—older than me who got burnt up. Ella—who is myself—then Alf—No Babe or Anna May is her right name—then Alf—then Mag then Isaiah then Freddie—Now I cant say for certain whether Freddie was born after or before Isaiah—I cant give the year any of them were born

It was common for men and women to lose not only their children but their spouses as well. Civil War pension files show that remarriage was frequent, if not inevitable, among widows and widowers. For example, James Hubbard, a veteran who lived along the banks of the Mississippi River after the Civil War, survived two wives and most of his children.

Excerpt from the Deposition of James Hubbard, May 29, 1911, Civil War Pension File of James Hubbard, 71st USCI and 70th USCI, RG 15:

> I was first married in the year 1868 about month of February, to a woman by the name Jane King, who was a widow with one child a girl, named Matilda King. By this marriage this woman, Jane King and I had nine children. Of these children four are living. One boy, Adolphus Hubbard now lives with me on Belt's Island Plantation [in Tensas Parish, La.], just about one-half a mile from Ashwood. This wife Jane died about the year of 1888, at Spring Hill Plantation, Adams County, Mississippi.

Jacob Overall (alias Hutchinson, alias Abraham I. J. Wright), 4th U.S. Colored Heavy Artillery

> I again married in March 1894 at Spring Hill Plantation, Adams County, Mississippi. This time I married a woman by the name of Mandy Davis who when I married her had three children. By this marriage we have had no children. We lived together about 15 years, when she died which was in December 1909.

Death was not the only thing that separated family members after the Civil War. The dangers of life for African Americans in the Jim Crow South are also manifest in the Civil War pension files from time to time. A case in point is the deposition of Mary Overall, who testified in the pension application of her husband. Overall had not seen her husband in many years. He had been implicated in the murder of a white man in a black bordello, and rather than stay to face arrest, possible lynching, and almost certain execution, he fled the jurisdiction and assumed a new identity. Being asked to testify for her husband was Overall's first indication since he disappeared that he was still alive. Hence, although he was technically still alive, for Overall, her husband, Jacob, or "Abraham" as he now called himself, had essentially been dead to her for years.

Extract from the Deposition of Mary Overall, Nov. 9, 1901, Civil War Pension File of Jacob Hutchison (alias Jacob Overall, alias Abraham I. J. Wright), 4th USCHA, RG 15:

> I don't know my age; I was old enough to marry before the war of 1861–5 and did marry Jacob Overall, who was Nace Overalls slave and was given by him to his daughter Lizzie who was the wife of Jim Hutchinson. I was slave of Sam Thomas a "Cumberland Presbyterian preacher," and I married Jacob Overall. My master married us; I was living when married on my owners farm & Jacob Overall was living near Franklin Tenn. with his owner Hutchinson and visiting his Parents, Joe & Sarah Overall, on Nace Overalls place, next to Thomas' farm, was how I met him. We lived near Yorkville, Tenn. at that time.
>
> Jacob Overall had by me 6 children, named Hiram, Newt, Joe, Cora, Francis & Jacob—Hiram, Newt, and Francis are living; the others are dead. . . .
>
> I had 4 children by said Jacob Overall before he went away in the Army and two, Francis & Jacob, after he came back from the Army.
>
> The last I knew of Jacob Overall my husband was when he left me on the Wm Jones farm near Halls Hill Tenn.; I don't know when that was; my said husband was with a party of negroes who killed a man named Lawing and "they put it on Jake" and he ran away and I never after that heard from nor of him.

Despite Jacob Overall's being a wanted man, the Pension Bureau personnel did not turn him in to Tennessee authorities for Lawing's murder. Instead, after verifying his identity, they approved his pension application, which he collected as a free man until his death. J. S. Patterson, a special examiner who investigated the case, no doubt typified the feelings of the bureaucrats in his 1902 report to the commissioner of pensions. "Lawing was a miserable white man who did need killing," he wrote, "& got it."[13]

In short, the case of Jacob Overall is an interesting, if exceptional, tale of a former slave in post–Civil War America. But in Civil War pension files can be found equally fascinating and much more typical stories of African American life during this period: stories that put a human face to larger trends in the black community during this period; stories of former slaves coping with poverty and the related lack of access to health care and high infant mortality; stories of former slaves adjusting to a new world of work, one with limited rewards, little security, and significant dangers of injury and even death; stories of former slaves on the move in search of a better life or clinging to the familiar in rural locales in which it was easier to live in the preindustrial manner to which they were accustomed. Still, pension files also are full of stories of former slaves who broke the mold of African American life following the Civil War, becoming land owners or business proprietors and in other ways defying established patterns. Inherent in all these stories, though, is the significance of black family in the postwar period. As indicated in the introduction, Civil War pension files are particularly strong in documenting the family life of ex-slaves, and it is to this topic that we now turn.

4

Marriage and Family

Former slaves' pension claims resonate with stories of family life both under slavery and after emancipation. Some scholars have argued that the pension system was America's first national system of social provision, one rooted in a vision of family as a constellation of dependents circling around a male head of household, or a male wage earner.[1] As a consequence, pension officials were often interested in claimants' familial relationships. The Pension Bureau expected widows and other relatives eligible for pension—children under sixteen years of age, mothers, fathers, or siblings—to be able to verify that they were indeed related to the soldier in some legitimate capacity. Recognizing that slaves' family relationships existed outside legal sanction, pension legislation was flexible in not requiring former slaves to prove that their relationships had been "legal," but it did hold them to proving them as binding.[2] As previously discussed, a lack of documentary evidence of such relationships often meant that pension officials relied on the testimony of claimants and corroborating witnesses to verify family relationships. In such testimony—a widow describing how she met her husband as a young slave, a former fellow slave recalling the events of a marriage ceremony, a former owner recounting the birth of one of his slaves—lies a rich history of family life among slaves and ex-slaves.

The marriage relation is especially prominent in the pension files because widows constituted the second-largest group of pension claimants after the soldiers themselves. As pension officials strove to determine which were legal marriages, they probed the intimate details of claimants' personal lives, often going beyond the bounds of their own concept of propriety to gather their information. In the case of widows' claims, in particular, pension officials often used their own sense of morality as the measure by which to determine the legitimacy of many relationships. Conversely, rooted as they were in white, middle-class Victorian culture, pension officials tended to operate under the belief that stable families—those sanctioned by law—promoted morality among former slaves and, as such, helped to make them more suitable members of American society. As much as it was the job of pension officials to ensure that the Bureau awarded pensions to legitimate relatives of Civil War soldiers, many of them clearly felt they had a secondary responsibility to instill in former slaves the morality that they believed was lacking in slavery. Widows' pension claims reveal the importance of marriage to slaves and ex-slaves. They also bear witness to a range of intimate relationships among them, from those that were marital in nature to those that clearly were not.

Former slaves' pension files also provide portraits of family life in general, though not nearly as explicitly or as exhaustively as those of intimate relationships between men and women. Still, in the files lay stories of parents, children, siblings, and other relatives and of the joys and tragedies of the lives they shared. Ultimately, former slaves' pension files speak to the significance of family to emotional and physical survival during slavery and after.[3]

Family Life under Slavery

A constant fact of slave life was the threat and often the reality of family separation. Sales of slaves, the death of an owner and the subsequent division of his or her estate, an owner making a gift of a slave to his or her children, and the lack of decent medical care all contributed to a strong element of uncertainty in slaves' family life. Charlotte Guinn of Hot Spring County, Arkansas, was eighty-two years old in 1890 when she made the affidavit that follows. Although brief, her account of losing several of her fifteen children through sale and death speaks volumes about the havoc slavery wrought on slaves' families. Priscilla Shorter's detailed account of slave family life in Tennessee includes the tragic story of her mother's loss of both a husband and a son to sale. In her story of her mother's remarriage and the birth of children by her new husband, Shorter also reveals the resilience necessary for survival under slavery.

Excerpt from the Affidavit of Charlotte Guinn, May 9, 1890, Civil War Pension File of Simon Peter (alias Miller), 57th USCI, RG 15:

I was the mother of fifteen children at that time—1862 some of whom were dead, and some two or three had been sold as slaves and carried away so that I do not or did not know whether they were living or not—I had living to my knowledge at that time Felix Guinn, John Miller, James Miller, Emily Meredith (ne Guinn) Anthony Miller, Henry Guinn, Edie Guinn and Tyler—I don't know their ages at that time—No taxes paid by colored people at that time—date of soldier's death—Family physician at that time is dead. My husband died 7 years ago next August—& I have never remarried. I depended on my own labor mostly for a living in 1863 & 5

Excerpt from the Deposition of Priscilla Shorter, Apr. 9, 1917, Civil War Pension File of Isaac Shorter, 14th USCI, RG 15:

My old mistress used to tell me that I was born along about the first part of September. I dont know the year of my birth or the day of the month thereof. I know that in September, 1861, I was said to be 15 years old. I live in my own home on East Main St., Lebanon, Tenn. . . . The only work I do is working a little plot of ground on my place. My full, correct name is Priscilla, but I am generally called Scilla. At the time of my birth, my mother, Barbary (phonetic) was living on the Moore plantation in Smith county. She was called Barbary Moore. My father's name was Charles Sadler. He lived on Billy Sadler's place. He was sold when I was a little baby and went south. I dont remember ever having seen him. After my father was sold, my mother married Abe Montgomery. This marriage took place in slave times. She had five or six children by him Three of them I know are dead and Jim and Scott Montgomery are living. After Emancipation, mother went with her son Scott on little Indian Creek and staid with him until her death, which occurred about five years back. Mother had a son by Charles Sadler, Ned Husden, who lives near Smithville. . . . All my sisters are dead. The three boys named are my only living relatives Scott and Jim are only half brothers to me, they are younger than me. Ned is older than me. He got his name Husden by being sold during slavery. My master's name was Richard Moore and his place was located near Indian Creek. His wife's name was Betsy Moore. . . . Both Richard and Betsy Moore are dead. . . .

I dont know of their being in existence any kind of a record showing the date of my birth. I never heard that there was any written record showing the date of my birth. All I know about my age, is that I was born

> sometime during the early part of the month of September, and that when I first married in September, 1861, my mistress told me I was then fifteen years old. I am quite positive that that is what she told me. I dont know a living soul who would know the date of my birth. Ned is right smart older than me but I dont know how much. Scott and Jim are younger than me, but I dont know how much. I lived on Richard Moore's place from birth until about a year after the war closed. He had about 100 acres of land and had 16 or 17 slaves. With mother in the year 1860 besides myself, were Jim, Amy, Annie, Mandy, Aby and Laura, and another one whose name I have forgotten. The others were mother's children—most of them have died. Mother lived on same plantation during the summer of the year 1850, but I cant tell you who were with her then, I was much too little to know. In September, 1861, I with my mistress's consent, married in slave custom, John Cowan, who belonged to Capt. Matt Cowan. Capt. Cowan's plantation adjoined ours. Yes, John got his master's consent to our marriage. Hodges Sadler, a colored man, who went around and married colored folks married John and I. After the marriage, John and I lived about a year on the Moore place, then we lived at different places, all on Indian Creek. After living together about six years, John was killed. . . . On Capt. Cowan's place, there was a cave in which it had been found gold. My husband went there digging try to find the mouth of the cave in which the most of the gold was supposed to be. He would work in the fields some and down at the cave at nights. One early morning while working there, a large rock fell and killed him.

A few pages from the Bible belonging to Ona Bibb's former owner offer readers the barest bones of her life history. We learn that she was born in 1823, that she married Reuben, a slave from another plantation, at the age of twenty-three, and that she had her first child at age twenty-four and had her ninth, and last, child at the age of thirty-nine. In addition to Ona's history, the entries in the Bible, which identify slave children by their mother, underscore the notion that from the perspective of slave owners, the central familial relationship among slaves was that of mother and child. The laws of slavery held that children inherited their status from their mother and that the mother's master owned her children as well. In the examples that follow, we see how these practices shaped slaves' family lives. We also see the persistence of slave owners' control over slaves' identity even decades after emancipation. In each of the following two examples it is the slave owner who possesses crucial information about his former slaves' family history. Bibb herself noted that "her idea of dates is not good and she is guided in the matter of fixing dates by the information she has secured from her former owner."[4]

Excerpt from "Exhibit H" Case of Ona Bibb, Apr. 18, 1878, Civil War Pension File of Reuben Bibb, 65th USCI, RG15:

> Labadie, Franklin Co. Mo. April 18, 1878
>
> I Arthur Shepherd a Special Agent of the Pension Office hereby certify that I have this day examined the family record in the possessions of Mr Flavins J. North, the Postmaster at this place. The record is quite old and full, five pages, extending back two generations. From it I quote the following:
>
> "Ona was born March 10 1823."
> "Ona and Reuben (slave of Judge Bibb) married February—1847"
> "Reuben (Ona's child) born Jany 10 1848."
> "Betsy Ann (Ona's child) born June 1st 1849."
> "John Wesley (Ona's child) born Aug 1 1850"
> "Walker Allen (Ona's child) born Jany 7 1854"
> "Scott (Ona's child) born Dec 1, 1855"
> "Sarah Jane (Ona's child) born Dec 8 1856"
> "Luther Reuben (Ona's child) born April 1 1858"
> "Phoebe Jane (Ona's child) born July 1 1860"
> William A (Ona's child) born Oct 1 1862"
>
> I would further certify that the child of different women viz "Kate, Marla, Georgianna" were identified by the mother's name in brackets as Ona's are identified above.

Excerpt from the Deposition of J. S. Womack, Oct. 20, 1892, Civil War Pension File of Henry Womack (alias Thompson), 40th USCI, RG 15:

> I am well acquainted with the claimant, as he belonged to me before the war. I owned his mother and after I bought his mother the claimant was born and he belonged to me from the date of his birth until freedom was declared. I bought his mother in about 1845, and I think that the claimant was born the following spring after I bought his mother, so that the claimant would now be about 46 years of age.

Marriage under Slavery

Although the laws of slavery did not recognize slave marriages, typically slaves "married" one another, procuring their owner's consent in lieu of any legal procedure. Most slaves married partners of their own choosing, though this was not always the case. Former slave General Walker claimed that he had never married but was "put together by my Old Mistress. . . . My old Mistress put me and my wife together that was in Smoke Bend Louisiana the year I do not know."[5] For their part, however, slave owners usually sanctioned voluntary slave marriages for a variety of reasons, including the belief that slaves in stable family units were more productive in their labor and in providing owners with more slaves. Slave owners also believed that they were instilling morals in their slaves by encouraging marriages among them. As Mississippi former owner Duncan Chamberlain noted in an 1890 deposition, "We always encouraged our slaves to marry and tried to inculcate some degree of morality."[6] In addition to procuring the master's consent, slaves often marked their marriages by some sort of ceremony presided over by a minister, who might have been either a fellow slave or a white clergyman. Slave owners often sponsored some sort of celebration as well, as in the two examples that follow.

In their pension files, former slaves often used the phrase "living together" as they described the circumstances of their slave marriages. The claim that a slave couple had "lived together" does not necessarily mean that they did so on a regular basis but often reflected the living arrangements of couples married "abroad," that is, married to slaves on other plantations. Depending on how far apart their owners lived, couples who married abroad saw each other anywhere from once to several times a week, whatever was most convenient for their owners (Sunday was a common visiting day). In most cases, the slave husband would travel on foot to see his wife and spend the night with her. For slaves who only lived a few miles apart, this was relatively easy to do. However, it was not unusual for couples married abroad to live many miles apart. Regardless of how little or how often slave couples were able to spend time together, they often referred to this living arrangement as "living together."

Excerpt from the Deposition of Fannie Price, Jan. 9, 1907, Civil War Pension File of Edward Price (alias Waiters), 135th USCI, RG 15:

I am about 66 years of age; my post-office address is #20 Spring Park, Columbia, Richland Co., S.C. I am a laundress.

I am the widow of Edward Price who served in the United States army during the war under the name of Edward Price, but I do not know what company and regiment he served in, I hand you his pension certificate which shows his service. . . .

I made the acquaintance of Edward Price when we were both children. He belonged to Dick Price whose wife was named Mrs. Emma Price, and I belonged to Harmon Coon.

I married Edward Price in February of the fine year the war started in Charleston. We were living in this county about seven or eight miles from Columbia when we were married. We were married by James DeBruhil a colored Baptist preacher. He is now dead. Among those present at our marriage were Wesley Adams, Isaac Green, Ellen Aiken, and Easter White all of Columbia. The preacher went through with the usual church ceremony, just the same thing that they do now. We first went to our owners and got their consent before we were married. We went to them just like we would to our parents. My owner gave us a large supper. There were more than two hundred people present at the marriage, so many that we had to stand out in the yard when the ceremony was performed. After we were married I lived at my owners place and Edward lived at his but he would come to see me once a week. He would come Saturday night and remain until Monday morning. We continued to live together in that way until he went into the army. He did not go into the army until toward the last of the war. . . .

We were both young when we got married and no one had any claim on us.

Edward Price came straight back to me after being discharged from the army and we lived together from that time until he died [1905], as husband and wife and were recognized as such by the community. We were never divorced or separated. We lived together all our days without being separated.

Excerpt from the Deposition of Hannah Brown, Aug. 6, 1896, Civil War Pension File of Lindsay Brown, 13th USCHA, RG 15:

Age: 65 years, Occupation, washerwoman; Residence and PO Address: Mexico, Andran Co., Mo

Am applicant for pension as widow of Lindsey Brown. I have none of his army papers and didn't preserve any of his letters to me. I cant say what Co. and Regt. he served in. A colored man, Jim London, found my husband's service for me from his army comrades. I don't think any of his comrades live around here.

I was born in Augusta Co., Va, and at eleven years of age was bought by the Heyser family and brought to Monroe Co Mo, two miles east of Santafee. Shortly before the war (I cant give the exact date) I married Lindsey Brown in my masters house near St Afee. Wm. Meadows, a colored Methodist preacher, married us. I had not been married before, but my husband had a slave wife in Virginia, from whom he had parted years before. I had given birth to two boys before I married Lindsey Brown. I had been engaged to a man belonging to Mr. Bob Sinclair and he was the father of my two boys, Marion and Charles, born before the war. They were good big boys when I married Lindsey Brown. Since war, they are known as Marion and Charley Brown. After I married Lindsey Brown my first child was William, who was born in cold weather. He died in Spring of the next year. My next child George Ann was born in Spring some two or three years before my husband went into the army. She is living now in Kansas City, Mo., the wife of N.S. Whaley at 1919 Vine St. She is the last child to whom I gave birth.

During the war I joined the Presbyterian church and was presented with a bible, in which have been set down entries of births and deaths of my family. . . .

My husband Lindsey Brown, belonged to James Trimble, who lived one mile from my owner's place. He came to see me when he pleased, by the consent of our owners. Mrs. Nancy Heizer, on near Santafee, Mo. witnessed my marriage, as did the wife of Charley Davis, a resident of this place. John Heizer, husband of Nancy Heizer, also witnessed the marriage, as did their daughter, now Mrs. Mary Davis. I was called Hannah Brown after my marriage, and we cohabited as man and wife and were so regarded by our owners and fellow servants.

In the last year of the war, just after the slaves had been declared free, my husband decided that it would be dangerous to remain in Monroe Co., Mo., so he packed up some clothes, took an axe and left for Illinois in the spring of the year. The next thing I heard of him he was in the service. He wrote me and told me he had gone into the service. He wrote me from several places. The last letter he wrote me was from Smithland, Ky., in which he told me they were going to move "but I know not where. Don't write until I write." I never heard from him again, and never received a letter from anyone relative to his death.

Not all slave couples "married" with a ceremony or some particular event to mark the occasion. Many "took up" together, a term indicating an informal beginning to a relationship that could have been considered a marriage or could have been an intimate relationship with no marital intent.[7] In Hagar Washington's case, the lack of a marriage ceremony or celebration clearly had no bearing on the marital nature of the relationship. That Hagar "remarried" her husband George when he was in the army suggests as much. In the case of George Jackson's claim for his father's pension, Jackson explained that his parents "took up" with each other. His case was reviewed by the Pension Bureau's Law Division to determine his status as the legitimate child of Henry Jackson, in question because Jackson noted that his parents had never married. Officials in the Law Division found his parents' relationship as one that was marital in nature because they had lived together for at least ten years and because they had gone to the trouble of having their child baptized. In the case of widow Willie Parker, it is revealed that Parker had an intimate relationship with a man whom she did not regard as her husband. Both the Jackson and Parker cases also bear witness to the practice among slaves of having children within relationships not considered as marriages. Given the nature of slavery, this practice often was one subject to neither shame nor scorn in slave communities.[8]

Excerpt from the Deposition of Hagar Washington, Dec. 29, 1894, Civil War Pension File of George Washington, 58th USCI, RG 15:

> My age is 55–60 years, servant, I live about one mile from Natchez, Miss. I claim a pension as widow of George Washington who served in Co E, 58 U.S.C.T. . . . Prior to the war I belonged to Col. Ben Pryor, and George Washington to Mr. Bingman, 2–3 miles from Natchez; Col. Pryor was a horse trainer for Mr. Bingman and George Washington attended to Mr. Bingman's horses. I had been bought by Mr. Pryor when I was a little child from the nigger traders on the "Forks of the Road", who raised me and kept me in his family as a nurse. I became acquainted with George Washington 3–4 years before our marriage 7–8 years before the war. We were not regularly married, just took up and lived together as man and wife; neither of us had ever been married prior to that time; and shortly after George Washington's enlistment in Co E, 58 U.S.C.T. we were married by Mr. Wright, Chaplain of the regiment. Every fall and winter Mr. Bingman used to send his horses to Col. Pryor for training and George Washington and I passed these seasons

together, while later in the spring and summer my husband had to go with the stock to the races. We were regarded by the people in the neighborhood as husband and wife. My maiden name was Hagar Johnson. At the time of my husband's enlistment I had three children, Virginia, Madison and Elizabeth Washington; Sarah, Francis and Richard Eugene all by the soldier, were born during his service. . . . I came to Natchez with my husband when my husband when he enlisted and I lived here all through the war. During the latter part of the war my husband was shot on the way from Brookhaven, Miss to Natchez, he did not die right away, but was picked up by the ambulance and died before he got to Natchez Miss. . . .

Excerpt from the Deposition of George Jackson, June 16, 1904, Civil War Pension File of Henry Jackson, 82nd USCI, RG 15:

My father was owned by a man named Squire John Smith and my mother was owned by John Miller they had plantations about half a mile apart, they took up with each other by slavery custom, there was no marriage between them and they lived together until he went away to the army where I was told afterwards that he was killed in the army. My mother after the war took up with a John Sam and lived with him and had a number of children by him five of whom I think are still living. My mothers name was Felice Miller and when she took up with Sam she went by the name of Felice Sam. She died in here in the year 1882 as near as I can come at it. . . . I was the only child of my father by his first and only wife.

Excerpt from the Deposition of Willie Parker, May 13, 1888, Civil War Pension File of Jonathan Parker, 11th USCI and 113th USCI, RG 15:

My name is Willie Parker. I am over 50 years old. I am a housekeeper and live [in] . . . Little Rock, Pulaski Co. Ark. . . . I was born in . . . North Carolina. I lived in that state until I was 12 or 13 years old when I was brought to this state. I was brought here by my Master Smith Wethers. I was called Willie Wethers before my marriage. Smith Wethers settled in Pope Co. about 5 miles from Adkins Sta. to the west. I lived there up to the time I married Jonathan Parker. I had one child a girl by a colored man named Sam Cunningham before my marriage to Jonathan Parker. I was not married to Sam Cunningham and did not consider myself his wife. I think he is alive—and has a large family. . . . This child whose name is Mary Rebecca Cunningham is now alive and is married to a man by the

> name of Albert Sypho. . . . This girl was about three years old at the time I married my husband Jonathan Parker. I was married to Jonathan Parker on the 25th day of Dec 1859 in Pope Co. Ark. I was first married by a man by the name of Jack Williams who was a colored man, who married the colored people. I suppose he was a minister but I did not know him. I was at the house of my husband master on the night I was married. My husbands master was Price Parker and after my marriage I went back to my master's place and my husband used to come every Saturday night and stay with me until Monday when he would go back to his work—Our plantations were six miles apart. After the war broke out and after we had been made free, my husband came and told me that he was going away to become a soldier. He came to my house and told me this.

Excerpt from the Deposition of Royal Embreo, May 16, 1888, Civil War Pension File of Jonathan Parker, 11th USCI and 113th USCI, RG 15:

> My name is Royal Embreo. I am 77 years old. Am a resident of Little Rock Pulaski Co. Ark. . . . I have no trade. I am now blind and can do no work. I was owned and lived with Col Ben Embreo at his place about 5 miles west of Adkins Sta in Pope Co. Ark. I have known this woman Willie Parker ever since her girlhood I knew her long before her marriage to Jonathan Parker. Her maiden name was Willie Wethers and her master's name was Wethers and his farm was not quite two miles from my master's place, and I was well acquainted with all her family—She was never married before her marriage to Jonathan Parker. Although she did have a girl baby by a man by the name of Sam Cunningham. He promised to marry Willie Wethers and under the promise of marriage he seduced Willie and she had a baby by him, but he never did marry her, but married another woman and raised a large family and is now living with his family. . . . After this Jonathan Parker, who was right smart older than Willie courted her and was married to her at Parker's place, about the year 1859, and I think this marriage was performed by a fellow servant by the name of Jack Williams who did this kind of work for the colored people
>
> Jonathan Parker and Willie lived together as man and wife and was so recognized by all their fellow servants from that date up to the day of his death about two years ago.

The following deposition from a former Kentucky slaveholder reveals that some masters let their slaves follow their own inclinations in choosing a mate, even trying to appease particular slaves by purchasing a favored partner. It also underscores the notion that informal relationships usually carried no stigma among many slaves and suggests, too, that such attitudes persisted in the black community following the war.

Excerpt from the Deposition of J. D. Butler Sr., Sept. 15, 1891, Civil War Pension File of Solomon Butler (alias Flood), 122nd USCI, RG 15:

> The clmt. Jincy Butler belonged to my father, in days of slavery. Prior to the war clmt had 3 or 4 different men and children by several of them. She was a great woman for the men. We bought a man—Sol. Flood—some time before the war, to please clmt as she seemed to think more of him than of any other man. She had several children by Sol. but left him after the war and married Reuben Kennedy and lived with him for a few years and then left and went to live with Jack Fuqua. Clmt left Reuben while they were cropping in our place. I do not know the cause of her leaving unless it was her natural propensity for a change

Mary Malonne, a native French speaker from the sugar-producing region of Louisiana, declared that she was "about 100 years" old when she claimed a pension on account of the service of her son, Octave Jessie.[9] Her own story is an interesting one. Malonne had a slave husband with whom she took up, apparently without a ceremony. Prior to her marriage, Malonne had a number of children by two different white men. Malonne did not testify as to the nature of those relationships, whether they were forced or voluntary. She claimed simply that she was not the wife of either man but that they stayed with her sometimes in her little cabin behind her master's house.[10] Malonne testified that her father was a white man named Halgaut and that she was owned as an adult by two brothers named Halgaut. Although there is no evidence to confirm it, it is entirely possible that Malonne's owners were her own brothers or otherwise related to her.

Excerpt from the Deposition of Mary Malonne, Sept. 11, 1893, Civil War Pension File of Octave Jessie, 96th USCI, RG 15:

> I had Octave Jessie by a colored man named Octave Theriot, who I took up with a long time before the war. Octave Theriot belonged to Susthene Theriot and lived in Convent. I belonged to Augustine Halgault who also

lived in Convent. I had three children by Octave Theriot, and their names were Octave Jessie, Alexander Colar and W[illiam] Colar. Alexander Colar lives here in Convent and I live with him, and W[m] Colar lives in N.O. All of said children were born in Convent. I do not know how old Octave Jessie was when he enlisted, but he was then quite a young man. He was a brown skinned fellow. . . .

The soldier belonged to the same man that I did before the war and he lived with me until he enlisted. After the war he lived in Careltin, La. until he died. . . .

Octave Theriot died in Convent right after the war. I lived with him as his wife from the time I took up with him until he died. I had a little cabin in the rear of my master's house, and Octave Theriot used to come and stay with me nights.

I had six children before I took up with Octave Theriot. I had my first child by . . . Dupa't a wealthy white man, and then I had five children by Joseph Michael, another white man. I did not live with either of these men as their wife, but they used to come and stay with me sometimes. . . .

Q. What was the soldier's occupation before he enlisted?

A. He worked on the sugar plantation doing regular farm work, such as plowing . . . and he sometimes did carpenter work.

Q. Who did you belong to before you belonged to Augustine Halgault?

A. I belonged to Alexander . . . Halgault, who was a brother of Augustine Halgault. When Alexander died I went to his brother Augustine.

Q. Who did you belong to when Octave was born?

A. I then belonged to Alexander . . . Hagault.

Q. What was the color of Octave Theriot?

A. He was a black man.

Q. Who was your father?

A. Michel Halgault a white man

Q. Who was your mother?

A. My mother was an Indian woman named Camille. . . .

I own no property of any kind, except a little house that my son Alexander Colar built for me. I am unable to work and am dependent upon my son Alexander for my living. I only saw the soldier once after he was discharged, and I then saw him in N.O., but I do not remember the year that I saw him.

Pension Bureau officials often asked for a widow's entire marital history in order to determine the legitimacy of her claim to a pension. For example, because Milley Hale had been married to another slave prior to her marriage to the soldier, Joseph Hale, pension officials sought to confirm that before she married Hale, Milley's slave marriage had ended. In order to attain this history, it was common for examiners to interrogate various family and community members in addition to the widow. When they recounted that history, as in the cases of Hale and Emeline Pipes, widows frequently shared stories of separation either from the soldier or from a past slave husband. The circumstances of separation in Pipes's story are quite clear, but the varied testimony in Hale's case underscores the diverse ways in which different parties involved may experience and understand the same event. Given the bureaucratic nature of the pension system and the formality of the interview process, former slaves' testimony often reads as if it lacks emotion. Little imagination is required, however, to conceive of the trauma and heartbreak that accompanied the experiences of separation so common among slave families.

Excerpt from the Deposition of Emeline Pipes, Oct. 3, 1893, Civil War Pension File of Irwin Pipes, 80th USCI, RG 15:

> I am an applicant for pension . . . as the widow of Irwin Pipes. . . .
>
> My first husbands name was Bolivar. We were married by masters consent. My maiden name was Neer. When our master Henry Dunn died, I fell to Miss Mary and Bolivar to Miss Amanda, daughters of Henry Dunn. Bolivar was taken away and we were separated. I have never lived with him since. After that I married one Jackson Dunn, a slave of Miss Mary's. I lived with him until he died which was before the war but I don't know just when it was. I then remained a widow until I married Irwin Pipes.

Excerpt from the Deposition of Andrew Nero, Oct. 3, 1893, Civil War Pension File of Irwin Pipes, 80th USCI, RG 15:

> I am a brother of the above named claimant and am a few years her senior. I have known her all her life. After my old master Captain Henry Dunn died Emeline fell to his daughter Miss Mary and she was taken about 15 miles away. Her first husband that she married in slavery times was named Bolivar. She lived with Bolivar three or four years when he was drawn by one of her masters sons in law, and taken away leaving Emiline with

Miss Mary Butler a daughter of Captain Henry. Bolivar never came back to Emiline again as he was taken too far away. After that Emiline took up with a man named Jackson, and they lived together until a short time before the war when he died on the Miss Mary Butler place. He died in slavery times. My sister had but one child a girl who was born before her marriage to Bolivar. After Jackson died, Emeline remained a widow until about a year after the soldiers were all mustered out when she married a man named Irwin Pipes

Excerpt from the Deposition of Mary Carney, Oct. 3, 1893, Civil War Pension File of Irwin Pipes, 80th USCI, RG 15:

I have known the above named claimant since my first recollection. She was a slave on the plantation of my father R.B. Dunn. She originally belonged to my grand-father Henry Dunn. I do not remember that she ever had a husband named Bolivar, but Aunt Amanda Pipes owned a number of slaves and there may have been one on the plantation of that name.

Her first husband of whom I have any recollection was a slave named Jack. Jack died about the outbreak of the war. He and Emeline had been living together some years when Jack died. Emeline remained a widow until after the close of the war when she married a colored man named Irwin Pipes, with whom she lived until he died.

Excerpt from the Deposition of Milley Hale, June 28, 1898, Civil War Pension File of Joseph Hale, 1st USCHA, RG 15:

My maiden name was Milley Whitecotton. Whitecotton was my fathers name. My last owner was Sam Queener who raised me from a child 8 years old. He lived near Jacksboro, Tenn. Ollie Queener, my mistress is still alive. I first married William Queener (who was owned by Jake Queener) before the war in slavery time but he was sold away into the south in the first part of the war, but a long time after the war, probably something like twenty years ago he came back to this country and was sent to the penitentiary from Clinton, Anderson Co. Tenn. . . . He and I were married in slavery time at Queener's by Gosh Queener whose whereabouts I don't know. He was old then.

Excerpt from the Deposition of Sarah Clotfelter, July 1, 1898, Civil War Pension File of Joseph Hale, 1st USCHA, RG 15:

I was well acquainted with Milley Queener, a negress. She belonged to my sister Ollie Queener with whom I stayed. I was present and saw Milley married to Will Queener by Gosh Queener a slave.

They were married according to slave custom which marriage held good as long as they were in reach and bounds of each other. When they were not within reach each was permitted to marry some one else. Milley had quite a big wedding and stood up just like people of today do and had their waiters and all and a regular ceremony was performed.

Along about the beginning of the war Will started to run away from here and they followed him and caught him but he eluded his captors and did escape. This is what I heard.

Excerpt from the Deposition of Ollie Queener, July 1, 1898, Civil War Pension File of Joseph Hale, 1st USCHA, RG 15:

I was well acquainted with Milley Hale. I raised her from a small child. She married Will Queener who was owned by Ann Queener widow of Jake Queener. They were married at my house I don't remember the date but it was before the war came up. It was quite a big wedding. Several white people were present. My husband would not allow any whites in the room but he and I stood in the door and saw Gosh Queener, a slave marry them. They were married according to the Methodist ceremony or discipline. Gosh Queener held the book and read off the ceremony to them. It was quite a nice ceremony. . . . These two negroes Millie and Will lived together all they could. Milley was sold to Mr. Gibson. Mr. Gibson ran her back over here in the time of the war to prevent them from getting her I suppose.

She finally went away and when she came back she told me she had been waiting on soldiers in small pox hospital but I don't know where. Before she left here though Will had gone but I don't know just how he came to get away.

Excerpt from the Deposition of J. C. Hunter, July 16, 1898, Civil War Pension File of Joseph Hale, 1st USCHA, RG 15:

I knew Will Queener a negro owned by Jacob Queener's heirs.

He was said to be married to Ann Hunter a negress owned by my mother and her heirs. He came to house of mother and it was said he was married to Ann. It was just a slave marriage.

> I hear that he afterward married Milley Whitecotton. He just left Ann I guess for Ann was here in this neighborhood and died only last summer.
>
> During the war about 1862 or '63 Will ran away from here and I was hired to go after him and found him at Gibsons where Milley was and hand cuffed him but he got away hand cuffs and all. Afterwards I learned he was at Cumberland Gap and went after him but don't know that I saw him there. I heard at Cumberland Gap that Will was at Flat Lick, Ky and went there and the union soldiers captured me and sent me to Johnson's Island in Lake Erie where I was kept nearly two years. I came home and never saw the negro Will Queener again to my knowledge although shortly after the war was over I heard that he was down here about Clinton, Anderson Co. Tenn. I don't know anything about Wills death.

Transitions

In his influential work on slave families, Herbert Gutman noted that nearly half of the slave couples in Virginia and North Carolina counties (that kept records) had legalized their marriages by 1866. Although Gutman's argument that former slaves desired to formalize their relationships is an important one, it does not consider the complexity of motives that compelled former slaves to take such action.[11] Former slaves' pension claims reveal a variety of reasons for legalizing marriages. Certainly, many former slave couples simply wanted the protection and formal recognition that legality afforded. Others responded to the legal requirements of the state in which they lived. A number of Southern states made special provisions in their Black Codes (laws passed by Southern legislatures in 1865 and 1866 designed to control former slaves' activities) that either automatically married former slave couples or required them to legalize their unions under penalty of a fine or imprisonment. Former slave couples also heeded the advice of army and government officials who believed in the ability of formal matrimony to instill moral values in ex-slaves.

Excerpt from the Deposition of Elizabeth Dallas, Nov. 26, 1881, Civil War Pension File of James Dallas, 76th USCI, RG 15:

> Two or three years before the war (1861) she was married by consent of owner to a fellow slave named James Dallas. . . . She continued to live in

Cohabitation with said husband on the plantation, until the U.S. Forces Captured Baton Rouge,[12] when upon their return to New Orleans her said husband went with them and enlisted at New Orleans as She understood. She cant give the date. Soldier (her husband) returned to Baton Rouge some time afterward a Soldier in Co "D" 4 La Guard, afterward 76 US Col Troops. She rejoined him at Baton Rouge, and Continued with him and the Regiment until they went from Baton Rouge to Fort Jackson, and thence to Port Hudson, (after the capture of Port Hudson) Affiant remained with the soldier at Port Hudson four or five months when she came to New Orleans, leaving said husband with his command. . . . She further declares that while at Baton Rouge in 1863 with her said husband, she was remarried to him by Chaplain Reed of his Regiment, the chaplain did not believe that the marriage in slavery was in accordance with religion and morality, hence he married them over.

Excerpt from the Affidavit of Kizzie Sexton, Mar. 5, 1898, Civil War Pension File of Henry Sexton, 65th and 67th USCI, RG 15:

I was first married to [Henry Sexton] on or about the day of December 1855, on a farm in Boone County, Missouri. When the late civil war came on he enlisted and went away, and returned to me right away after his discharge, and we lived together as husband and wife until in the month of September 1869 We were remarried at St. Louis Missouri by Rev. Spottswood Rice, minister of the A.M.E. church. This second marriage was advised by friends as a protection to myself and the children. That neither myself nor husband had been previously married. I further declare that I was never divorced from said Henry Sexton but continued to live with him as his lawful wife until the date of his death, which occurred on the 3rd day of September 1897.

Affidavit of Spottswood Rice, December 15, 1897, Civil War Pension File of Henry Sexton, 65th and 67th USCI, RG 15:

I, Spottswood Rice, a regularly ordained minister of the gospel. of the County of El-Paso, and State of Colorado, former of St-Louis County and State of Missouri, being first duly sworn does upon oath depose and say, That he re-married one Henry Sexton and Kizzie Sexton, at the City of St-Louis, and State of Missouri sometime during the month of September 1869. under the then existing laws of said State, I further declare that I have no interest directly or indirectly in the Widows claim for pension, and am not concerned in its prosecution.

Excerpt from the Affidavit of Lucinda Sibley, Jan. 11, 1893, Civil War Pension File of Solomon Sibley, 63rd USCI, RG 15:

> I was owned by Hamilton Sibley of Hinds Co. Miss. . . . He also owned my husband. Neither myself nor said Solomon Sibley had been married to any one else but each other. I was married to said Solomon in my masters House in Hinds Co Miss. I do not know the date of our marriage—but I lived with him 40 years before he died. After his enlistment in Co D 63 USC Inf—there was a general impression that our old slave marriages were not valid and we were advised to marry again under the United States regulations. and on the 15 day of May 1864 we were again married by Rev. J.K. Locke an Army chaplain. I have the certificate given us, which I herewith file and make a part of this affidavit.

Excerpt from Thomas Hodges's Pension Bureau Questionnaire, Sept. 7, 1897, Civil War Pension File of Thomas Hodges, 92nd USCI, RG 15:

> No. 1. Are you a married man? If so, please state your wife's full name, and her maiden name. Answer: Yes Fanny Hodges Fanny Briscoe
>
> No. 2. When, where, and by whom were you married? Answer: Aug 17 1889 in St. James Ph La by Rev Thomas Allen. . . .
>
> No. 5. . . . I lived with my wife 30 years but only lawfully married her in 18– according to the laws I am recognize the same if I had married her thirty years ago

Excerpt from the Affidavit of John Lawrence, Oct. 12, 1869, Civil War Pension File of Green Colyar (alias Collier), 15th USCI, RG 15:

> On or about the 25th day of Nov. 1865, I joined in marriage Green Colyar of Co. "G" 15 U.S.C.T. and Essabelle Carr. I was Chaplain of the Regiment at the time to which Colyar belonged, and advised all colored persons, who proposed to live together as husband and wife, to be married in the most solemn and legal way that was practicable. The Laws of Tennessee did not provide for the issuance of license to persons in their condition until May 1866. I regarded the parties above named as mar-

ried in accordance with the law of God and common law of the land. Such marriage is legal in this state as the Supreme Court has repeatedly decided.

In this time of transition, former slaves' family lives represented a blending of old and new practices, as exemplified in the pension claim of Georgia Evans, widow of Osborne Evans (see earlier excerpts from her testimony in chapter 3). Although the lived experience of combining old and new practices raised little concern among former slaves, the phenomenon confounded Pension Bureau officials who were responsible for categorizing former slaves' relationships according to conventional legal definitions. In his report to the commissioner of pensions, special examiner Eugene B. Payne measured relationships by three standards: slave practices; the laws of the particular Southern state in which the claimant lived (in Evans's case, Missouri); and the norms of middle-class, Northern, white society.

Excerpt from the Affidavit of Georgia Evans, July 20, 1893, Civil War Pension File of Osborne Evans, 18th USCI, RG 15:

> I had been acquainted with the soldier about two or three years before our marriage. I was married to the soldier on the 21st day of January 1872 at Huntsville Mo. by S.P. Lindley a preacher. I never had but one owner while a slave and he was Theophilus Eddings at whose place I was born near Huntsville Mo. I was free when I was married to the soldier. I was past known, while a slave, by the name of Georgia Eddings, taking the surname of my master. After being set free in 1865, I was known as Georgia Miles, that being the name taken by my mother at freedom, though she had been known as Eddings after her owner. . . .
>
> I don't know where the soldier was born. He said he was born in the state of Kentucky. . . . I know nothing of him before his enlistment. I do not know his age. He said he was 55 a short time before he died. He was a barber by occupation. . . . He said he was the slave of Henry Evans when he enlisted—heard of no other before. He was free when I married him and he never had any other wife or name that I know of.

Excerpt from Eugene B. Payne, Special Examiner, Chillicothe, Mo., to the Commissioner of Pensions, Washington, D.C., Dec. 23, 1893, Civil War Pension File of Osborne Evans, 18th USCI, RG 15:

The proof shows that claimant had never been married before.
Soldier had been married.

In 1862 in Randolph Co. Mo. the soldier and Sarah (Sally) McCampbell, both slaves, were married, slave fashion ie with the consent of masters—They lived together until soldier enlisted After discharge the soldier returned to Macon Mo. & lived with his slave wife five (5) years, when they separated forever They had only one child which died at 9 months old—Soldier then went to Brookfield Mo. and lived with a prostitute a short time, possibly a year, and then he went to Huntsville & married claimant. Sarah McCampbell the slave wife died in winter of 1879 and 1880.

The state of Mo. passed in 1865 an act governing and regulating slave marriages and prescribing the manner in which colored people could *legally* live and cohabit together—called "An Act in relation to the marital rights" and children of colored persons" app Feb 20" 1865. And this law was in force until repealed by the general act passed in 1881 governing all marriages both white & black and requiring *license* & a record of same—The following are some of the provisions of said act of 1865

Sec. 1. In all cases where persons of color heretofore held as slaves in the state of Missouri, have cohabited together as husband and wife, it shall be the *duty* of persons thus cohabiting to appear before a Justice of the Township where they reside, or before any other officer authorized to solemnize marriages, And it shall be the duty of such officer to join in marriage the persons applying and to keep a record of same Sec. 3 Requires such officer under a penalty of $50 to send a certificate of such marriage to the county recorder & sec. 4 requires Recorder to docket same in a book and keep said Record

Sec. 6. "All persons of color living or cohabiting together as husband and wife without being married according to the provisions of this chapter *shall be liable to a criminal prosecution as now provided by law.*"

I searched the records of Macon County Mo. at Macon but could find no record of the marriage of soldier to Sarah or Sally McCampbell. And her mother and brother both testified that—as they called it, Osborne and Sarah were never married "under the new constitution"

So that the living together of soldier after the war was an *adulterous* cohabitation and *not legal* according to the law of Mo. . . .

Therefore Sarah McCampbell the slave wife ceased to be the wife of soldier Feb 20th 1865 (date of approval of law)—And his marriage to the claimant was legal under the law of Mo. But supposing our office refuses

> to be governed by the law of Mo. but says a legal slave marriage is always a marriage for pension purposes while the parties live. Then another principle steps in and says soldiers marriage to claimant was legal.
>
> It will be observed that the slave wife *died* in the winter of 1869 [actually 1879] and the prostitute . . . was never his wife.—Now a ceremony having been performed between soldier and claimant *according to law*, in Jan 1872, the moment the legal impediment (ie the slave wife) was removed by death (in 1879) there arose an instantaneous legal marriage between soldier and claimant see 1st Bishop on Marriage and Divorce sec 505
>
> Then again, soldier and claimant (as shown by the proof) lived and cohabited together as man and wife and held themselves out to the Public as such from 1879 (death of slave wife) to 1893 when soldier died—or at least from 1879 to 1881 (date of the enactment of a general statute requiring a license &c) and this, under the discussions of the Mo. courts constituted a valid marriage. . . .

The pension claim of widow Julia Clark is representative of countless claims of former slaves who met, fell in love, and married after the war. Theirs were often legal marriages, performed in the church or by a government official, which took full advantage of the opportunity that freedom provided to pursue relationships that were both recognized and protected by law. Clark's inability to afford the $1.50 copy of her marriage certificate offers some insight into her financial condition in the 1890s.

Excerpt from the Deposition of Julia Clark, Dec. 30, 1893, Civil War Pension File of Mark Clark, 2nd USCLA, RG 15:

> I am the widow of Mark Clark. . . . I first made his acquaintance in 1865 just as the war closed. My maiden name was Julia Steward I was a slave and belonged to Enoch Steward, he lived first in Lagrange Fayette Co. Tenn. and he moved to Coahoma Co. Miss. and we lived there 9 years before the late war commenced. I came to Helena Ark. the next day after the fight at Big Creek. I came with my two sisters and their husbands we slipped away and came over here.
>
> I was married here in Phillip Co. 10 miles from Helena on the widow Suttons place, by a Methodist preacher named Rev. Williams. I did not know his first name we were married in 1868. I cannot now remember

> the day and month. I have been told that it is recorded here at the Court House, but I am not able to pay the $1.50 to get a copy of it. . . .
>
> No, Sir, I have never been married since the death of Mark Clark and I have not lived with any man as his wife since his death. He died 16 miles from here Dec. 16, 1880. he was accidentally shot and died. Frank Bragg shot him and he was sent to the Penitentiary for one year.
>
> No Sir When Mark Clark was killed he left no property of any kind, and I have not owned any property since his death. and I have not now and have not had any income from any source whatever except from my daily labor.

Marriage and Female Morality

At thirty-nine years old in 1899, Eliza Ann Winslow was a member of the generation of African Americans who came of age under Reconstruction. Winslow had been married twice by the age of thirty-nine, once to the veteran Luke Riddick and later to a man she met when he came to work a crop for her. Both of Winslow's marriages were legal. In the case of all widows, but especially African American women, Pension Bureau officials paid careful attention to a widow's degree of morality in her actions and in her relationships; a woman deemed immoral was often also deemed undeserving of a pension.[13] Accordingly, special examiners often conducted exhaustive investigations into the intimate relationships of both white and black women and frequently asked female claimants personal questions that seem now to overstep the bounds of Victorian propriety. Questions about when Winslow began having a sexual relationship with the man who became her second husband arose because she had a child after only six months of marriage to him. Special examiner E. H. Carver reported that Winslow "got in a 'delicate' state and the people compelled them to marry."[14] Winslow herself was careful to delineate the nature her relationship to her second husband, no doubt in response to the question of its morality.

Excerpt from the Deposition of Eliza Ann Winslow, May 4, 1899, Civil War Pension File of Luke Riddick (alias White), 38th USCI, RG 15:

> I am now the wife of David Winslow. I was formerly the wife of Luke Riddick, who served in Co. B, 38 U.S. C. Troops. . . .

> I married David Winslow Nov. 13, 1898 at this place by J.B. Roach a minister. There is a record of my marriage at Hertford, N.C. . . .
>
> I lived with him [Luke Riddick] as his wife from the time I married him up to the time he died. We were never separated or divorced. He died Nov. 8, 1895. He died of what Dr. White said was heart disease. . . . He drew the pension under the name of Luke Riddick. He married me under the name of Luke White. He was formerly a slave of Riddicks. He belonged to Willis Riddick. . . .
>
> I kept house myself after my husband Luke White died and did not marry any one until I married David Winslow. David Winslow came here last March to attend a crop for me. I never occupied the same bed with him until after I married him, but we were intimate from the latter part of last summer. I have had one child born by him. It was born last night.

In the case of Elizabeth Vass, widow of Henry Vass, a reprimand from the Zion Baptist Church, of which she was a member, compelled her to legalize her marriage. As in Eliza Ann Winslow's case, Vass too was subject to an invasion of her private life, asked personal questions about whether she had a sexual relationship with the soldier in the years prior to their legal marriage. Vass was frank in her explanation of her relationship to the soldier. She considered herself to be Henry Vass's wife, although she acknowledged that theirs had not been a legal union for many years. Although special examiner John W. Hall considered the years prior to Vass's legal marriage to the soldier as "illicit" (what the church called "adulterous"), Vass seemed perfectly content to live as such, only changing her mind when she found herself unable to rejoin the church. Her interpretation of her experience stands in contrast to that of Winslow, who made it very clear that her relationship with her second husband was legitimate and morally sound.

Excerpt from the Deposition of Elizabeth Vass, May 19, 1903, Civil War Pension File of Henry Vass, 2nd USCC, RG 15:

> I am about 55 years of age . . . occupation domestic. . . . I first met the soldier about 1870, and was married to him in Washington D.C. on July 3 1890 by the Rev. Wm J. Howard, at 718 3d St. S.W. my maiden name was Elizabeth Conway. I was born in King George County Virginia and resided there until I came to Washington about 1870. I had not been married prior to my marriage to the soldier. I do not know whether the soldier had been

previously, but my understanding was he had not been. Soldier died in Washington D.C. February 17, 1900. From the time of my marriage to the soldier until the date of his death I lived with him continuously as his wife. No sir, there was never any divorce granted to either the soldier or myself. About eight yrs prior to my ceremonial marriage to the soldier I began to cohabit and live with him as his wife. For something more than two years prior thereto I began keeping house for him—he owned a little home and was a single man. I did not live there all the time but went back and forward. It was when I first went there to keep house for him that we began to have carnal knowledge of one another. That intimacy and the relation continued . . . until I moved to his house about eight years prior to my marriage to him. When I went there about 1882 it was for the purpose of establishing myself permanently as his housekeeper he being then a single man and I an unmarried woman. There was no discussion of the question of marriage between us until just prior to the time we were married by the Rev. W.J. Howard, a copy of certificate of such marriage was furnished the Bureau. There had never been any agreement that there should be a marriage between us until just prior to the time the marriage was performed—about two months prior thereto.—I had got tired of living with him in the capacity of a wife without being married to him. Some four or five years prior to our marriage I had been "turned out" of the church for living with him without being married to him. I wanted to rejoin the church and could not do so until I was lawfully married to him. It was the Zion Baptist church . . . from which I was expelled, Rev. W.J. Howard, the pastor. Yes sir, I was expelled from the church for the reason that I was leading an adulterous life with the soldier. Yes sir, I was a member of the church when I first met the soldier and I was known to the members of the church and congregation as Elizabeth Conway. Yes, my name was borne on the records of the church as Elizabeth Conway at the time I was expelled from the church. . . . Yes sir, during the eight years that I lived with soldier as his wife prior to my marriage to him I was known and went by the name of Elizabeth Conway—Conway was the name of my father and mother. No sir, I was not introduced by the soldier to his friends and acquaintances as Mrs. Vass until after my marriage July 3, 1890. I was at times called Elizabeth Vass or Mrs. Vass by some who knew I was living with him in the capacity of wife. Yes sir, I had two children by him the older Edward and the younger John Henry they were both born before my marriage to him, they are both living and have always been known by the name of the father. . . . I can neither read nor write and cannot identify the certificate of birth . . . which you show me but it must refer to John Henry. Edward is about 19 years old. I have had but ten children in all, five are living and five dead. Eight of these children were born prior to the time I began living with Henry Vass. Their father being Spencer Conway who is now dead.

The widow's claim of Harriet Booker proves an interesting case because it documents three different kinds of intimate relationships: a slave marriage; an informal marriage formed after emancipation; and finally, a formal, or legal, marriage. Special examiner O. M. Goodwin paid particular attention to the fact that Booker had a child, "Lizzie," in a fourth relationship, one that Booker did not consider marital in nature. As we have seen, having children outside a marital relationship was common during slavery. Booker's claim reveals that, among former slaves, children born out of wedlock were treated with the same level of acceptability after emancipation.

Excerpt from the Deposition of Harriet Booker, Dec. 18, 1908, Civil War Pension File of Glenn Booker, 2nd USCLA, RG 15:

I am the widow of Glenn Booker He was a soldier, but I did not know him till after the War so I can't tell what company and regiment he was in. . . .

I was raised a slave for Dr. Rand near Tuscumbia, Ala. . . .

A long time before the War I married a man named Berry. Don't remember his other name and don't know his master's name. They lived "Back from Tuscumbia farther than we did" but I don't know which direction. . . . After Berry and I lived together two or three years we had three children and all died "Before the Wah"—his owner moved to Mississippi but to what place I do not know and I have not seen or heard from Berry since then. We "couldn't keep the number of the years then" but it was a long time before the War that his folks moved to Mississippi.

All that was required for a slave marriage was the consent of the owners and that marriage only lasted till one or the other of the owners sold the slave and then the marriage was ended and either one was at liberty to marriage again.

This was my only slave marriage and after the War I married Henry Jackson. Married him on "The Preston Place." Old Man Sam Dixon, a Colored Preacher married us directly after the War.

Henry Rollie and his wife Margaret Rollie would know of this marriage. Margaret Rollie is a grand daughter of Henry Jackson I lived with

Henry Jackson till he died on the Preston Place in this county. We did not have to have a license then.

I had one daughter by him, Dillie wife of Wilson Buford and she lives in town

After the death of Henry Jackson I married Glenn Booker. We went to Helena and were married but were living on the Preston Place. I lived with him from that time till Glenn Booker died about two years ago or a little more—two years last October. I have never [re]married.

Excerpt from O. M. Goodwin, Special Examiner, Pine Bluff, Ark., to the Commissioner of Pensions, Washington, D.C., Dec. 30, 1908, Civil War Pension File of Glenn Booker, 2nd USCLA, RG 15:

Claimant made no effort to conceal the child Lizzie when asked about her and told her story freely. I am sure she did not tell me of Lizzie herself as she considered that "An Accident" and with these people these "Accidents don't count nohow."

I could not find any record of her marriage to Henry Jackson but it was plantation knowledge and the child, Delia Buford, is proof of it. The child Lizzie was born prior to her marriage to Jackson, and he, Jackson, was dead and she had married the soldier prior to the passage of the Act of Aug. 7, 1882.[15]

There is no evidence here to be secured in regard to her "Slave Marriage" to "Berry" and she is utterly unable to give me any data by which that can be proved or disproved. But she says his master went away to Mississippi and she thought that with the freedom of the slaves later cancelled that marriage. It is possible that some of the family of Dr. Rand, Ned Rand, or Jerry Rand may be located at Tuscumbia, Ala. but I don't think it worth the effort so I shall recommend consideration by the chief of the Board of Review.

Informality

In spite of the opportunity to formalize marriages under the laws of the states in which they lived, many former slaves simply chose not to do so. They preferred instead to continue the practice of an informal system of marriage that characterized relationships under slavery for over two hundred years. For many ex-slaves, informal marriages were as committed and lasting as those that were legalized; for others, informal marriage allowed more flexibility in beginning and ending relationships.[16] The testimony of witnesses Morgan Black and Clem Willis in the pension claim of Josephine Bellfield gives readers insight into the persistence of this practice as well as its acceptance within communities of former slaves.

Affidavit of Morgan Black and Clem Willis, May 16, 1891, Civil War Pension File of Phillip Bellfield, 63rd USCI, RG 15:

> We have known the applicant all her life—know when she was born—and we knew the late Philip Bellfield ever since 1845—Philip's first wife was named May she died in 1876—leaving no issue—in 1880 Philip married the claimant. The fact is that he was not legally married to the claimant, but simply married her as was formerly prevalent among slaves—he took her to his home and gave notice to all his friends & acquaintances that she was his wife. Every body, white and black, who knew them, regarded them as man and wife—She bore him 8 children 5 of premature death—one died in infancy and 2 are now living—Philip spoke of these children as his—There can be [no] doubt of this fact that the claimant was his wife—socially and morally—if not legally—We lived on adjoining places to Philip & his wife for 50 years.

The practice of informal marriage created flexible boundaries around intimate relationships. Without legal sanction clearly delineating which relationships were marital in nature and which were not, there was room for both in an informal system of marriage. As a witness in the pension claim of Mary Malonne, Rose Baptiste had occasion to describe her relationship to veteran Octave Jessie, Malonne's son. Baptiste maintained that she had had a long-term intimate relationship with Jessie, one that spanned two decades and existed, for a time, alongside the soldier's legal marriage to another woman. Baptiste referred to herself as Jessie's "wife" and indicated that friends and neighbors recognized her as such, but she made it clear that she and Jessie had not been formally married.

Excerpt from the Deposition of Rose Baptiste, Sept. 19, 1893, Civil War Pension File of Octave Jessie, 96th USCI, RG 15:

> I am about 50 years of age, occupation laundress. . . .
>
> I was well acquainted with Octave Jessie. I first met him in Carrollton (N.O.) La. soon after he was discharged from the army. I took up with him when I first met him and I lived with him off and on thereafter until he died.

After I lived with him a long time, I cannot say how many years, he married a woman named Mary Ann McCray, a sister of Henderson McCray. She died after she married him. I cannot say how long they had been married when she died, but I do not think she lived a year after she married him. He staid with me about as often as he staid with her while he was married to her. He used to come around to see me while he was living with her and I used to try to drive him away, but he would not go. When his wife died, he lived with me right along until he died.

I was out to [illegible] when I heard that Octave was going to marry Mary Ann, and I raised a big fuss, and they "sneaked off unbeknown to me and got married."

I lived with him as his wife, but I never went by his name. I would not go by his name as I was not married to him. The people used to call me by his name, but I would always correct them and tell them that my name was not Rose Jessie. He promised to marry me when we first took up with each other, but he never married me. Do not know why he did not marry me. I did not push him to marry me. I had but one child by him—a girl. I had said child by him before he married Mary Ann. The child only lived to be two weeks old.

I always paid the rent while he lived with me, but he used to buy "rations" for the house sometimes. I claimed him as my husband while I lived with him, and he claimed me for his wife. I never called him my husband. I always used to refer to him as my old man or Octave. He is the only man that I have lived with since the war. . . .

I never lived with a man named Baptiste. That is my father's name. I had three sons before I took up with him (Octave) I had the two oldest boys by a man named Edmund [illegible], but he went away during the war and I have never seen him since. I had my youngest son by a married man. My youngest son was a baby when I took up with Octave Jessie.

Informality was also evident in the termination of relationships, whether voluntary on the part of both partners or the sole decision of one partner. Within an informal system of marriage, just as marriages began without legal sanction, they ended without legal divorce proceedings. As the case of Rebecca Saulsbury exemplifies, many couples "quit" their marriages, as they had done in slavery, by simply separating.[17]

Excerpt from the Deposition of Rebecca Saulsbury, Apr. 18, 1898, Civil War Pension File of Calvin Saulisberry, 51st USCI, RG 15:

My age is 51 years. . . .

I am an applicant for pension as the widow of Calvin Saulsbury who was a soldier in the late war but I do not know his company & regiment.

He died in October 1894 & I have not married again nor lived with any man. . . .

My first husband was George Jackson who was bred and born in this parish [Iberville, La]. He and I were married on the Avery plantation just about the close of the war. We were married by a colored preacher named John Robinson.

I lived with George Jackson seven or eight years and had five children by him. We parted because he treated me bad and was a man who ran about after other women. We did not have any license to marry and we did not get any divorce. He went off up the river after we quit and I don't know whether he is alive or dead.

No I do not know where he is. He went away before I married Calvin Saulsbury and I have not heard from him since.

I remained single five years then Calvin Saulsbury & I were married on the Avery plantation and I lived with him till he died and I buried him.

I don't own anything but a house & lot worth about one hundred dollars. I have no income from any source and am dependent on my own labor for a support.

Calvin's first wife was named Lizzie. They had been separated before Calvin & I married. She was living out on the Bayou when we (Calvin and I) were married. She lived some time after our marriage but I do not know how long.

Q. Why did you swear that you had not been married prior to your marriage to Calvin Saulsbury?

A. Because George Jackson and I had no license. . . .

Q. Where did you and George Jackson separate?

A. Up the river in Miss. but I was a stranger and do not know the place. . . .

I do not know the county. We lived away back in the interior but I can't tell on whose plantation. I can't tell at all where it is. He put me out and I came back to my father. I have not seen George Jackson nor heard from him since.

Laura Fogee did not acquire a widow's pension because she could not satisfactorily reconcile conflicting evidence in her claim. A key factor in the denial was the insistence by one man that he had been married to

Fogee and her assertion that he had not. Another strike against Fogee may have been the nature of her relationships with three different men prior to her marriage to the soldier. Finally, the fact that Fogee had six children from what she considered to be nonmarital relationships may have influenced the conclusion of special examiner George G. Hoover. Ultimately, Hoover pointed to the fact that Fogee had been legally married to another man whom she did not legally divorce as the source of her ineligibility for a pension as Henry Fogee's widow. Whether legal or not, it is clear that Fogee believed she had the right to be treated well and thus the right to "quit" her prior relationships.

Excerpt from the Deposition of Laura Fogee, June 11, 1907, Civil War Pension File of Henry Fogee, 84th USCI and 79th USCI, RG 15:

> I am the widow Henry Fogee. . . . I knew him only two or three years before I married him and I married him fourteen or fifteen years ago and with a license from the clerks office at the Court House and Elder Josiah Jones who was in the army with Henry performed the ceremony. . . . Henry Fogee and I did not separate or get a divorce from each other during his life time but we lived together as husband and wife from the day we were married until his death, and I have not married again since he died. . . . I had no children by Henry Fogee but I had six before I married him and only three are living. . . .
>
> Henry Redmond, Nat Wright, and Archie Jones were the father of those children but I wasnt married to them lawfully and Nat only is alive and stays near Ruston somewhere. I have cohabited with no other men in my life but these and Henry Fogee, and I have had no other children. Henry Redmond was my slavery times husband and I had one child by him and we parted the year before freedom and he died soon after that on the place of Mr. James Kidd our owner in Jackson Parish La near Vernon P.O. I was born and raised there and never left Mr. Kidd until the second year following the surrender when I went to Ruston to stay and from there on down here. I was on Mr Jim Roans place at Ruston. Down here I have lived on the place of Mr John Parker on the Bayou east of town "ceptin" when I was here in Monroe. I just visits Pine Bluff when there with my children. Well I guess I lived with Nat Wright two or three years as near as I can come at it and with Arch Jones a little longer than that and it was all on that Mr Kidds place this happened and I was just a country nigger and let them stay in my cabin to help me work and thats all there is to it. No I

was not considered their wife by the white & black folks on the place. I picked up and left them when I got ready and nobody said a word about it. I picked up and left them because I got tired of them.

Excerpt from the Deposition of Nat Wright, June 20, 1907, Civil War Pension File of Henry Fogee, 84th USCI and 79th USCI, RG 15:

> I married Laura Fogee in the spring of 1868 on the place of Mr James Kidd (dead) in Jackson Parish La near the town of Vernon and a colored preacher named —— performed the ceremony. . . . I got a license to marry Laura with from Vernon the Parish seat and lived with her from that time—the spring of 1868—until some time in 71 or 72 when we parted because she got contrary. . . . Laura then went by the name of Laura Wallace—No, not as Laura Watson but as Laura Wallace. Her brother (dead) was named Sam Wallace but I dont know the names of her parents. . . . I have never been divorced from Laura Wallace. She ran off and left me so I just thought I would let her go.

Excerpt from the Deposition of Laura Fogee, June 21, 1907, Civil War Pension File of Henry Fogee, 84th USCI and 79th USCI, RG 15:

> I was not lawfully married to Nat Wright and I was not lawfully married to Archie Jones I dont care who says so, and that marriage record dont refer to me for I never did go by the name of Laura Wallace.
>
> Yes I had a brother named Sam Wallace, and I had a brother named John Singleton (both dead) but my name was always Laura Watson after the man my Ma said was my daddy—Lewis Watson (dead.) My mother had children by Lewis Watson, old man Sam Wallace Sr. and the father of John Singleton whoever he was but I dont know who was her lawful husband or whether she ever had one. She had three other children but I dont know who was their daddy. My brother Sam Wallace was the only child she had going by the name of Wallace and if folks ever called me Laura Wallace it was because he was my brother. They had no right to do it and it wasnt my right name and I was never married under any such name. I dont know who that marriage record refers to. . . . I lived with Archie Jones but I was not married to him lawfully and I was not married to Nat Wright who is swearing to a lie in this case. I left Nat because he had another woman. I left Archie Jones because he was so mean to me. . . .

Family Support Networks

Civil War pension files demonstrate that marriage and family played an important role in how ex-slaves dealt with the vicissitudes of black life in the postwar period. Former slaves' pension files also show a tendency toward living in multigenerational households, which were essential to daily survival. Margaret Fields, a sixty-nine-year-old Kentucky widow, suggested the mutuality in such arrangements in her explanation of her living situation: "I live with my married daughter. I help keep house."[18] What follows are examples of applicants for pensions living with their children in their old age because they had no other means of support. Sometimes this phenomenon emerged in the testimony of the applicants themselves and sometimes in the reports of special examiners. In either case, they demonstrate the importance of family in coping with the difficulties of poverty and aging in post–Civil War black communities.

Excerpt from the Deposition of Harriet Booker, Dec. 18, 1908, Civil War Pension File of Glenn Booker, 2nd USCLA, RG 15:

> Q. What property did he [Glenn Booker] leave and what have you had from which an income or support could have been derived during the years 1907 and 1908?
>
> Ans. He left no property only our bed. We were living with my daughter and her husband and I have made my home with them ever since. I have no money or property of any kind and am not able to work so have lived on this daughter and have had no income, and no support except from her.

Excerpt from A. R. Smith, Special Examiner, Nashville, Tenn., to the Commissioner of Pensions, Washington, D.C., May 23, 1917, Civil War Pension File of Isaac Shorter, 14th USCI, RG 15:

> With this report, I have the honor to return herewith all papers of the above entitled claim for pension [by Priscilla Shorter, widow of Isaac Shorter]. . . .
>
> The claim was referred for special examination [to] determine whether claimant is soldier's legal widow. . . .

> I made careful and painstaking inquiry in Lebanon [Tenn.] and could learn nothing to indicate that claimant had violated the provisions of the act of August 7, 1882 since soldier's death.[19] Her home is a very poor place just on the outskirts of the town, looks like it is about ready to fall down and the interior was about the worst sight I ever saw. She has living with her soldier's son Adam and his children. She is highly spoken of by the white people seen by me and is especially well regarded by soldier's relatives, who said that she proved to be one of the very best wives and mothers possible, having raised soldier's children by his former wife Henrietta and had quite a family by him herself.

Just as aged parents were sometimes dependent on their adult children, the reverse could also be true. Adult children or even grandchildren were at times dependent on older family members who were Civil War pensioners. This phenomenon appears to have been particularly prevalent during the Great Depression of the 1930s and is documented in the excerpts of the following two contact reports written by representatives of the Veterans Administration (VA), who visited aged veterans to inquire after their welfare. (The VA subsumed the functions of the Pension Bureau in 1930, including administering Civil War pensions.) In the first case, the VA representative found the arrangement to be mutually beneficial. In the second case, the investigator believed that the veteran's grandchildren were exploiting him (the pension file does not contain the grandchildren's side of the story). In both cases, it appears that having an aged Civil War veteran was a godsend for African Americans thrown out of work during the Great Depression.

Excerpt from Examiner's Contact Report, J. H. Holladay, Associate Attorney, Indianapolis, Ind., Apr. 30, 1936, Civil War Pension File of George Winlock, 115th USCI, RG 15:

> This veteran, who is a colored man, is eighty-nine years of age and resides at 418 S.E. 5th Street, Evansville, Indiana, with his son-in-law and daughter, Mr. and Mrs. P.T. Miller. They live in a nice home, reasonably well furnished, and the veteran was well dressed. He is getting pretty feeble, but his mind appears to be clear. His daughter and her husband were former school teachers, but they are both unemployed at present. The Millers have a daughter who is teaching. Mrs. Miller, the daughter, frankly admitted that

she and her husband had not had much work in the last few years, but states that he draws a pension from the School Board and that the veteran has helped them some and he has helped his grandchildren a great deal. She states that if it had not been for the veteran's pension, she does not know what they would have done. The Millers, however, appear to be very high classed colored people and it is very clear that they are very attentive to this veteran and are giving him the best of care. He states that if it had not been for his daughter giving him such good care, he would have been dead.

Excerpt from Examiner's Contact Report, E. F. Fewell, Field Examiner, Millen, Ga., May 28, 1936, Civil War Pension File of Alexander Daughtry, 135th USCI, RG 15:

Contact was had with this veteran at his home near Egypt, Ga. He says he is 89 years old and he is probably older. He bears an excellent reputation among both white and colored he is a colored man, and is well known in the community where he has made his home for the past 50 years. I have seldom seen a colored man who bears a better reputation. He is considered a quiet, honest and well behaved old Negro.

Veteran own a farm of about 67 acres and there are several houses on the place. He is unmarried now but states he has had four wives, all of whom are dead. He has no living children but has four or five grandchildren and a half brother. He lives in a poor shack, little better than a pig pen, and an old woman lives in the house and is supposed to take care of him. He has no bedding or furniture worthy of the name and the poorest sort of clothes. Inquiry developed the fact that his grandchildren and his half brother are all living off him and keeping him in abject poverty. Although he is able to cash his own pension check the veteran is mentally and physically incompetent to handle his own affairs and he does not even know the exact amount of his pension. The woman who takes care of him receives $6 per month and her board and although she seems to have the interests of the veteran at heart she is neither physically nor mentally fitted for the position. With his farm and his pension this man should be able to live in comfort and in his position and surroundings in something like luxury. Instead of that he has nothing but a bare existence owing to his grandchildren who take everything he has.

This man should be under guardianship and such arrangements should be made with all speed.

With their emphasis on confirming family relationships, the Civil War pension claims made by African American soldiers' family members offer readers rich documentation of family life during and after slavery. Stories from former slaves' pension files confirm that family life under slavery was fraught with uncertainty and sadness, particularly because of the ever-present threat of separation. Since slave families lacked legal sanction under Southern laws, slave owners had full control over slaves' family life. Yet the pension files suggest that it would be a mistake to see only the negative experiences of family life under slavery. A number of families—husbands and wives, parents and children, single parents and children, extended families—stayed intact during slavery. These stories also reveal slaves' resilience and flexibility as they started families anew after separation, blended existing families with new, or found ways to be together even when separated by many miles. The lack of legal sanction also allowed for more fluid boundaries of intimate relationships between men and women; slave communities viewed intimate relationships not considered matrimonial as perfectly acceptable. We can imagine that ceremonies marking the marriage of a slave couple were filled with great joy. Similarly, we can imagine the love that characterized relationships among family members.

Former slaves' pension files demonstrate a complexity of family practices after emancipation, especially in the case of marriage. The transition from slavery to freedom promised ex-slave families the very legal protection that slavery had denied. Many couples happily embraced the opportunity to formalize existing relationships or to begin new relationships under legal sanction. Also, some did so because the laws in their state compelled them to. In theory, such legal protection meant the end of forced separation.[20] Many former slaves simply continued to keep their relationships informal, some because they preferred the old ways and others because the expense and the bureaucratic procedures of formal marriage—the processes for beginning and ending marriages—were too much to bear. Beyond the marriage relationship, the pension files also shed light on the importance of family support networks to daily survival in the decades following the war.

In their focus on familial relationships, and marriage in particular, former slaves' pension files reveal the degree to which white, middle-class, Victorian attitudes toward morality shaped the way pension officials went about their work. They used their own sense of morality as a means to test the soundness of the relationships they encountered, often ignoring the slaves' and former slaves' own values. In addition to providing an invaluable window onto the experiences of African Americans during slavery, the Civil War, and after, former slaves' Civil War pension files vividly bring to life the challenges of the pension process itself for both pension officials and for former slaves. These challenges no doubt were replicated in many other bureaucratic processes in which former slaves engaged as they made their way from slavery into freedom.

Appendix

Complete Sample Documents

Voices of Emancipation began by offering readers a glimpse of Charles Franklin Crosby's testimony in his Civil War pension file.[1] We used Crosby's testimony, like the other excerpts featured in this book, to make a specific point about the kind of information, themes, and stories readers might find in former slaves' Civil War pension files. At first glance, reading Civil War pension files can seem a daunting, laborious task, especially if one sees them in their original form in the National Archives. Even transcribed documents can seem impenetrable at first. Once readers begin to make their way through the files, however, they discover the richness of the documentation, its vibrancy, and its insight into the lives of African Americans and middle-class Northern whites in the eras of slavery, emancipation, the Civil War, Reconstruction, and beyond. We designed *Voices of Emancipation* to serve as an introduction and a guide to these pension files. We used excerpts of former slaves' testimony to emphasize important themes that emerge from the files—those of family and identity, for example—and to bring to light former slaves' individual experiences during some of America's most tumultuous and transformative times.

Missing from this introductory approach to former slaves' Civil War pension files is the wonderful sense of raw discovery one experiences when reading such documents for the first time. Also, this approach does not give readers an overall sense of the documents or the context from which the insights they offer emerge. The purpose of this appendix is to present a number of complete transcriptions of testimony from special examinations and to allow readers to uncover their riches for themselves. We have chosen to present a selection of the more comprehensive special examinations in our possession, with an emphasis on those not excerpted extensively elsewhere in this book. We offer no introductory or explanatory comments, preferring that readers draw on their experiences with the earlier text to reach their own conclusions. Readers will encounter many of the themes we have pointed out in the text and will note that many of the documents contain multiple themes. The appendix starts where *Voices of Emancipation* began, with the deposition of Charles Franklin Crosby.

Document 1

Deposition of Charles Franklin Crosby (see photograph on page xii), June 19, 1914, Civil War Pension File of Frank Nunn (alias Charles Franklin Crosby), 86th USCI, RG 15:

I reckon I am about 67 years old. I do not know my age but that is as near as I can get at it. My address is Box 289, Eagle Pass, Texas. I am a laborer.

I served in the civil war in Cos. A & K, 86th La. Inf. as they called it in those days. I never served in any other company or regiment and was never in the navy.

I am claiming a pension on account of said service.

I was born in Kentucky as well as I remember. They told me I was born in Lexington, Ky. I was raised in Florida near Geneva, Ala. I enlisted in Barrancas, Fla. I was a slave. My owner was Eli Nunn. No, the name was not Nearn, it was Nunn. He lived in Florida near the Alabama line and Geneva, Ala. was his nearest town. He is dead and had no children. I am satisfied all his family are dead and he had no children. Q. Who were in the family? A. Just his wife. Her name was Polly. No sir, they had no children nor any white children with them. My mother's name was Jane and she was called Jane Nunn because she belonged to the Nunns. My father's name was John Crosby and he lived in the town of Geneva, Ala. Both my parents are dead. I had two brothers and one sister. They were Nelson Nunn and George Nunn and they may have changed their names to Crosby too for they were my father's childrenm and Martha Ann who was unmarried the last I knew of her. All these were still near Geneva Ala. (on the Florida side) the last I knew of them but that was before I enlisted. No sir, I have not heard from them since except that I have heard in some way they are dead.

I enlisted in 1863 and I think it was in the fall of the year. I enlisted under the name Frank Nunn. That was the name I had been known by all the time. My father and mother did not live together an I was known by master's name.

I was not free at the time of my enlistment. I ran away and enlisted. No sir they did not examine me much. Just asked me my age and I told them I was eighteen but I was not that old. I told them that because I wanted to get into the army. Q. How old were you at that time? A. Somewhere between twelve and thirteen years of age but I was big for my age. I can't tell how tall I was but not near as tall as I am now. I do not know how tall I am now. (Looks to be about five feet, 10 or 11 inches. F. C. Spl. Exmr) I was pretty dark in color and had black hair and eyes. I was kind of on the tall order but was a kind of big husky boy too. I had no marks or scars by which I might be known or remembered. I have never been able to read or write. I had a photograph but I sent it to Washington. I don't know to whom I sent it, the Pension Commissioner, I think. It was a recent photograph. I have no old ones.

They swore me in and gave me my blue uniform and gun and drilled me. That was at Barrancas. My gun was a Springfield. When I was discharged, I turned it in. It used a cap and ball and we had to bite the end off the cartridge. I cannot tell how long we stayed at Barrancas. I had been in the service probably one week when we had a battle. It was at a place called Pollard, Ala. That was not much of a fight, just kind of brush but after we started back to Barrancas, we had a fight that lasted two hours and a half at Pine Bairn, a creek. I do not know, but I was told that there were only 1200 of the enemy and that we killed 800 of them, including their general, Clanton. We had only about five killed and wounded, I do not know how many of each. No sir, we lost no officers then. We went back to Barrancas from Pine Bairn. I cannot tell how long we stayed but when we left there we went to Ft. Blakely on the Alabama River in the rear of Mobile. We went there to take the fort and we took it. It took us a week to take the fort. We started against it—that is, started our attack—at six o'clock one Sunday morning and at four o'clock the next Sunday afternoon, we charged the place and took it. I cannot tell what our losses were at Ft. Blakely. I think we lost a good many men there. One officer, Major Mercer or Murcher or some such name, was killed. I do not remember whether any officers were wounded there or not.

From Ft. Blakely, we went by steamboat to Montgomery, Ala. intending to attack and take it and we had got our pontoon bridges put down across the Alabama river and were getting ready to cross and attack when they ran up the white flag and surrendered. No, we did not take any prisoners. They had evacuated the town and when we got over there there was nobody there to fight with.

Then we came back down to Mobile and lay in camp for quite a time, but I cannot tell how long. Then we were sent to Ft. Morgan Ala. to take charge of that place relieving some soldiers that were there but I do not know what organization it was. We did nothing there but guard duty and drilling. We stayed there quite a while and were ordered back to Mobile where we stayed awhile and then to Fort Gaines, Ala. and stayed there until we were ordered to Mobile to be mustered out and then we went to New Orleans and were discharged at Greenville, La. and I cannot tell whether that was in 1865 or 1866 but I think it was in April. Yes sir, when we went to Louisiana to be discharged, is the first time I had ever been in La.

Capt. Jenkins was my captain all the way through. Other officers were Col. Yarrington. We had no lieutenants in our company. I don't know why. Our 1st Sgt was . . . Wright; there was sgt Mabrum Jones, corporal George Rice and there was a captain of another company named McCloan, of B company. I remember him because he was an Irishman and used to have a good deal of fun with the men. I do not know where any of these men are nor whether or not they are living.

I can remember the names of some members of the company but the Pension Bureau tells me they are dead. The Bureau sent me the addresses of some men of the company and they could remember me they wrote, but I couldn't remember them. I was a private all through my service. I have no discharge certificate, it got lost at New Orleans by my having left my grip with some people where I roomed and when I came back they had moved and I never found them nor my grip nor my discharge certificate. I don't remember their name.

Q. I will now read you the surnames of some men from this list. Tell me whether you remember them and if so, what sort of looking men they were:

Alfred Adams? A. I don't remember him.

Q. Hogans? A. Yes sir. First name is Stephen. I have had some correspondence with him and says he recognizes me. Mr. Bonnet now says he sent him my picture but I did not know that until just now. Q. Roberts. A. Don't remember him. Q. Edward Washington and Nelson Williams? A. No sir, don't remember them. I recall Frank Cecil who used to take care of the colonels horse. No, I don't know whether he is living or not. I do not know where any of my comrades are if living, except those whose names the Bureau sent me.

Q. How long were you in the army? A. I think it was three years. I enlisted in 1863 and was discharged in 1865 or 1866.

Q. What is your correct name in full?

A. My correct name in full is Charles Franklin Crosby.

Q. By what name are you known here [in Eagle Pass, Texas]?

A. By Charley Crosby, only. The people here do not know that I was ever known by any other name. I did not know what was my father's name until after the war and I learned it by writing to my brothers at Geneva, Ala. and they told me my real name was Crosby and I commenced using that name instead of Nunn. I had always known that my name was Charley Franklin but they called me Frank instead of Charley. So when I took the name of Crosby, I went to the Charley part too so the whole name would be right.

I was not sick nor injured or wounded in the service.

After discharge I lived in New Orleans, La. until 1867 and then came to Texas and lived around about New Braunfels and worked for the German farmers up there and in and out of there until 1886 or 1887 when I went to old Mexico and have lived there ever since until last June when I came to this place and have lived here ever since.

Q. Can you name any person anywhere that has known you by both Nunn and Crosby? A. No sir. I made the change in New Orleans and I cannot now name anyone who knew me there.

I am married. My wife is a Mexican and had not been married before she married me. Her maiden name was Francisca Robia. We were married in Victoria, Mex. by a magistrate that they call a civil judge. I think it was in 1892 that we were married. I had not been married before. Yes sir I was old enough to have been married before but that was my first marriage. I had lived with a woman, Easter Eatons, in San Antonio before this but we were not married and we separated. I had no children by Easter. Franscisca and I have lived together without separation or divorce ever since our marriage. We have had six children. But four of them are living. They are Guillerma Crosby, born Feb. 10, 1891; Carlos Crosby, born Feb. 18, 1893; Albina Crosby born just about two years and two months later but I cannot give the date; and Adela Crosby born—I forget when but she is going on 13 years of age. No sir, none of these children was born before my marriage and if the dates show that, I have made some mistake but I can't tell what it is. No, I can't say whether I was married earlier than 1891 or not.

I have no attorney. In 1900, I was living in Monterey, Mex. In 1890, somewhere in Mexico. In 1880, I was in Texas but was not permanent anywhere as I was engaged in driving cattle to market before they began shipping them to market on the railroads. I used to drive from Texas to Kansas. In 1870, I was probably up about New Braunfels, Texas, but I cannot tell with whom I was staying at that time. Q. Did you ever live in Georgia? A. No sir, not that I know of. If I did it was before my recollection.

I have heard my statement read. I heard from my brothers after I came out from the army but not after I left New Orleans.

Stephen Hogans was a kind of brown-skinned fellow as I remember him medium height and little on the slender order.

My name on the [army] rolls was Frank Nunn. No sir, it was not Frank Nearn. If that is on the rolls anywhere it is a mistake made by the two names sounding so much alike.

I have heard the above and foregoing read, I fully understand its contents and my answers and statements are correctly written.

Document 2

Deposition of Mary Jane Taylor, May 13, 1919, Civil War Pension File of Samuel Taylor, 45th USCI, RG 15:

My age is 69: residence and post-office address 1516 West Breckenridge Alley, Louisville, Ky.

I am the same woman who is claiming pension as the widow of Samuel Taylor who was in the army during the Civil War in Co. A 45th U.S. Col. Inf., and who died here in this city October 11, 1895. No, I cannot give the dates of his enlistment and discharge, but have some papers showing same I think. I know that Samuel Taylor was a soldier because he always said so and he got a pension at time he died. He was never in the military service of the United States but the one time that I ever heard of.

Yes, sir, I do claim that I am the lawful widow of Samuel Taylor: I was regularly married under license here in Louisville: the license was got at the Court House and he and I were married at the home of Brother Gaddie, pastor of the Green St. Baptist Church: we were married at Mr. Gaddie's house on Clay St. Rose Slaughter was there as a witness and Julia, I forget her last name: Yes, there were others there too: Henry Mount and Sam Morrison were there. There is a record of our marriage at the Court House because it was got once and sent to Washington.

No, sir, I had no legal husband living at date I married Sam Taylor and he had no legal wife living at all. He had been married before and so had I. My first husband was Bill White and he was alive when I married Sam Taylor, but he and I parted a number of years before I married soldier, and he was not my legal husband at all.

Q. Why not?

A. Why he and I were married under the Old Constitution by slave custom and we didn't have to get any divorce at all they said. We weren't regularly married at all. He had married after we parted, that is regularly under a license, before ever I married Sam Taylor; Bill married Ann Finley up in Oldham County and I think that she died before I married Sam Taylor; then he married again. No, I never tried to get any divorce from Bill White and he never did from me at all. Yes, I am sure of that.

Q. When you married Bill White weren't you married by ceremony, that is by a regular preacher?

A. Yes, by Preacher Sneeden: we were married here in this county on the place of Norborne Artterburn, who was my master in slavery days: yes, that was after Freedom I am sure. It was the next year after Freedom I think.

Q. How did it happen that you married under slavery custom if it was after Freedom? How could you so marry then?

A. I don't know but that was way it happened. Why we didn't really know that we were free until long after Freedom. I know that others married in same way even after slaves were free. I will tell you all about it. I was born on place of Norborne Arterburn: my mother was Mary Eliza Jackson and my father Reuben Jackson. My mother was given to Miss Bettie Arterburn and others of the white children had other slaves and children of the slaves belonged to their young white mistress. My father belonged to Robert Bates who also lived in same neighborhood: up on Muddy Fork in this county: the Bates family bought his mother and him in Virginia. My father came to see my mother about every night. I had four brothers, Silas, Tom, Sam and one born dead: had sisters Dinah, Adeline, and Roseanna. I always lived on the Arterburne place until after Freedom: it was fully a year after Freedom before we really knew we were free: I was raised right there on that place and was never anywhere else before we came here to Louisville after Freedom. I first knew Bill White there on the place of my master: he came there when the soldiers came with Sherman's Army from the south: Col. Perry and Major Johnson came to our place to board, that is to the home of my master and Bill White was their servant and waited on them. No, I don't think he was a regular soldier at all: he was just a servant. I don't remember whether he wore a uniform or not. There were lots of white and colored soldiers camped in Muddy Fork Woods near our place and they got mustered out there. Col. Perry and Major Johnson went away and Bill White stayed there and hired out to my master: he was hired out for $25 a month. It was after the soldiers had gone that he and I were married. We were staying there just like we had in slavery days: as we had from time I can remember anything. Bill White and I were married right there: I was only a girl about 16: my mistress had told me that I was born Sept. 9, 1849: she had it down in a book, and I have always remembered that date as that of my birth. No, Bill White and I did not have any license to marry at all: we just got married by a colored preacher like they always had: my young mistress gave her consent. Bill White had been a slave he said down at Florence, Ala. and had followed the soldiers off: he had no master there: that was way he and I was married: We stayed there a year after Freedom and our old master made presents at Christmas to those that stayed: gave some $12 and some more. Then he told us we were free. I remember Bill White used to say to us "don't you know you are free"? My father who had run away to Indianapolis and made $2 a day came back and hired us all out there as I remember it: then we came here to Louisville and lived in rooms awhile until father started to build this very place where I now live. He had a little money when we come here and bought this ground and put up a little cabin and then it was added to gradually from time to time: this was home of my father until he died and of my mother until she died. Bill White came with the rest of us when we come here, and he and I lived together for a number of years: we had three children, two boys and a girl: Bill White was born first and then a boy who was born dead and then Josephine my girl: these are children I have ever had. Of same only Josephine is living: she married a John Woodward and he died and she has married again but I don't really know her name now: haven't seen her for two years: she cooked for Dr. Allen on Fields Ave., Crescent Hill last I knew of her: she doesn't come around me for she drinks like her father and I won't have it. Bill White was an awful drinker: he would get drunk often and come home and want to fight and we did. We separated three different times and then he would come back and want me to live with him and I would: all my children were born in this city, and Josephine was about ten years old when Bill White and I parted for good. The last place he and I lived together was at 15th and Southgate here. Josephine is now 46 years old.

No, sir, I never lived with Bill White at 312 East Green: I lived in rear there with my son Bill White (now dead) and my daughter, and lived on East Market St. with them, but Bill White, my slave husband, and I had then quit for good.

After I came here with my father and mother I worked out as cook right along even when living with Bill White. And after we quit I cooked right along too. I cooked on Washington St. for Mrs. O'Heal and cooked there while living on East Market too. I can't remember all the places by years, but I know that right along after Bill White and I quit I cooked and made a home for my son and daughter.

No, sir, I did not marry any man after Bill White and I separated until I married Sam Taylor: I have never had but two husbands Bill White and Sam Taylor. No, I have never at any time or place lived with or been known as the wife of any other man. I have never had but three names in my life, Mary Jane Jackson, Mary Jane White and Mary Jane Taylor. Those are all. No, sir, I was never married under license to any other man at any time but Sam Taylor: that is true.

Q. Did you ever know a man by name of Harrison Smith?

A. I never did to my knowledge.

Q. Did you ever know George Boswell?

A. I never did.

Q. The Marriage Records of this county, the records where they put all marriages of Colored Persons show that Mary Jane White married Harrison Smith Feb. 5, 1868 and that Mary Jane White married George Boswell in June 1874, were you or were you not ever married to either one or both?

A. I never was: that is some other Mary Jane White who married them. I was never married anywhere to anybody but Bill White and Sam Taylor. I wouldn't tell you a lie: I was raised that way.

No, sir, I never at any time married any man by the name of Manuel Mills or any man by name of Samuel L. Day or David Miles. It was Sarah Johnson that Bill White married after Annie Finley died and he was never so far as I know married in this county to any woman named

Georgia Brachett, or Mary Williams or Mahala Ann Oldham. He got married up in Oldham County where he lived mostly after we parted. He died up there three or four years ago. I never married any man at time named Aaron Barbour.

Q. How many times was Samuel Taylor married before he married you?

A. Twice: his first wife was his cousin Fannie Taylor: I knew her when I was a small girl: she belonged in slavery or her mother did to Gen. Taylor's people and lived across road from my master's place. I don't know when Sam Taylor married her but he always said it was in slavery: they parted and she later lived with Brian Craven and Joe Shipp, and was living with him when she died: she died here and was buried here: I really don't know whether she died before or after Sam Taylor and I were married. He had married Susan Fountain under license after Fannie and he separated and Susan had died before he and I were married: I did not know Susan but got acquainted with some of her kin afterwards: I raised Sam's little girl by Susan. No, Sam never got any divorce from Fannie I am sure: she was his slave wife and they just separated like Bill White and I did without any divorce.

Yes, I am sure that Sam Taylor did not marry any woman from time that Susan Fountain died until he married me. No, I never heard or knew in any way that he got a license to marry a woman named Alice Fishback. Yes, I have heard of other Sam Taylors here but never knew anybody else by that name.

No, sir, Bill White and I never went to the Court House after Freedom or any time and declared that we wished our slave marriage made legal. No, I never heard in any way that Sam Taylor and Fannie Taylor made their slave marriage legal in that way. No, Sir, Bill White and I never went anywhere and got a license and got married over again regularly by law.

Q. Did you live with Sam Taylor continuously from very day you married until day he died?

A. Yes, sir, and we always lived fine together: never any trouble or fights as with Bill White. Yes, I was living with him day he died and he and I were never separated at all. We were never divorced. When he died I took him to Taylortown to bury him beside his mother just as he wanted it to be. Watson was the undertaker.

Q. Exactly where have you lived since he died, that is since October 11, 1895?

A. I made my home right here, that is is this was place always came back to, except that for quite a time I kept home at 645 Russell Alley. I always have cooked out since Sam Taylor died until two years ago when I came here to cook and keep house for my brother whose wife had died. I stayed for some years after Sam Taylor died at the white people where I worked. I cooked for 4 years for Mr. and Mrs. John Tilford in country above Pewee Valley, and then I cooked different places around country, each summer for twelve years at Camp Meeting Grounds up above Pewee Valley, where white folks lived in summers. I lived at 717 Jefferson St. awhile and cooked for Captain Parker who lived there on that street. I also cooked for Mrs. Shouse on Frankfort Ave about two years.

Q. Who is there that has known you ever since you were a girl in slavery?

A. My sister Rosey Taylor, wife of Rufus, who lives near corner Shelby & Jackson, my brother Sam Jackson with whom I live and Joe Lewis who lives down here on Gallagher Street. My cousin Fannie Anderson who lives in alley between Market and Jefferson and Shelby & Clay and her mother Kitty Trowell who lives in Portland at 24th & Lighter. They belonged in same family in slavery.

Q. What witnesses can you name to show that you never married after you and Bill White parted until you married Sam Taylor and that you lived with latter, without divorce, until he died and that you have married no man since?

A. All those named know that Minnie Hopalite and Lena Mayman, white, near here: their father ran a grocery over here and they knew us forty years. Mattie Cox has known me since she was a girl: she lives over here on Breckenridge Street.

Q. By what witnesses can you show that soldier was legally married to you, that is that he was not married before except as you have made oath and that he had a right to marry you?

A. His brothers Abner Taylor at Taylortown, Ky above Worlington and Ras Taylor on Coke Street here in Louisville know that. I got a record of death of Susan Taylor at City Health Office I know. There are plenty here who know she died before I married Sam Taylor.

None of my white folks are alive yet except one, Mrs. John Hardin who lives somewhere up in Oldham County.

While I lived on Russell Alley rented of Mr. Neff and Mattie Forbes and Mary Lewis knew me: latter now lives here, that is rents room of me and is here Sundays: she cooks out: my brother guves me money from that room.

No, I have not made any agreement with anyone to pay a fee if my claim is allowed. No, I have not paid any fee to anyone. I have paid small amounts for drawing up papers and notary's fees.

I do not wish to be present or represented during taking of testimony in my claim. I understand your explanation of my rights as to that.

If I was made to swear in my original application for pension under this new law that I was divorced from Bill White they put it down wrong for I never was divorced from him at all.

Document 3

Deposition of Charles Washington, Dec. 18, 1905, Civil War Pension File of Charles Washington, 47th USCI, RG 15:

I am 89 years old. My post office address is Lake Providence, East Carroll Parish, La., Occupation farming. I am the same Charles Washington who enlisted some time in May 1863, at Stoneman's plantation, near Lake Providence, La., in Co. E 47th U.S.C. Inf., and served until the regiment was mustered out at Baton Rouge, La., in 1866. Do not remember what month I was mustered out, but it was when the whole regiment was mustered out. I am now an applicant for a pension, but do not know under what law my claim is filed All I know about what grounds that I am claiming a pension, because I understand that all old soldiers are entitled to a pension. I was born in the state of Flordida, and lived there until I was quite a lad of a boy and then I was sold to a man by the name of Thompson, who sold me to a man by the name of Randolph, and was then put into the traders yard at New Orleans, La., and there a man by the name of Dr. Vincent, who lived on Joe's Bayou, who lived eighteen miles from Lake Providence, and he owned me for a long time, until I was a grown man, and had a wife and three children, and th then Dr. Vincent, or Dr. Vinson, sold me to Mr. James Berry, who livnd on the Mississippi River, up Lake Providence, not far from Longwood plantation. He lived there, but he owned the Vincent plantation. I never lived on the place where Mr. Berry lived. I was there on the place sometimes, would go there to take his wife home when she would come down to the plantation, and would occasionally drive his carriage home, when he would be on the plantation. I had been the slave of Mr. Berry for about four years when I went into the service, and he was my owner when I enlisted. Mr. Berry bought Dr. Vinson's plantation and all of his slaves. Did not any one of his slaves who went into the army with me. After I left home to go into the army, Mr. Be[rry] carried all of his slaves who had remained at home, to the state of Texas, and I have never heard of any of them. I was a married man, and had three children and he carried them to Texas, and I have never heard of them since. My wife was called Julia Ruffin all the time, but my boys went by the name Washington. When I enlisted I did not personally know any member of my company before I enlisted. I was not asked how old I was when I enlisted, if they did I have forgotten it. They asked me who owned me. They did not tell me how tall I was when they measured me, and do not know how tall I was. Do not know what year I was born. Question. How then do you arrive at your age. Answer. My mother told me one Christmas, that I was twelve years old, and I have been trying to keep my age as near as I could ever since. Do not know how long I had been married before I went into the service, but had been married long enough to be the father of three children when I left home. Have no idea how old I was when I was married. I think I was a slave of Dr. Vinson about thrity or forty years, and he bought me as a boy eleven years old. No sir, I did not have any peculiar marks about me. My color was light brown. When I enlisted I had a little mustasche, and some chin whiskers, but they had not "growed" to do any good, "they have growed out since." I have never shaved but one time, and never had shaved when I enlisted. No sir, I have not got a photograph or picture of myself. Do not know of any one who knew me before I went into the service. The colonel of my regiment was Schofield, Peeples was Lt. Col. Crump was Major, Summer Green was Adjutant. Think that when I enlisted the surgeon was Adams, but when I was mustered out the doctor we had then was called Fitts. My captain was Hathaway, who was a spare made, of ordinary size, and his hair was dark. He did not wear a muotasce [mustache], or whiskers. Do not know where he was from. The First Lt., of the company, was Lt. Lymons who was a small man, and had a brownish colored mustasc [mustache]. Weightman was 2nd Lt. He was tolerably tall, and did not have any whiskers at all. My orderly sergeant at first was a man by the name of Fish, who was a white man, and they removed him, and put William Foreman as orderly sergeant. He was a small, dark brown colored man, and did not have any mustache, or whiskers. Robert Anderson was the first duty sergeant.

He belonged to Mr. Berry and lived on the upper place, he never lived on the place he bought of Dr. Vinson. Yes sir, he had a wife. Her name was Emiline. She was with the regiment at times. Yes sir, she knew me before I enlisted. She lived on Mr. Berry's upper place an belonged to him before he bought the Vinson place. I heard he was shot and killed at Vicksburg, Miss. I was next duty sergeant. No sir, I did not have any wife with me. A young fellow by the name of James Nish was a sergeant, but they took his stripes off of him, and put him back in the ranks but do not know why they did that. Do not think they put any one in his place. I bunked alone. There were two or three fellows in the tent with me but do not remember their names. I did not have any special bunk mate, when we were on a march we had dog tents and two men would join together. Did not have any special one. Question. Name every member of your company, whose name you can recall. Answer. Adam Shepherd, Henderson Stevens. No sir, he was not called Henson Stevenson, or Stevens. The captain always called him Henderson Stevens. A fellow by the name of Nat, do not remember the other part of his name, another fellow by the name of Julius—one by the name of Sampson. Another one they called Abram. Ross Thompson, Nelson Owens, Asberry Lee, Eli Piles, Lawrence Brown, and those [illegible] dead. Do not know where Nelson Owens lives, but he lives somewhere up the Mississippi River. Adam Shepherd, Henderson Stevens and Ross Thompson all live in this parish and all know me well and they know that I am the same Charles Washington who served in Co. E, 47th U.S.C. Inf., If my regiment was ever called anything but the 47th U.S.C. Inf, I do not remember it. The first year after I was discharged, I lived up on the Davis place up Lake Providence, near old river I have lived witin three miles of the first place I lived after coming home ever since the war. The regiment was near Lake Providence when I enlisted and we went from there to Goodrich Landing, was there a month or more, and then we went to Vicksburg, and was there two or three weeks, and from there we went to Haynes' Bluff, Miss., was there about a month and then we went up White River, and from there we came back to Vicksburg, and was there for two or three days, and then we took a boat, name forgotten, and went to New Orleans, was there a week, and then we went to a place called Brancas, Fla., think that was what they called it. We then went to Ft. Blakeley, Ala., where we had a fight, and that was the last battle we had. We had a little battle at Yazoo City. A fellow by the name of Jo was the only member of my company who was killed. Robert Anderson got a scratch on his thigh in that battle. That and the battle of Ft. Blakeley were the only two battles we had, but we were in some skirmishes. We h d a skirmish at Grand Gulf, Miss. One or two white cavalrymen were killed. But no one of my regiment, that I know of. There was not a member of my company killed in battle of Fort Blakeley, nor was any one wounded. Several in the regiment were wounded and some killed but I did not know of them. From Ft. Blakeley we went to Mobile, Ala., and from there to Selma, Ala., nd from there back to Mobile, and from there to Pineville, on Red River, and from there to Baton Rouge, La. where we were mustered out. I can prove by Adam Shepherd, Henderson Stevens and Ross Thompson that I am the same man who served under the name of Charley Washington. I was called Charles Washington while a soldier. No sir I have not got my certificate of discharge. I sent it to Mr. Fletcher of Washington, and he has not returned it. I have heard you read the list of comrades with the papers in this case. I remember Lawrence Brown, Wince Herndon, Capt Hataway, but did not remember his given name. Adam Shepherd Ross Thompson and Charles Wheeler, but do not remember the others on that list. Lawrence Brown was a dark brown colored man, or darker than I am. Charles Wheeler was a low chunky brown colored man. No sir, I have never at Pilcher's Point, No sir, I have never claimed that as my post office address. Yes sir, I know a Minister by the name of Powell. His name is Henry Powell. He is the first man, who ever did anything in my pension claim. Yes sir, I had my mail sent in his care, but I do not know where his post office was. If I ever had a man by the name of Wills for my Attorney I do not remember him. Since you have asked me about it, I remember I have a claim before Mr. Gilmore. Do not remember his given name. Do not remember now who were witnesses for me. The next claim I filed I went before Mr. Hamley, Elder Bell wrote the papers for me. Do not remember who witnessed my mark. No sir, I did not tell Mr. Hamley that I belonged to Dr. Vincent when I enlisted, but I told him that I was living on the Vincent plantation. I want Adam Shepherd and Henderson Stevens examined to prove that I am the same Charles Washington who served in Co. E 47th U.S.C. Inf. They are the only two I want examined. Question. There was not any one in your company, who was borne on the rolls, under the name of Henderson Stevens, what have you to say to that. Answer. That is what the captain called him. No sir he did not call him Henson Stevens, he called him Henderson Stevens. No sir, I do not care to be present or represented by attorney, either here or elsewhere during the further examination of my claim. The first woman I had for a wife after I came home from the army was Cherry Green. We were married in this parish in 1870 by Mr. Goff, who an officer of some kind. She is living yet. Yes sir, she is the only one I have had for a wife or lived with since I was a soldier. . . . Have not got any child living. This deposition has been read to me. I thoroughly understood your questions and my answers thereto are correctly recorded.

Document 4

Deposition of Louis Jourdan, May 27, 1915, Civil War Pension File of Louis Jourdan, 77th USCI and 10th USCHA, RG 15:

I am 75 years of age; my post-office address is No. 1920 St. Anthony Street, New Orleans, La. Occupation—laborer. I am pensioned under Cert. No. 839,270 under name of Jourdan, Louis Jourdan for service in Co. F, 77" U.S.C.I. and Co. K, 10" U.S.C.H.A.

I was born in Washington Co., Md. near Boonsborough, I was only a few miles from Hagerstown too. I was born the slave of Ed Butler My father was George Jourdan and my mother was Millie Jourdan, both were slaves of Butler. There were ten children of us in all, the whole family was sold to the slave traders about five years before I enlisted in the army and were brought here, no that is wrong only three were brought here to New Orleans, viz. my brothers, Nelson Jourdan, John Jourdan and myself, we were sold to Dr. Martin whose plantation was about a mile below Paicourtville, Assumption Parish, La. My age was given as 18 when I was sold, John's age was given as 19, and Nelson's as 20 past. I remained on the Martin place until about the time there was a battle near Paincoutville, I then went with the soldiers to Thibodaux, I was then a married man and had four children, my slave wife was named Ellen Thomas, my children then were Alfred, Solomon, and two dead. From Thibodaux I came with my family to Algiers, and was in the Contraband Camp and living here awhile, my wife belonged to Madam Lestree, and she came or sent some one to the Contraband Camp and took my wife and children back to Bayou Lafourche, later I went out to visit them and while there the Confederates run in on us and took me with them and made me dig trenches and breastworks, I escaped from them just this side of Morgan City and came back to Thibodaux via of Houma, then I came on back to this city and when down to the Tauro Building and enlisted in Co. F, 77" U.S.C.I. my first captain was Bickers, he went to Co. M, 10" H.A. later, I do not remember the other Co. officers, yes I do too we had a Lieut. called Curzon (Henry Curzon, 2" Lt.), Ephriam Noah was our 1" Sergt. and he went with me to the 10" H.A. and was my sergt. there too and later became Sergt. Major, we had a sergt. named Smith too (Victor Smith); James Smothers, John Redman, Samson Matthews, David Johnson, George Washington, Henderson Carroll, Pleasant Gaines, Jules Felix, Henry Carter, William Clifton, George Aleck were all with me in same Co. in the 77". I cannot give the date of my enlistment in the 77" and I was in that regiment a little over a year then my regiment was consolidated with the 10" U.S.C.H.A. and I served in that regiment in Co. K, for a year or more and was discharged at Baton Rouge. I forget who my captain in the 10" H.A. was but while we were at Ship Island, Capt. Fettis had charge of the post and Lt. Night had charge of our Co. (George Knight, 1" & 2" Lt. Co. K), I forget the names of the other officers. Andrew Williams was with me in the 10" H.A. so was Jim Smothers, George Washington, and John Spencer.

While in the 77" we were at Ft. St. Philip most of the time but we came here once and were at Camp Parapet awhile, it was here twice, we were out at Pearl River once too. While in the 10" H.A. we were at Ship Island most of the time, we were at Baton Rouge a month or two before discharge too. I have here a certificate of service which shows that I enlisted on Sept. 1, 1864 and was discharged on Feb. 22, 1867. I am about 5ft 4in tall, my hair is black and kinky, my eyes are black, am dark brown in color.

After my discharge I went out to Bayou Lafourche and got my slave wife and brought her here and lived with her until she died, this wife died in the Charity Hospital in this city I cannot give the date but she died a year before I married my second wife and I have here my original Marriage Certificate to my second wife and this reads as follows:

"MARRIAGE CERTIFICATE
"STATE OF LOUISIANA
"Parish of Orleans, September 14, 1879,
"I do hereby certify that I have this day joined together in the BONDS OF
"MATRIMONY Mr. Lewis Jordan and Mrs. Martha Barew according to
"the usage of the Baptist Churches, and in conformity to the laws of the
"state of Louisiana.
"Rev. Robert Joseph
"4th Justice Pastor of the St. John's Baptist of the Peace Church

I had this marriage recorded in the Board of Health on Sept. 22, 1879, here is the receipt. I got the license from the Fourth Justice of the Peace.

I have lived with this wife ever since our marriage and we have never been separated nor divorced. These two are the only wives I have ever had and they are the only women I have ever lived with.

My second wife's maiden name was Martha Taylor, she was the widow of Pass Burrow when I married here, he served as a corporal in Co. A, 10" U.S.C.H.A. and my wife drew his bounty money or filed a claim for it anyhow, has not drawn it I think. Pass Burrow was the way his name was on the Rolls of his Co. but his right name I think was Bazile Barrow I think. My wife lived with Burrow until he died, I knew him well, he died about a year before I married my wife (his widow), these are the only two marriages my present wife ever had so far as I know or ever heard. I have no children by last wife, never had any but a son by the first wife, Alfred Jordan lives here in town, the other son, Solomon Jordan may be living but if so I do not know where he is. All my other children are dead.

I have lived in here in New Orleans all the time since my discharge. I never have used any name except Louis Jordan or Jourdan, I call myself as though it were spelled Jur-den.

I have understood the questions asked, I have heard this statement read and it is correct.

The words "below" line 12, "them" line 24 and "Martha" line 63 inserted before signing.

Document 5

Deposition of Dick Lewis Barnett (see photograph on page 28), May 17, 1911, Civil War Pension File of Lewis Smith (alias Dick Lewis Barnett), 77th USCI and 10th USCHA, RG 15:

I am 65 years of age; my post office address is Okmulgee Okla. I am a farmer.

My full name is Dick Lewis Barnett. I am the applicant for pension on account of having served in Co. B. 77th U.S. Col Inf and Co. D. U.S. Col H Art under the name Lewis Smith which was the name I wore before the days of slavery were over. I am the identical person who served in the said companies under the name of Lewis Smith. I am the identical person who was named called and known as Dick Lewis Smith before the Civil War and during the Civil War and until I returned home after my military service.

I enlisted in April 1864 at the Turo Building New Orleans, La. In Co. B 77 U.S. Col. Inf. (La. Troops) and served with that company until the whole company was transferred to Co. D. 10th U.S.C. Heavy Artillery. We were transferred in October, 1865, and I served till my discharge Feb. 20, 1867, at Baton Rouge La. I enlisted as Lewis Smith and served as a "musicianer" and my duty was to beat a drum. A drummer and musicianer are the same things. My fifer was James Harrison; I camped right with my company all the time.

During all my service we were stationed at New Orleans and between Baton Rouge, La. and Frt. St. Philip, and at Camp Parapet.

I was born in Montgomery Co. Ala. the child of Phillis Houston, slave of Sol Smith. When I was born my mother was known as Phillis Smith and I took the name of Smith too. I was called mostly Lewis Smith till after the war, although I was named Dick Lewis Smith—Dick was the brother of John Barnett whom I learned was my father after I got back from the war, when my mother told me that John Barnett was my father.

I was raised on Sol Smith's plantation near Montgomery Ala. and I stayed there till December 1862, when I went to Cedar Key Fla. 60 miles from Key West Fla. with Jacob Smith, my master's son and from there I went to New Orleans La. Christmas 1863, and the next February 1864 or March 1864 I enlisted in the U.S. service in Co. B. 77 Col. Inf. but I was not sworn in until April 1864. I had no Confederate service.

Lt. Marshall of Co. B. and D. got me to enlist.

My Colonel was Charles A. Hartwell. My Lt. Col. was named Street, but he did not stay with us after our transfer because he said something about the army which Gen'l Butler proposed to court marshall him for, and we did not see him anymore.

I cannot name any majors nor any surgeons. I have forgotten the name of my captain in Co. B.

Q. Was it Baiston, Parker, Bicker, Fettis, Wingate, Gordale, or Allgourn.

Ans. I cannot say. Wingate was captain of Co. A.

My captain in Co. D. was Charles Bailey, and my lieutenant was named Dunham. Lt. Marshall was a different person.

Q. Name some of your comrades?

Ans. George Abbott, Moberly Mo. Peter Grant, Steven's Store Calaway Co. Mo. (both of whom I saw last February) Solomon Sylvester
John Robinson, Sgt., James Harrison
E. King Sgt., Thomas Brown
Ben Ballard Ogees George (a Creole)
George Mitchell Austin French
George Hatten Curly Simmons.

I was a stranger to my comrades when I enlisted; after the service I saw none of them until last February when I called on Abbott and Grant to get their affidavits for use in my pension claim.

When I got home after the war, I was wearing the name of Lewis Smith, but I found that the negroes after freedom, were taking the names of their father like the white folks. So I asked my mother and she told me my father was John Barnett, a white man, and I took up the name of Barnett.

Q. Give your personal description in service.

Ans. I was a mulatto; brown eyes, black hair, 17 years of age, I think; and my height was very near 5 ft; place of birth was Montgomery Ala; and occupation was tending cattle and working about the house of my master, Sol Smith. I had an army discharge and I kept it for years and years; we kept it with other papers in a bureau drawer, and we kept the papers for so long, and so long that we took some of the papers out of Bureau and they got scattered and the army discharge got lost.

I hear read the list of comrades and I recall all of them except Nelson alias Foxwell. Some were Creoles—a great many were unable to talk English plainly.

Geo. Kiles, deceased, Montgomery Ala. was in Co. K. 77 U.S. and I knew him before service. James Harrison (fifer) was my bunk mate. During my service I was sunstruck, in first march about a month after I was sworn in, and I had a fever with sunstroke and did not get over it by the time I was transferred. After my enlistment my company was stationed at New Orleans La. for about 5 weeks, and then we marched to Camp Chalmet, 3 miles south of New Orleans for 4 days and then we went up the river to Camp Parapet where we stayed till our transfer to artillery. I was sick all the time at Parapet, La. and I was taken to a hospital but I escaped after a day and went back to my tent for so many men were dying. From Parapet we went to Fort St. Philip and stayed there 6 or 8 months—till about July 1866 when we were called to fight the rioters in New Orleans, and on our way up the river to New Orleans, La. the boat we were on sank, and Lt. Dunham took the wheel and ran the boat to shore and we jumped off and I fell in the water with my drum on me. After we got to New Orleans, our regiment lost a white major (name forgotten) through sickness, and a private named Henry Dupree died on account of eating too much ice cream. I was in no battle or engagement with the enemy but at Parapet the 11th Rhode Island Artillery got into a row with men in my regiment and several volleys were fired without anyone being hurt.

Soon after I enlisted it was proposed that my company go to Texas to fight Indians or Mexicans, but our people opposed it and we did not go.

I have only been married once. I married Eliza Henson Nov. 14, 1868, by a ceremony performed by Rev. Crowell (white Methodist preacher) near Mathews Station, Montgomery Co. Alabama, at Merrill Plantation in the presence of Randall Werder and James Bailey. My wife had never been married before; we had a marriage license recorded at Montgomery Ala. After my service, I resided in Montgomery Co. Ala. at Panther and Downing Ala. till I came here 6 years ago; and I worked for Columbus Baker, James Armstrong, Miss Helen Vincent on their plantations. I was known there by Wash Hood, Barbara Hood (now here), Dr. C.C. Baker, and Andy L. Barnett, Panther Ala; and Richard Barnett (my half brother) at Cecil Ala.

I was born July 22 1846. My full name is Dick Lewis Barnett. Q. You have stated that you were born on July 22, 1847? Ans. I can't say which is right. I have tried to give the best I can. I forget what age old Misses Smith told me I was when I used to go and see her. When I enlisted I did not know that I gave in my age at all; I was wanted as drummer by Gen Day, fifer, and he gave in my description; I know of no record or writing or witness who could testify or prove my age. After I got older and talked more to my mother about my age, I got the idea that I was born not later than July 22, 1847. When I stated today that was born in 1846, I did then think and still think that that was possibly the year of my birth.

Q. What was your physical condition in Aug. 1909 and ever since?

Ans. I was suffering from results of sunstrokes—I have had about 4 strokes since the one I had in the army. Dr. Thigpin, Montgomery Ala. examined me thoroughly 6 years ago and told me to keep out of the sun and that I should leave Alabama on account of my health, and it was on his advice I came here. I have also suffered from rheumatism ever since said August 1909, and ever since said date I have been able to perform only a few chores and I cannot do any part of an able bodied man's labor in the summer time. Being a farmer by occupation and not knowing any other trade or occupation, I am unable to earn a living by my labor. I have one son who works land and my wife works too. I have had no medical treatment here.

I waive my right to be present, represented by attorney, or notified on account of any further special examination of this my pension claim.

I have heard the above read. I understand the questions asked me.

Q. Did you enlist April 9, 1864 or April 25 65?

Ans. I can't tell now.

Q. by Attorney James: From what you know about the time you were born and what you figure therefrom, would you say that your exact age April 25, 1865 was 17 years, 9 months, 3 days.

Ans. Yes.

I have heard the above read. I understand the questions asked of me. My answers are correctly recorded as written.

Document 6a

Deposition of Ellen Wade, Nov. 21, 1906, Civil War Pension File of Walker Bettlesworth (alias Wade), 116th USCI, RG 15:

I am 60 odd years of age; my post-office is Farmdale, Franklin Co., Ky. Housekeeper. Pensioned as widow of Walker Wade, who enlisted under name of Walker Bettlesworth, the name of man he belonged to He served in Co "A" 116 USC Inf. I cant tell dates of enlistment or discharge, he lost his original discharge and suit and got another. He never had but the one service, he was a Corporal after being a private for awhile. Walker Wade was born & raised in Anderson Co, Ky, at Lawrenceburg, Ky. He was born in the Lillard family and Mrs. Bettlesworth was his young mistress, Martha Lillard and she married a Jennings first & then after Jennings got killed she married John Bettlesworth, and Walker fell to her & went from Mrs Martha Bettlesworth when he went to the army. I often heard Walker talk of his officers & comrades, but I forget the names. I believe all the men who were in army with Walker are dead. I belonged in Anderson Co., to Mobala Lane and was a slave & so was Walker Wade. I was never married to any one before I married Walker Wade, I had a man Charley Carter in slavery, he belonged to Sam Wilson and we first took up in slavery, but we had no marriage ceremony. We took up a short time before the war & had two children John & Mollie born before Charley Carter went to the army. Charley Carter went to the army from me & came back to me after he got out of the army. We had one more baby born dead & then we parted. We lived together about 12 years altogether. I cant tell dates correctly, but I went to Ohio on a visit & stayed five months & when I came back, he came & stayed a few days & then left for Frankfort & never did come back to me. We never had any marriage & we never went to Clerks office or had our taking up made legal. Charley Carter later married Julia that belonged to Nick Green & they are both dead now. Charley & I never married even in slavery so I never counted that as a marriage & I was never married but one time & that to Walker Wade who served as Walker Bettlesworth in Co A 116 USC Inf. Charley Carter drew a pension, but I don't remember his Co & Regiment, he has been dead about ten years perhaps & Julia his widow drew a pension till she died. After I parted from Charley Carter I married Walker Wade who served in Co "A" 116th USC Inf. Walker Wade had never had a legal or lawful marriage, I will tell you the truth about this, Walker waited on me when we were young & my owners made me take up with Charley Carter, but I never loved Charley & I did love Walker Wade as a girl & on up to today & I never cared for any other man. Alice Red, she belonged to Dan Parker, her father was Lewis Red, was a slave that had a baby before she ever had any slave husband, Harry Carter was that child & is dead, Harry's father was John Carter, brother to Charley Carter, my man. Walker Wade got Alice in a family way & her owner said if Alice had another baby without marrying that he would sell her south and as he had gotten her into this fix, he married her to save her. I don't know how many children they had, but several died or were born dead, but Sam Wade her son by Walker Wade lives here next door to me. Walker & Alice did have the ceremony of marriage at her owner's house, Old man Abe Story or Wallace a colored preacher married them, this was before the war and Walker lived with her up till he went to the army & came back to Alice for a time, but she was a drinking woman & Walker & Alice parted, Walker said he stood it as long as he could & he left her. After Walker parted from Alice she went to Kansas in August 1879, 27 years ago and Walker and I had married May 25th 1879 and Alice talked about making a fuss then, but Mr Blackmore now dead told Alice she could not do a thing for she & Walker had not made their slave marriage legal. Walker Wade and Alice never married by any License &

never went to the Clerk's office to make their slave marriage legal & so I stated when I applied for pension that neither Walker nor myself had ever been married except to each other, for the Law did not consider living together or a slave marriage as legal. Alice went to Atchison Kansas & had a girl baby by Bob Wallace out there, this girl was Anna Wallace & graduated in High School at Atchison Kansas and died at 22 years old, Alice wrote this to her son Sam Wade & my grandson read the letters & I heard them read. Alice had been away from Aug 1879 till she came back this summer on the Home Coming & then went back to Kansas & made a claim for pension as I understood & she has now come back here the last two or three weeks to live with her son Sam & Lucy his wife, but she is not pleasant & is now working out. My husband's father, Sam Wade lived in Atchison & owned a home there & when he died he left it to my husband, his son Walker Wade & my husband deeded it to Alice & her son Jim Wade, who was my husband's youngest son. It was just a little two or three room house on a little lot, but as Alice had his youngest child he gave them this house. Jim was only child of Walker Wade Alice had to raise, Sam Walker was raised here by white people. No body knows where Jim Wade is, but he went off & left his mother Alice. So far as I know Alice never married, but I heard she & Bob Wallace would have married if he had not died. No sir, Bob Wallace was not a soldier, he was the son of Abe Wallace, who performed the slave marriage for Alice and Walker. Reuben Butler, Sam Wade Alice's son and most any of the old people about here know the facts as I have told you. Alice herself will have to tell the same thing for she knows that Walker & herself had not had a lawful marriage or she have would have done some thing at the time, for she did a lot of cutting up at the time we married & the fact she was not legally married to Walker Wade is the only reason she did not make trouble then, she was a bad drinking woman then & got worse but I don't think she is so bad now has not been drunk since she came back but takes her draw. Alice told Lucy or some of her people that she was disgusted with whiskey & Green Thurman and Wm Bush know all about this, they know I had Charley Carter & was not married to him & they also know Walker Wade & were in the army with him & know he & Alice had a slave marriage but no lawful marriage after the war & had parted. Walker Wade never left here, he never went to Kansas, but Anderson & Franklin Counties Ky was his home up till he died & he & I moved into this house in Jan 1880 & I have not remarried or lived with any man as his wife since Walker Wade my husband died. I have just this little house, after Walker Wade died I sold 1 5/6 acres of land I think to pay his burial expenses & I am still paying on his Doctor Bill. This place is not worth $200 and I have no means of support except my pension. I draw $8 per month, payable at Louisville Agency & my check comes to Farmdale, Franklin Co Ky & not to Alton Station, but some times I am at my son's, John Carters & draw pension there for old pensioners there know me well. I have no especial witnesses to be seen, but Alice & the comrades will have to tell the facts as I tell you. She cant deny this, but if she does the old neighbors can tell the facts as I have told you. Walker & I lived in Anderson Co Ky at the time we married & we got the License at Lawrenceburg Ky, I was with him at the time, Frank Carter I think was a witness on the Mage Bond. I have no Attorney & dont care for any. I do not care to be present when the witnesses are seen here or elsewhere. I have no complaint to make of the conduct, manner or fairness of your examination. Have heard this read, fully understand your questions and am correctly recorded.

Document 6b

Deposition of Alice Bettlesworth (alias Wade), Nov. 21, 1906, Civil War Pension File of Walker Bettlesworth (alias Wade), 116th USCI, RG 15:

I am about 65 years of age; my post-office is Farmdale, Frankfort Co, Ky Occupation Domestic for Mrs Tips McCowan I am the Alice Bettlesworth who was in Atchison Kansas and I went to see Mr Adams a Lawyer there & told him about Walker Wade my husband who served—Co A 116th USC Inf as Walker Bettlesworth & deserted me for Ellen Carter & then Mr Adams & his partner filed a claim for me as the widow of Walker Wade or Bettlesworth. I only had a slave marriage to Walker Wade alias Bettlesworth, that was in the parlor of Jas D Parker my owner, some years before the war and Abram Wallace married us, he was also called Abe Story for his owner. I only had the slave marriage to & did not remarry & go to the County Clerk after the war for Walker Wade would not go with me. At first when he got home out of the army & came back I thought the slave marriage was all right & after a little while he got to running after Ellen Carter who was living with Charley Carter. I did not at first think about needing to make the slave marriage legal, but when I was baptized & went to join the Church the Minister told us I should have Walker Wade go with me & make our marriage legal & Walker would not do it he was then running after Ellen Carter. Wade kept getting worse with Ellen & they led me a dogs life for 6 or 7 years & finally the house Walker & I lived in burned down on Tuesday & on Saturday he ran off, said he was going to Frankfort & I did not see him again for five months but I found that Walker Wade & Ellen Carter were up in Ohio at her sisters. He left me without shelter & in a delicate situation & this baby Jim Wade was born April 8th, 1878 and about time Jim was born, soon after Ellen & Walker came back but I never spoke to him again. Charley Carter took Ellen back but she would not stay with him & the next May, a year, May 1879 Walker Wade and Ellen married. I was not present but my son was there & I know it was true, so I left here in Aug 1879, soon after this marriage & did not come back till last June on a visit & when I got back to Kansas I went to see Mr Adams & he said he would try & see what could be done. He did not say I could or could not get it, but I made an application for pension on his advice but I have not gotten my claim number. Lewis Rennicks, at Atchison Kansas was in the service with my husband & he knew of Walker writing & getting letters from me & of eating at our house after Walker got back from the army. I dont know what Mr Adams did do, but I was sworn to the paper, I guess I was mistaken about that, he just asked me about it & wrote one letter, but he had not gotten an answer from them so did not do anything more, but he has my address at Farmdale Ky & he promised to write as soon as he would get a letter. He never got any pay from me. I have paid nothing to any one. I told you I had made a claim but I guess I was mistaken for I did not swear to a statement & have it signed & witnessed, I just showed him some letters from my people & he read them out & had a young lady write it down. I thought from what he & others said that I might be allowed a pension, but I knew that Walker Wade & I never made our slave marriage legal for he would not go with me & do so, and I knew that he did marry this Ellen Carter & deserted me for her and she had deserted Charley Carter for Walker Wade & I did not think such meanness as that ought to be rewarded. As soon as they married &, I could, I left this country to be away from them and I stayed away till home coming last June. Then my son wanted me to come back here to live, but I am sorry I came back, but I had no relations out there. My son Jim is gone & I don't know where he is now. Walker Wade gave our baby boy a home in Atchison that his father James Wade, my boy's grandfather owned, but Jim sold this. I own no property. No sir, I have never married since Walker Wade deserted me. I went by the name of Wade out in Kansas. Yes, I lived in Atchison Kansas from time I went away till I came back here. I had a child, Annie Wallace by Bob Wallace while I was out there, but we never lived together, I got down sick & he helped me & that was the result. Bob was a son of Abram Wallace who married me to Walker Wade back in Slavery. My daughter Annie Wallace died at 22 years & 9 months there at Atchison Kansas. She was a graduate of High School there, she died April 5th 1906. I have no Atty more than I told you. I have told you just the straight of every thing Mr Parker & Creasy Ross can tell the same & I don't dispute what Ellen says except they drove me to drink. The marriage to Wade was never made legal & so I will drop this. Have heard this read & same is fully understood & correctly recorded herein.

Document 7

Deposition of Hiram Kirkland (see photograph on page 19), Nov. 26, 1902, Civil War Pension File of Hiram Kirkland, 101st and 110th USCI, RG 15:

I am on the rise of 80 years of age. I dont know my exact age. I live on Saffarans St near Alabama St. [in Nashville, Tenn.] I was a grown man and I had three boys and three girls when I enlisted I was a common laborer when I was able to work. I am now so old and stiff that I am not able to work at all. My son Andrew Kirkland supports me. I live with him.

I served in Co G 101 U.S.C. Inf. in the Civil War. I enlisted in Co G 110 U.S.C. Inf under Capt Canady and was transferred to Co G 101 U.S.C. Inf.

I enlisted at Prospect Tenn. and was mustered out in Nashville Tenn.

The only time I was in the hospital was when I had the small pox here in Nashville. I was taken from the hospital to be mustered out. I didn't know where the hospital was nor its number.

While we were in Ala near Athens, and before I was transferred to the 101 U.S.C. Inf I had the measles and was treated by Dr. "Dinklog" who was our surgeon. I was sick a long time; they thought that I would die. I was mistaken when I called the doctor Dinklog: he was a Lieutenant.

The 110 USCI was captured at Athens, Ala. but I was not with it when it was captured. I came to Nashville about a week before the 110th was captured I was, while here in Nashville, transferred to the 101 U.S.C. Inf. which regiment did not do any fighting, but guarded the railroads and bridges.

My correct name is Hiram Kirkland. Some persons call me Harry and others call me Henry, but neither is my correct name.

My first master was John Casson. I was born "low down in Miss. My next master was Mr Lively. Milton McClure was my next after him came Latham then Hamilton Pickens who sold me to James Kirkland for $1700^{00} Mr Kirkland (decd) lived 2 1/2 miles from Culleoka, Tenn. on the Cornersville road. I had been living in Tenn for 15 or 16 years at the time I joined the army

James Kirkland had a brother John.

No sir: there was not any Joseph Kirkland connected with the family. I never belonged to Joseph Kirkland

Mr Kirkland did not have any children old enough to know anything about me.

Mr Kirkland owned only three negroes, myself wife (decd) and Don Bishop. Don Bishop was still living with the old master when I was down there about 20 years ago

Don Bishop was the only person besides my old master and mistress living when I was there 20 years ago, whom I knew before the war.

George Bebee was capt of Co G, 101 U. S. C. Inf. Dinklog was 1st Lt. I don't know name of 2d Lt.

Parks and Turner were the Corporals Orderly Sgt was "Ben" He was a cross eyed fellow from Miss.

Other members of my company were, as follows: Reuben Vanlear, Wm Fitzpatrick (who lived at Mooresville before the war) also Hark Moore of same place, General Townsel, Fountain Townsel, Plato Watkins, Caleb Thomas, Coleman Garrison, Joseph Stark (Corpl) Martin Townsend & Wm Holt.

I don't know where any of the comrades live Reuben Vanlear was living in Maury County Tenn when I left there.

Of the names you have read from the list I know the following:

Starling Butler, Wm Fitzgerald, Wesley Gilbert John Harville, Wm Holt, Columbus Sykes, Aaron White, Joseph Stark, Martin Townshend & Reuben Vanlear

I am the identical Hiram Kirkland who claims pension for service in Co G 101 U S C Inf under the name Hiram Kirkland. I was living at

Spring Hill Tenn when I put in my claim. Reuben Vanlear of my company was living near Spring Hill at the time and he put in his claim a few days before I put in mine. I think that he is the Reuben Vanlear who served in my company; but I am not sure as to that.

I have no wife nor any children under 16 years of age

I never had more than one wife. Her name was Mandy Kirkland. She died twenty years ago. She was the only wife I ever had.

I am the only Hiram Kirkland who served in Co G 101 U.S.C. Vol. Inf. I have never rendered any military service except as above stated. I have never served in the Navy or in the Marine Corps.

I can prove my identity by the testimony of the men I knew in the service and whose names I have stated above.

I do not care to be present nor to be represented by an attorney in the examination of my claim.

The varicose veins came on both my legs soon after the war and the sores were there when I first put in my claim at Spring Hill Tenn.

I worked for Mr McCampbell of Spring Hill Tenn for 3 years. He raised race horses. He called me Uncle Henry. I don't know whether or not he knows that I had varicose veins. I could not give the names of any person who knows that I had the varicose veins. I never complained to my associates about the varicose veins. I also worked for "Cane" Brown (decd) & Col Brown (near Columbia)

My statement is correctly recorded.

Document 8a

Deposition of Emma Frederick, June 2, 1899, Civil War Pension File of Clement Frederick, 70th and 71st USCI, RG 15:

I am about 68 years of age; my post-office address is No. 1726 No Rochblave St. New Orleans, La., occupation washing.

I am an applicant for pension as the widow of Clement Frederick. I don't remember what regiment he served in, but I have his discharge paper, which he gave me when he was dying. (Orig. disch. cert. produced same shows that Clement Frederick Pvt of Capt. Samuel Manly's Co. E, 70 U.S.C. Inf, was enrolled Mch 19/64, to serve three years, and was discharged Mch 7/66 at Vicksburg, Miss, and gives personal descrip. same as in record. Exr)

He enlisted only once.

I applied for pension a long time ago, don't know the date. I first went to Gross on Exchange alley he did n't do nothing for me, then I got a man named Lobre to do my writing. I swore to my application here in the Custom House before a Mr. "Gray" (Craig) I am sure he swore me, had me hold my right hand and touch the pen.

Q. Did you know what you were swearing to.

A. Yes to the truth that I was the widow of Clement Frederick and had not married again.

Q. Who were your witnesses if any at that time.

A. Octave "Lauvon" (Lanes) he was sworn and signed his name.

Q. Was any other person present.

A. "Marcelley" Baptiste, she came in afterwards was sworn and touched the pen. Mr. "Gray" hold the pen. She is dead now.

Etienne Villers, my brother in law, now dead, made an affidavit in my case, with "Marcelley" Baptiste.

The only other witness who have testified in case are Martha White and her mother Lucy "Seymore," that's been lately. I did not go with them when they were sworn. Simon Lyon, Wash^{n} D.C. is now my atty, don't know who was my attorney before him, don't remember hearing the name Addison G Du Bois. "I never tell him, Lyon, nothing about paying."

Q. What have you paid Lobre.

A. I have paid him for every paper he made out, the first one two dollars, and since then a dollars, and sometimes since less.

Q. Has he asked you to pay him anything if your claim is allowed.

A. He told me if he gains the case that I am to give him \$25.^{00} I said that could not count the chickens before they the eggs were hatched. I aint going to pay it.

He said that more than a year ago.

The soldier was born in Washington, came to St. Jame's Par. La. a young man I was his first wife, that's what he said. I had a slave husband named Reubin, he died before I took up with Clem. I took up with Clem long before the war and had 7 children by him before he went into the army.

I was married to him "under the flag," by an officer of Clem's regiment. That was in St James Par. after he enlisted before he went off.

He came back to me after muster out and two months afterwards we moved to this city. We were never divorced, lived together as husband

and wife until he died in Charity Hosp'l don't know the date. I had him buried in St. Roch Cemetery.

He has been dead 6 or 7 years. No sir, I have not remarried or lived or cohabitated with any man as his wife since his death. My true and correct name is Emma Frederick and that is the only name I have been known by since the war. My master was my father his name was St. Martin Michael. I don't know near what post office I lived in St. James Par.

I don't know what the officers name was who married me to the soldier, don't know if he was a chaplain or not. That was the first time I saw any soldier. It was a colored Regt that came through, the regiment my husband enlisted in.

The officer gave me a paper, but it fell in the fire and got burned.

I have no property of any kind and no income except what I can earn myself.

All of my children are dead.

I fully and thoroughly understand your questions and my answers thereto are correctly recorded herein.

Document 8b

Deposition of Emma Frederick, Mar. 12, 1903, Civil War Pension File of Clement Frederick, 70th and 71st USCI, RG 15:

I am 94 years of age; my post-office address is #2817 Maurepas St., New Orleans, La.; occupation I do such house-work as I am able to do.

I am claiming pension as the widow of Clement Frederick who served in the Co. and Regt. that is shown in this discharge certificate (Exhibits original discharge of Clement Frederick of Co. E 70 Regt. U.S.C. Inf.—Capt. Samuel Manly's Co—showing that soldier enlisted Mar. 19, 1864 and was discharged Mar. 7, 1866—that he was born in Washington, D.C., 37 years of age complexion and hair black—E. L. W. Sp. Ex.) The soldier only had one service, military or naval. The soldier and I belonged to the same man before the war. His slave wife was named Celestine who belonged to Francois Boudois who owned a plantation two or three plantations from ours.

I belonged in slavery to Marin Rain of Bonnet Carre, St. John the Baptist parish, La. He had two sons, Jules and Charles Rain, and one daughter,

Adele Rain, but they are all dead. Adele Rain married Lucien Montagut. Celestine, the soldiers slave wife, belonged to Francois Boudois. I don't know the names of any of the comrades of soldier except Andrew—I think his full name was Andrew Lewis. I do not know where he resides. I do not remember the names of many of the slaves on our plantation except John Baptist, John Pierre and a man called Henry. My slave husband was named Reuben Ward. He died three or four years before the war. Reuben Ward belonged to the same owner in slavery that I belonged to. While the soldier, Clement Frederick, had a slave wife named Celestine before the war yet he was intimate with me before he enlisted and when he enlisted I was with child by him (was three months gone) and I had had three children by him before he enlisted. The soldier had no children by his wife, Celestine. No, I do not know whether Celestine went with the soldier when he enlisted or whether she lived with him in Natchez, Miss. No, I never heard that the soldier, Clement Frederick, was married to this woman Celestine "under the flag" during the war. I never heard that He never told me what he did. After he came back from the war he came to my house and rested three weeks and then he went to look for his wife Celestine and found her with a man named Willis. He then came back to me and lived with me as husband and wife until he died. We left the country about six months after his discharge and came to this city where we lived until he died and where I have lived ever since.

Q- Before the war you considered that Celestine was his wife and that he was simply "taking up" with you?

A- Yes, sir.

Q- Did you ever have a ceremony performed uniting or purporting to unite you and the soldier in the bonds of matrimony?

A- Yes, after his return from the army—after his discharge—a minister named John Bull (colored) had a kind of ceremony with a broom-stick. My sister, Estelle, and her husband, Etienne Villers, saw us married by this colored minister but they are both dead. No, my sister was not married at the same time I was. She was married at St. Bonaface's church (Catholic) on Claiborne St. in this city. No one else was present when I was married to the soldier. I was married to the soldier after his discharge and before we moved to this city. Yes, the soldier's wife, Celestine, was living at that time but she was living with a man named Willis as his wife. No, the soldier never went into court and got a divorce from Celestine, and she never got a divorce from him to my knowledge. She was alive when I married the soldier but died afterwards. I never went back to the country after I left there six months or so after the soldier's discharge but my husband, the soldier, went back to get shoat and some chickens about three months after we left and he told me that she was dead

The soldier lost one eye while in the service He said he lost it by sticking the ram-rod in his eye while cleaning his gun.

I do not know anyone in the country who would yet know me except Paul Lewis and his children Pauline, Evaline and Marie Lewis

A woman named Aimee (don't know her other name) and Lulu Eugene have known me ever since I have been here. A number of other people have known me since I have been in the city but I do not know their names. I will bring them to you or will bring you their addresses on a piece of paper.

I do not care to be present at the examination of the witnesses.

I lived with the soldier until he died. He died on Friday in the hospital. He died of old age. When he was taken to the hospital I told them if anything happened to give me his body. When he died they gave me his body and I got a white man (Eugene Ravin) to bury him for me. He furnished the money, as I was working for him at the time. Both Eugene Ravin and his wife are dead. I do not know how many years ago it is that he died but I think it was about four years ago.

Yes, I remember testifying before Special Examiners Montgomery and Teicher

Q- Did you not tell them that you were married to the soldier under the flag?

A- Yes, I did.

Q- Why did you tell them that?

A- They bothered me so much. We were laughing and talking. They did not think I was a colored woman I was so light

Q- As a matter of fact you were not married to the soldier "under the flag" were you?

A- No, I was not. What I have told you today is the truth.

I have not remarried or lived with any man as his wife since the soldier died.

I have not owned any property since the soldier died and have been wholly dependent upon my own labor for support ever since the said soldier died.

I have heard this deposition read I have understood the questions asked and my answers have been correctly recorded. The words, "I have known me ever" and "both" stricken out before signing.

Celestine was a small brown skinned woman. She was rather good looking woman but had short hair. By short hair I mean kinky hair She was a young woman—much younger than I was.

I, J. P. Wootin, Special Examiner, am witness to the fact that the foregoing was carefully and fully read to and freely acknowledged under oath and signed by Emma Frederick in my presence

Document 8c

Deposition of Emma Frederick, Mar. 31, 1903, Civil War Pension File of Clement Frederick, 70th and 71st USCI, RG 15:

Yes, I had a sister named Estelle. Estelle had a daughter named Helena who married Paul Lewis.

I have heard the depositions of Paul Lewis and Amilie Ganff read. Yes, they are mistaken. I did not live with Reuben after the war.

Q- Where did Reuben die?

A- He had the small pox and they put him in the small pox hospital on Elysian Fields St. Yes, I lived with Reuben until he died.

Q- You told me before that Reuben died in the country three or four years before the war Now you say he died in this city on Elysian Fields St. Will you explain?

A- I don't know just when he died but he died before I took up with Clement Frederick.

Q- By whom can you prove the fact and date of Reuben's death?

A- I do not know but I will try and find some one.

Q- When and where did the soldier's wife, Celestine, die?

A- I do not know. I never saw her. All I know is that Clement Frederick told me she was dead.

My right name is Emma but they called me Aimee because I was born in May.

I have heard this deposition read and my answers have been correctly recorded.

Document 8d

Deposition of Emma Frederick, Apr. 11, 1903, Civil War Pension File of Clement Frederick, 70th and 71st USCI, RG 15:

I am the claimant in this case. I have testified before you two different times before.

I do not know what has has become of the soldiers first wife, Celestine, except that I heard that she was dead. A year or two after I took up with and began living with the soldier, Clement Frederick, he did not come home one night and I asked him where he had been and he told me that Celestine was dead—that he had been sitting up with her to see the last of her. She, Celestine, was living with a man named Willis as his wife when she died. I never saw Celestine or Willis and do not know when or where Celestine died. I do not know whether Celestine died in this city. I do not know what has become of Willis. I do not know of anyone by whom I can prove the death of Celestine. No, Clement Frederick was never divorced from Celestine to my knowledge.

Yes, Reuben Ward my first husband died in this city on St. Bernard St. We were living in a home we rented from Mr. Sick. Jules Ward is right about that. He remembers better than I do. Yes, I know I said he died of the small pox. It is true that he had recovered from the small pox when he died but he was still suffering from the effects of it. It was about one year after Reuben Ward died that I took up with the soldier, Clement Frederick. No, Clement Frederick and I never had any marriage ceremony performed but we lived together happily and he was very good to me. I called him “papa” and he called me “mama.”

Q- What agreement did you make with the soldier, Clement Frederick, when you first began living with him?

A- I told him that if he would take me for his bosom wife that I would not allow any man to come between him and me—that I would not have any thing to do with any other man, and he promised that he would not have any other woman than me.

Q- Did you know that his wife Celestine was living when you began living with Clement Frederick and made this agreement to live with him?

A- Yes, he told me about her and said that she was living with another man.

Q- Jules Ward stated that his father died in the year 1873—about eight years after peace was declared. Is that your recollection of the fact?

A- I suppose that he is right. His recollection is better than my own.

I have heard the deposition of Jules Ward read. His statement is all true to the best of my knowledge. I have also heard read the deposition of Elizabeth Faquier. It is also correct as far as I know.

I have heard this deposition read I have understood the questions asked and my answers have been correctly recorded

We James E. Flyner, 120 So Claiborne St. and Wm E. Bernard, #924 Cadiz St. New Orleans, La., are witness to the fact that the above and foregoing statement was fully read to claimant and freely acknowledged under oath by her before signing.

Document 9

Deposition of Thomas W. Wilbourn, Apr. 14, 1909, Civil War Pension File of Thomas Wilbert (alias Thomas W. Wilbourn), 122nd USCI, RG 15:

I am 62 years of age next month; my post-office address is Wharton, Texas; occupation, minister. I am the identical person who served under the name of Thomas Wilbert in Co. B, 122 U.S.C. Inf. I enlisted in latter part of 1864 and was discharged in 1866 I served as a private and drummer, I had no other U.S. military service and was never in the U.S. Navy or Marine Corps. I am not a pensioner but am an applicant for pension. I filed my claim I think first about 12 years ago. (Ques.) The first declaration on file amongst the papers in your case was filed Nov. 9, 1904. (Ans.) It seems to me I applied before that date, but I cannot remember dates. I was born May 10, 1847, at Atlanta, Georgia. There is no Bible record or public record or other record of my birth that I know of. I was born in slavery times and was born a slave. L. J. Gottrell was my master. My father's name was George Wilbourn. My mother was Jane. She was raised by the Gideons and was Emancipated. But I don't know anything about it. I heard that afterwards. I think I was about 17 years old when I ran away from home and went to Louisville where I enlisted. I can't tell you how long I was in Louisville before I enlisted. I was living in Atlanta, Ga., when I ran away. I had always lived there. My father and mother are both dead. I know my mother is and expect my father is too. I think I had 5 or 6 brothers and I believe 3 sisters. They are all older than I am. I have no knowledge of them and know nothing about them. The last I knew of them they were in Atlanta, Ga. I haven't seen any of them since 1864. I had one brother named Van another Isam. I think one named Wash. I can't think of the names of the others. One sister is named America, another named Georgeann, Eliza, dead, is another. I don't know whether any of them are living.

I don't know whether my master L. G. Gottrell is living I been trying to study his wife's name was but am not sure whether her name was Fanny or not. He had a boy named Joe, one named Barto, and Henry was another. Seems to me there was a girl, but I can't say sure. James Evans a cousin of min enlisted when I did and was put in the same Company. He was arrested in this state and put in the penitentiary at Huntsville many years ago. I heard he got away, but I don't know anything about where he is. He knew me before I enlisted. Another man who knew me before I went into the army and who enlisted when I did was John Dunlap and Henry Wright. But I only knew Dunlap and Wright a short time prior to my Enlistment. I think Dunlap was in H Company and Wright in K Company. I am not sure of that. I know they were in the same regiment. I do not know where Dunlap is. Wright was in Little Rock, Ark., the last I knew of him. Wright knew me as Tom Wilbert. Then after the war he knew me as Thomas W. Wilbourn here in Texas all up and down the H.&T.C R.R. Evans knew me in the army as Thomas Wilbert, and he knew me since the war as Thomas W. Wilbourn. Evans and I worked in Galveston together.

Dunlap never knew me under any name but my army name Thos. Wilbert. (Ques.) By what name were you known before you enlisted? (Ans.) When I enlisted I thought my name was Thomas Wilbert, and I gave that as my name. After the war I wrote back to my mother in care of W. H. Quarles, I think the initials were W. H., who was a preacher. My mother belonged to his church. He wrote me that my mother was dead, and that her name was Jane Wilbourn and not Wilbert. That was 42 years ago or about that time. Rev. Quarles is dead. His church was in Atlanta, Ga. My father's name was Wilbourn. That is where the name came from. From the time Rev. Quarles wrote me I have always gone by the name of Thomas W. Wilbourn and have always signed my name in that way, No sir, I do not know any one in Texas who was in the army with me.

At enlistment my skin, hair, and eyes were black. I was small and weighed only about 125 pounds. I think my height was given as 5 ft. 5 in. (Ques.) Did you have any marks or scars at enlistment? (Ans.) I have as scar just above my left knee. That was caused by cutting myself with a knife while making a pop gun when I was a boy. Then I had a scar on my fore head just above the root of my nose. That was caused by a boy hitting me with a stick in a fight. (Scar not now visible. H.J.) No sir, I had no other scar or mark when I enlisted that I know of. My Captain was Keys. We had a lieutenant at one time by the name of Casey. He was an officer, and I do not know whether he was a lieutenant or captain. I have never been able to think of the name of a single Sergt. or of any of the Corporals. (Ques.) Can you recall any of your regimental officers? (Ans.) A fellow name Lehman. I think he was a lieutenant Colonel. Then there was a Mr. Shedirick. I don't know whether he was a quartermaster or what he was. A man named Davidson was another officer in the regiment somewhere. Then there was a man named Tillison, who I think was a regimental officer. James Evans and I tented together. It may have been about 1869 somewhere that he was sent to the penitentiary. I think he was sent from Galveston for stealing. I heard that he afterward escaped. I've never seen him since he was sent to prison. Other members of my Company I do not believe I can name. (Names read from list. H. J.) Seems to me the name of Bryant is familiar. I remember Brown. John B. Keys. Geo. Trotter. The names of the others you read me sound familiar. I enlisted at Louisville, Ky. I don't know how long I was assigned to Co. B, 122 U.S.C. Inf there. Yes sir, I think we went away from there with the whole outfit. From there we went by boat, don't know the name, up the Ohio River up to where I think the B&O R.R. crosses the river. We there climbed up the bank and waited for the train. We got in the train and went from there to the union depot in Baltimore I think. That same evening we got off the train and went to a big barracks about 5 miles from the depot or from some particular part of the city. (Ques.) What was the name of the barracks? (Ans.) I understood it was Federal Hill or something of that kind. It was a fine big barracks. Plenty of stoves and big buildings. I don't know how long we stayed there. I don't think we did anything there but wait for orders to move. It was cold and some were frost bitten. I remember I washed my feet in the snow and was told not to go near the fire. I don't remember that we did any drilling there. We were not there so very long. From there we went by boat on Chesapeake Bay to some point in Virginia, but can't think of the name of the place.

I don't think we stayed there very long. Then we went up some river, I think it was the Washita into North Carolina. I can't say whether the town was Wilberton [Wilmington?] or Newbin [New Bern?]. We didn't stay there very long. Then we came right back down to some little place I thought was Norfolk but it don't seem to me that it was Norfolk. We brought some colored people down from North Carolina. Seems to me we landed them right opposite Norfolk. We stayed at Newport News for several weeks I think. We guarded prisoners (Ques.) Then where did you go? (Ans.) I can't say whether it was Fortress Monroe or not. But anyway we got on a large vessel there and came all the way by water to Texas—to Corpus Christi. I think it was low tide and we stuck on a sand bar. It was water melon time. We were stuck on the sand bar until the tide rose I think. Anyhow a steamboat came and pulled us off. We were taken off the big boat in small boats and were landed on a bar a few miles from Corpus Christi. We stayed there in Camp and drilled and did camp duty until they mustered us out. (Ques.) Were you in any battles? (Ans.) No sir, the only thing was going up the river into North Carolina there was a fort on one bank. They fired on us but there was a gun boat behind us, and they fired a few shots only. It was at Corpus Christi that they put me to beating a tenor drum in the drum Corps.

(Ques.) Can you recall any incident or experience you or any of your Company had while in service? (Ans.) No sir, nothing special. Up in North Carolina where we went there were some large Negroes chained out in the woods. Then it seems to me there were some colored women fastened up in a smokehouse. When we stopped at Cincinnati going up the river there was a man, seemed to me his name was Saddler, who caught the guard's gun and escaped from the boat and was never caught.

I think I had the mumps in service. I think it was the mumps. But it didn't stop me. I was never in the hospital. I think that was about all the sickness I had. (Ques.) By whom do you expect to prove that you are the identical person who served in Co. B, 122 U.S.C. Inf. under the name Thomas Wilbert? (Ans.) Now sir, I just can't tell you. Henry Wright is the only one who has identified me. I do not know what Capt. Keys could do. When I was in the army I was a small man. Now I am a big man weighing 226 pounds. I could not write in the army. I commenced studying in 1874. This picture of myself that you show me (see circular attached to B. J.) was taken in 1895. That is a cut made from a picture taken in 1895. I have a large framed picture taken along about 1884. That is the oldest picture of my self that I have. I have no smaller picture of myself. Since my discharge I have lived in Texas all the time. Have been in all parts of the State. Have lived in Galveston 2 or 3 years, Waxahachie 7 yrs., Corsicana about 2 yrs., Celeburne 1 year, Ft. Worth about 15 years, Marshall about 1 year, here [Wharton] since 1896. I have been preaching almost 30 years. Before that I was a barber. I have been married but once. My wife is still living with me. She was previously married to a man named Douglass who died in the Indian Nation [Oklahoma]—so reported but I don't when or where. He died before I married her her name was Annie Elizabeth Douglass. I forget the date I married her but it was in Waxahachie, Tex. There is a record of our marriage. We have no children. (Ques.) Your declaration for pension was filed Nov. 9, 1904. What was your physical condition at that time? (Ans.) I had shortness of breath, soreness over the lungs, and from each side of the small of my back down around in front and down into the groins I had pain. Then I have pain over my rectum. That condition has continued ever since. No sir, I reckon there is nothing else. Have had sick spells more than at times I get blind spells and short of breath. As far as doing manual labor is concerned, I could have done some but not very much. I couldn't have made a livelihood at it. I do not know how much I have been able to do. If a man just had to work, he might be able to do more than he otherwise would do. I have rheumatism in both shoulders but worse in my right shoulder. Sometimes I can hardly raise the right arm Have been bothered with that about 12 or 14 years but it has been growing upon me. Then I have Constipation and have had it about 6 years. No sir, I don't think I have anything else the matter with me except failure of the sexual organs that I told you about.

(Ques.) Can you give me the names of any witnesses who will know that you have suffered from the disabilities you have mentioned? (Ans.) Dr. Ben Covington, colored, Houston, Tex., but can't give you his city address, has prescribed for me. Dr. Nichols, colored, here in Wharton has given me several prescriptions. No sir, I don't know of any one else outside of my family who would know that I have suffered from the disabilities I have named. I have traveled a good deal for years. (Ques.) How much of the time have you been at home for the last four years? (Ans.) I hardly know. Sometimes I am at home 3 or 4 days in the week then I go away Friday or Saturday, and come back Monday or Tuesday. Then again I am away longer than that. Sometimes I am away two weeks at a time. I am in and out. I do not care particularly to be present when the witnesses are examined here or elsewhere. I've never said much about my disabilities. Dr. Nichols has not treated me very much. I think I am now using his third prescription. I don't know what he had prescribed for me. I told him I thought it might be dry pills. So he gave me a prescription. He first prescribed for me about 14 or 16 months ago. It hasn't been very long. I am financially unable to be present at any further examination of my case. Dr. Covington left here my wife says in about 1901 or 1902. I am not certain but I think he gave me a prescription once in Houston about 6 or 7 years ago, since he left here. I have made no contract to pay a fee that I know of, and I have paid no fees in this case. My attorney is Wills in Washington, D.C. I expect I have understood your questions. Have heard this Statement read. I think you have my answer set down right. I preached in Marlin, Tex., in 1906 and 1907, and as my wife states in her deposition, Dr. Clark examined me and treated me several times for loss of vital power, and said I had kidney trouble. He is a colored doctor who runs a bath house there. He is not running the bath house now, but he is still there. Am correctly recorded.

Notes

NOTES TO THE INTRODUCTION

1. Deposition of Charles Franklin Crosby, June 19, 1914, Civil War Pension File of Frank Nunn (alias Charles Franklin Crosby), 86th USCI, RG 15.

2. Ibid.

3. Ibid.

4. For more information on the WPA narratives, see Norman R. Yetman, "The Background of the Slave Narrative Collection, *American Quarterly* 19 (fall 1967): 534–53; George P. Rawick, *The American Slave: A Composite Autobiography*, vol. 1, *From Sundown to Sunup: The Making of the Black Community* (Westport, Conn.: Greenwood, 1972), xiii–xxi; John W. Blassingame, "Using the Testimony of Ex-Slaves: Approaches and Problems," in *Revisiting Blassingame's "The Slave Community": The Scholar's Respond*, ed. Al-Tony Gilmore (Westport, Conn.: Greenwood, 1978), 169–93; Paul D. Escott, "The Art and Science of Reading WPA Slave Narratives," in *The Slave Narrative*, ed. Charles T. Davis and Henry Louis Gates (New York: Oxford University Press, 1985), 41–58.

5. James M. McPherson, *Battle Cry of Freedom: The Civil War Era* (New York: Oxford University Press, 1988), 306n.

6. Maris Vinovskis, "Have Social Historians Lost the Civil War? Some Preliminary Demographic Speculations," *Journal of American History* 76 (June 1989): 54.

7. "CIA—World Fact Book—United States," http://198.81.129.100/cia/publications/factbook/geos/us.html.

8. Donald R. Shaffer, *After the Glory: The Struggles of Black Civil War Veterans* (Lawrence: University Press of Kansas, 2004), 133.

9. Ibid., 129.

NOTES TO CHAPTER 1

1. Frederick Douglass, *My Bondage and My Freedom* (New York: Miller, Orton, and Mulligan, 1855; repr., New York: Dover, 1969), 35.

2. John W. Blassingame, *The Slave Community: Plantation Life in the Antebellum South* (New York: Oxford University Press, 1972; revised and enlarged ed., 1979), xi.

3. A useful bibliographic overview of this particular era in the historiography of slavery can be found in Peter J. Parish, *Slavery: History and Historians* (New York: Harper and Row, 1989), 175–78.

4. Charles Joyner, *Down by the Riverside: A South Carolina Slave Community* (Chicago: University of Illinois Press, 1984), 41.

5. Pension Bureau Questionnaire 3-474, Sept. 26, 1901, Civil War Pension File of Hiram Kirkland, 101st and 110th USCI, RG 15.

6. For more on the practice of taking a former owner's name, see Elizabeth Regosin, *Freedom's Promise: Ex-Slave Families and Citizenship in the Age of Emancipation* (Charlottesville: University Press of Virginia, 2002), 67–73.

7. Regardless of the reason, when soldiers had more than one name, the Pension Bureau listed them all as aliases for record-keeping purposes.

8. Deposition of Thomas Wilbourn, Apr. 14, 1909, Civil War Pension File of Thomas Wilbourn, 122nd USCI, RG 15.

9. Affidavit of Benjamin Courtney, June 6, 1908, Civil War Pension File of Benjamin Courtney, 51st USCI, RG 15.

10. U.S. Pension Bureau, *General Instructions to Special Examiners of the U.S. Pension Bureau* (Washington, D.C.: GPO, 1882), 24. Printed initially in 1881, *General Instructions* was revised in 1882, 1886, and 1897. In the 1897 version of the booklet, there was no longer a separate section on "colored claimants." See Regosin, *Freedom's Promise*, 40, 194n. 43.

11. Lawrence W. Levine, *Black Culture and Black Consciousness: Afro-American Folk Thought from Slavery to Freedom* (New York: Oxford University Press, 1977), 158.

12. Donald R. Shaffer, "'I Do Not Suppose That Uncle Sam Looks at the Skin': African Americans and the Civil War Pension System," *Civil War History* 46, no. 2 (June 2000): 132–47.

13. Deposition of David Edwards, Nov. 14, 1911, Civil War Pension File of David Edwards, 88th USCI, 9th USCHA and 3rd USCHA, RG 15.

14. For more on antebellum manumission, see Ira Berlin, *Slaves without Masters: The Free Negro in the Antebellum South* (New York: Pantheon Books, 1974; repr., New York: Oxford University Press, 1981), 138–57.

15. Ibid., 136.

16. Ibid., 316–17.

17. Ibid., 218.

18. Peter Kolchin, *American Slavery: 1619–1877* (New York: Hill and Wang, 1993), 157–59.

NOTES TO CHAPTER 2

1. For published primary sources written by black soldiers, see Ira Berlin, Joseph P. Reidy, and Leslie S. Rowland, eds., *Freedom: A Documentary History of Emancipation, 1861–1867, Series II: The Black Military Experience* (Cambridge: Cambridge University Press, 1982); Edwin S. Redkey, *A Grand Army of Black Men: Letters from African American Soldiers in the Union Army, 1861–1865* (Cambridge: Cambridge University Press, 1982); Virginia M. Adams, ed., *On the Altar of Freedom: A Black Soldier's Civil War Letters from the Front, James Henry Gooding* (Amherst: University of Massachusetts Press, 1991).

For the autobiographies of black Civil War veterans, see Elijah P. Marrs, *Life and History of the Rev. Elijah P. Marrs* (Louisville, Ky.: Bradley and Gilbert, 1885); Allen Parker, *Recollections of Slavery Times* (Worcester, Mass.: Charles W. Burbank, 1895); Alexander H. Newton, *Out of the Briars: An Autobiography and Sketch of the Twenty-ninth Regiment Connecticut Volunteers* (Philadelphia: A.M.E. Book Concern, 1910); Peter Bruner, *A Slave's Adventures toward Freedom: Not Fiction, but the True Story of a Struggle* (Oxford, Ohio: by the author, 1925); Robert Anderson, *From Slavery to Affluence: Memoirs of Robert Anderson, Ex-Slave* (Hemingford, Neb.: Hemingford Ledger, 1927).

2. Camilla A. Quinn, "Soldiers on Our Streets: The Effects of a Civil War Military Camp on the Springfield Community," *Illinois Historical Journal* 86 (winter 1993): 245–56; Patricia Richard, "'A Great Crying Evil': Civil War Soldiers' Experiences in Milwaukee, Wisconsin," *Milwaukee History* 22 (1999): 16–30; Thomas P. Lowry, "Research Note: New Access to a Civil War Resource," *Civil War History* 49 (2003): 52–63; Brad R. Clampitt, "The Breakup: The Collapse of the Confederate Trans-Mississippi Army in Texas," *Southwestern Historical Quarterly* 108 (April 2005): 499–534.

3. Ward is referring to another deposition taken by the Pension Bureau two months before, when he told them he had been married only once and had not named Minerva as his wife. See Deposition of Alfred Ward, Feb. 11, 1901, Civil War Pension File of Alfred Barksdale (alias Ward), 63rd USCI, RG 15.

4. Even after the passage of the 1890 pension law, which allowed pensions for disabilities that were not service related, veterans still could apply for pensions under the original 1862 Civil War pension act, referred to as either the "old" or "general" law, if they could prove a war-related disability. The incentive was that pension rates under the 1862 law were more generous and that

under the provisions of the 1879 Arrears Act, they could collect a lump-sum payment for the pension that they should have been receiving since the date they incurred the disability during the Civil War. It was not until the passage of the 1912 pension law that non-war-related pensions became potentially more generous than 1862 law pensions, and surviving veterans pensioned under that law hastened to get off the 1862 rolls and onto the disability rolls under the 1912 law.

5. For more information on this incident, see Kip Lindbergh and Matt Matthews, "'It Haunts Me Night and Day': The Baxter Springs Massacre," *North and South* 4 (June 2001): 42–53.

6. By "warp," Waters is no doubt referring to kindling wood to start a fire.

7. Bell Irvin Wiley, *The Life of Billy Yank: The Common Soldier of the Union* (New York: Bobbs-Merrill, 1952; repr., New York: Doubleday, 1971), 23.

8. See DeAnne Blanton and Lauren M. Cook, *They Fought like Demons: Women Soldiers in the American Civil War* (New York: Vintage Books, 2003); Jane E. Schultz, *Women at the Front: Hospital Workers in Civil War America* (Chapel Hill: University of North Carolina Press, 2004); Mark H. Dunkleman, "Hoop Skirts in Camp: When Women Visited the Front," *North and South* 7 (November 2004): 36–43; Richard H. Hall, *Women on the Civil War Battlefront* (Lawrence: University Press of Kansas, 2006).

9. Jack Rudolph, "The Grand Review: 'They March like the Lords of the World,'" *Civil War Times Illustrated* 19 (November 1980): 42.

10. Berlin, Reidy, and Rowland, eds., *Freedom, Series II: Black Military Experience,* 484–87.

11. Revel Garrison's pension file is an example of a belated claim under the 1862 law that was accepted, although it should be noted that he made his application before the passage of the groundbreaking 1890 pension law.

12. Johnson's service record indicates that he was mustered into the Union army on May 1, 1865, and mustered out of service on January 4, 1866. See Civil War Service Record of Wiley Johnson, 136th USCI, RG 94.

13. Newton, *Out of the Briars,* 69–89.

14. It is interesting to note that at the time this investigation occurred Henry Ford (alias Charles Newton, alias Newton Charles) already had been a pensioner under the 1890 law for over a decade. In fact, the veteran was not under investigation in this deposition. The Pension Bureau was investigating pension fraud in the Norfolk, Virginia, area, and the facts revealed came out because of the question track taken by the special examiner in his cross-examination. It is also worthwhile noting that Ford was not dropped as a pensioner despite the facts uncovered and that he continued to collect a pension until his death in 1921. His pension eligibility was opened by an act of Congress

passed July 5, 1884. This law made it possible for a finding of desertion to be removed for a volunteer soldier in the Civil War provided that it had not taken place prior to May 1, 1865.

NOTES TO CHAPTER 3

1. U.S. Census Bureau, *Compendium of the Eleventh Census: 1890, Part III* (Washington, D.C.: GPO, 1897), 473.

2. Loren Schweninger, *Black Property Owners of the South, 1790–1915* (Urbana: University of Illinois Press, 1990), 183.

3. U.S. Census Bureau, *Negro Population, 1790–1915* (Washington, D.C.: GPO, 1918), 298.

4. Nell Irvin Painter, *Exodusters: Black Migration to Kansas after Reconstruction* (New York: Knopf, 1977).

5. Shaffer, *After the Glory*, 46–47.

6. Eric Foner, *Reconstruction: America's Unfinished Revolution, 1863–1877* (New York: Harper and Row, 1988), 81.

7. *Compendium of the Eleventh Census*, 540–79. At this time, the U.S. Census Bureau defined a town or city as urban if it had eight thousand residents or more.

8. Porter is no doubt referring to Goodrich's Landing, Louisiana, which was also the site of a Civil War battle in late June 1863 in which Confederate raiders defeated two newly raised black regiments. See Noah Andre Trudeau, *Like Men of War: Black Troops in the Civil War, 1862–1865* (Edison, N.J.: Castle Books, 2002), 97–102.

9. The phrase "vicious habits" is taken directly from the law of June 27, 1890, that authorized pensions for disabled veterans regardless of whether their disability was war related. Exempted from eligibility were disabilities caused by the ex-soldiers' "vicious habits." See *United States Statutes at Large,* vol. 26 (Washington, D.C.: GPO, 1890), 182.

10. Patrick J. Kelly, *Creating a National Home: Building the Veterans' Welfare State* (Cambridge, Mass.: Harvard University Press, 1997).

11. To be fair, the Pension Bureau came to realize the preindustrial view of time held by many ex-slaves and created a special procedure to approximate vital dates by ascertaining their association with events whose dates were known. As noted in chapter 1, a Bureau manual on special examination instructed pension agents, "it will generally be necessary to call attention to the witnesses to some important event, holiday, &c., to enable them to testify with any approach to accuracy in regard to dates." See *General Instructions to Special Examiners of the U.S. Pension Bureau*, 24.

12. Sirag Eldin Hassan Suliman, "Estimation of Levels and Trends of the U.S. Adult Black Mortality during the Period 1870–1900" (Ph.D. diss., University of Pennsylvania, 1983), 170. Suliman's exact estimates of life expectancy of white and black males at age ten, by decade, were as follows: 1870–80, white men, 49.2, black men, 42.54; 1880–90, white men, 49.75, black men, 41.0; 1890–1900, white men, 50.31, black men, 40.84.

13. J. S. Patterson, Special Examiner, Washington, Lebanon, Tenn., to the Commissioner of Pensions, Washington, D.C., Nov. 9, 1901, Civil War Pension File of Jacob Hutchison (alias Jacob Overall, alias Abraham I. J. Wright), 4th USCHA, RG 15.

NOTES TO CHAPTER 4

1. Most notable among these scholars is Theda Skocpol, *Protecting Soldiers and Mothers: The Political Origins of Social Policy in the United States* (Cambridge, Mass.: Belknap Press, 1992).

2. U.S. Pension Bureau, *A Treatise on the Practice of the Pension Bureau Governing the Adjudication of Army and Navy Pensions* (Washington, D.C.: GPO, 1898), 55, 75. The booklet stated, "Special provision is made concerning proof of marriage of colored and Indian soldiers by section 4705 of the Revised Statutes, under which marriage is proven by showing the parties 'were joined in marriage by some ceremony deemed by them obligatory, or habitually recognized each other as husband and wife, and were so recognized by their neighbors, and lived together as such up to the date of enlistment, when soldier or sailor died in service, or if otherwise, to the date of death.'"

3. For more on slave and ex-slave family life, see Laura Edwards, *Gendered Strife and Confusion: The Political Culture of Reconstruction* (Urbana: University of Illinois Press, 1997); Noralee Frankel, *Freedom's Women: Black Women and Families in Civil War Era Mississippi* (Bloomington: Indiana University Press, 1999); Herbert Gutman, *The Black Family in Slavery and Freedom, 1750–1925* (New York: Pantheon Books, 1976); Jacqueline Jones, *Labor of Love, Labor of Sorrow: Black Women, Work, and the Family from Slavery to the Present* (New York: Basic Books, 1985); Regosin, *Freedom's Promise;* Leslie Schwalm, *A Hard Fight for We: Women's Transition from Slavery to Freedom in South Carolina* (Urbana: University of Illinois Press, 1997); Shaffer, *After the Glory.*

4. Deposition of Ona Bibb, Apr. 15, 1878, Civil War Pension File of Reuben Bibb, 65th USCI, RG 15.

5. Bureau of Pensions Questionnaires, May 1898 and Apr. 13, 1899, Civil War Pension file of General Walker, 88th USCI, RG 15.

6. Deposition of Duncan H. Chamberlain, May 7, 1890, Civil War Pension File of Ellis Bowdel, 50th USCI, RG 15.

7. Frankel, *Freedom's Women*, 90–92; Shaffer, *After the Glory*, 102–3.

8. Deborah Gray White, *Ar'n't I a Woman? Female Slaves in the Plantation South* (New York: Norton, 1985), 97–98, 106–8.

9. Although Malonne claimed to be about one hundred years old, special examiner Charles L. Grannis noted, "This claimant is very old and feeble, although I do not think she is as old as she claims to be." Charles L. Grannis, Special Examiner, to William Loehren, Commissioner of Pensions, Sept. 25, 1893, Civil War Pension file of Octave Jessie, 96th USCI, RG 15.

10. Malonne's situation calls to mind that of Celia, a slave whose story Melton McLaurin recounts in *Celia, a Slave* (Athens: University of Georgia Press, 1991). McLaurin notes that Celia's master built her a cabin of her own so that he could have ready and private access to her. McLaurin catalogs Celia's sexual abuse from the time she was fourteen until she murdered her master at age nineteen.

11. Gutman, *Black Family in Slavery and Freedom*, 412–18. For a critique of Gutman's analysis, see Shaffer, *After the Glory*, 103.

12. Baton Rouge, Louisiana, fell to federal forces on April 25, 1862.

13. See also Megan J. McClintock, "Civil War Pensions and the Reconstruction of Union Families," *Journal of American History* 83, no. 2 (September 1996): 471–79.

14. E. H. Carver, Special Examiner, Hertford, N.C., to the Commissioner of Pensions, Washington, D.C., May 9, 1899, Civil War Pension File of Luke Riddick (alias White), 38th USCI, RG 15.

15. The law of August 7, 1882, sought, among other things, to disqualify widows who were living with men outside marriage in an effort to retain their pension, since women who remarried lost their eligibility. The exact language of the law stated, "the open and notorious adulterous cohabitation of a widow who is a pensioner shall operate to terminate her pension from the commencement of such cohabitation." See *Statutes at Large of the United States of America*, vol. 22 (Washington, D.C.: GPO, 1883), 345.

16. Ibid., 91; Shaffer, *After the Glory*, 104–13.

17. Frankel, *Freedom's Women*, 104–9; Shaffer, *After the Glory*, 106–7.

18. Deposition of Margaret Fields, Feb. 1, 1889, Civil War Pension File of John Fields, 118th USCT, RG 15.

19. Regarding the law of 1882, see note 15 to this chapter.

20. In reality, during the first decade of Reconstruction, ex-slave families with children struggled against the practice of apprenticeship, whereby white Southern authorities would find legal means to take children from their parents and to "apprentice" them—or bind them out—to white families. This sample of Civil War pension files does not address that phenomenon. For more on the

practice of apprenticeship and the efforts of African Americans to end it, see Peter Bardaglio, *Reconstructing the Household: Families, Sex, and the Law in the Nineteenth-Century South* (Chapel Hill: University of North Carolina Press, 1995), 161–63.

NOTES TO THE APPENDIX

1. Recall that during slavery and in the service, Crosby was known as Frank Nunn.

Index

Boldface entries indicates names of claimants taken from the U.S. Pension Bureau files; page numbers in italic indicate illustrations.

About the Authors

ELIZABETH A. REGOSIN is an associate professor of history at St. Lawrence University and the author of *Freedom's Promise: Ex-Slave Families and Citizenship in the Age of Emancipation.*

DONALD R. SHAFFER is an assistant professor of history at Upper Iowa University and the author of *After the Glory: The Struggles of Black Civil War Veterans*, which won the 2005 Peter Seaborg Award for Civil War Scholarship.